The Witch C'oxol / El aj-iitz C'oxol

**Also by James D. Sexton and Pedro Cholotío Temó:**

*Son of Tecún Umán: A Maya Indian Tells His Life Story* (1981, republished in 1990)

*Campesino: The Diary of a Guatemalan Indian* (1985)

*Ignacio: The Diary of a Maya Indian of Guatemala* (1992a)

*Mayan Folktales: Folklore from Lake Atitlan, Guatemala* (1992b, republished in 1999)

*Heart of Heaven, Heart of Earth and Other Mayan Folktales* (1999)

*Joseño: Another Mayan Voice Speaks from Guatemala* (2001)

*The Dog Who Spoke and More Mayan Folktales / El perro que habló y más cuentos mayas* (2010)

**Also by James D. Sexton:**

*Education and Inovation in a Guatemala Community: San Juan la Laguna* (1972)

*An Anthropologist Goes to the Vietnam War* (2016)

# The Witch C'oxol / El aj-iitz C'oxol

*An Ancient Legend and Other Mayan Folktales / Una leyenda antigua y otros cuentos mayas*

PEDRO CHOLOTÍO TEMÓ

EDITED AND TRANSLATED BY JAMES D. SEXTON

UNIVERSITY OF NEW MEXICO PRESS | ALBUQUERQUE

Printed in the United States of America

Library of Congress Cataloging-in-Publication Data
Names: Temó, Pedro Cholotío, author. | Sexton, James D., translator, editor.
Title: The witch C'oxol: an ancient legend and other Mayan folktales / stories told in Spanish by Pedro Cholotío Temó; translated and edited by James D. Sexton.
Description: Albuquerque: University of New Mexico Press, 2025. | Includes bibliographical references.
Identifiers: LCCN 2025006783 (print) | LCCN 2025006784 (ebook) | ISBN 9780826368287 (cloth) | ISBN 9780826368294 (paperback) | ISBN 9780826368300 (epub)
Subjects: LCSH: Mayas—Folklore. | Mayas—Folklore. | Tales—Guatemala. | LCGFT: Folk tales.
Classification: LCC F1435.3.F6 T468 2025 (print) | LCC F1435.3.F6 (ebook) | DDC 398.2097281--dc23/eng/20250218
LC record available at https://lccn.loc.gov/2025006783
LC ebook record available at https://lccn.loc.gov/2025006784

Founded in 1889, the University of New Mexico sits on the traditional homelands of the Pueblo of Sandia. The original peoples of New Mexico—Pueblo, Navajo, and Apache—since time immemorial have deep connections to the land and have made significant contributions to the broader community statewide. We honor the land itself and those who remain stewards of this land throughout the generations and also acknowledge our committed relationship to Indigenous peoples. We gratefully recognize our history.

Cover illustration: courtesy of the author
Designed by Felicia Cedillos
Composed in Adobe Jenson Pro

# Contents / El contenido



## FOLKTALES / CUENTOS

# Illustrations / Ilustraciones

# Preface

Pedro Cholotío Temó is a Tz'utujil who has lived his entire life of eighty-four years in San Juan la Laguna, Sololá, Guatemala. His town is above the shore of Lake Atitlán, one of the most magnificent lakes in the world.

Pedro is *primer principal* (first elder or dignitary), which is the highest traditional office in the civil-religious hierarchy of San Juan. Although the mayor and municipal secretary have more civil power, their offices are not necessarily the most prestigious. As I have said in *Joseño,* Pedro has served in a number of civil and religious offices in his town. His religious service includes a year as the *alcalde* (head) of the *cofradías* (religious brotherhoods) of María Concepción and

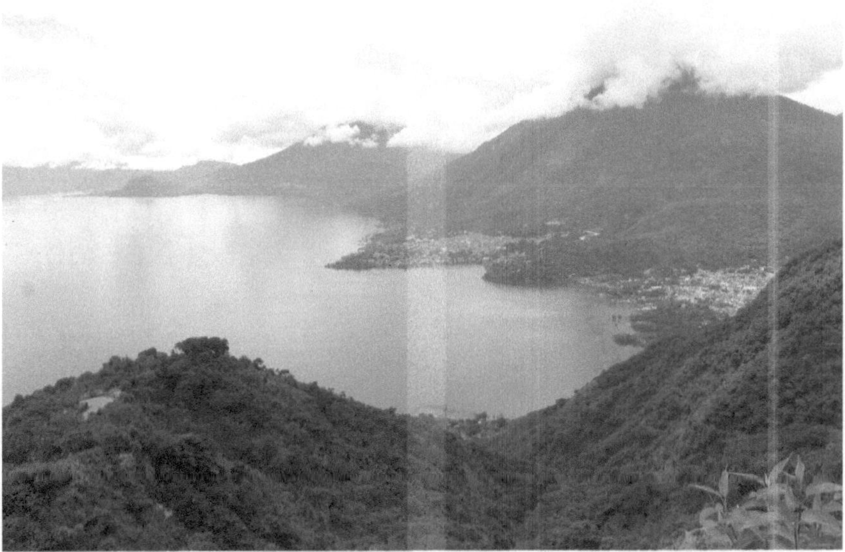

*Figure* 1. View of San Juan la Laguna to the far right of the photo, with San Pedro to the immediate right, and Santiago Atitlánin in the distance / Vista de San Juna la Laguna al extremo derecho de la foto, San Pedro a la derecha inmediata, y Santiago Atitlán en la distancia

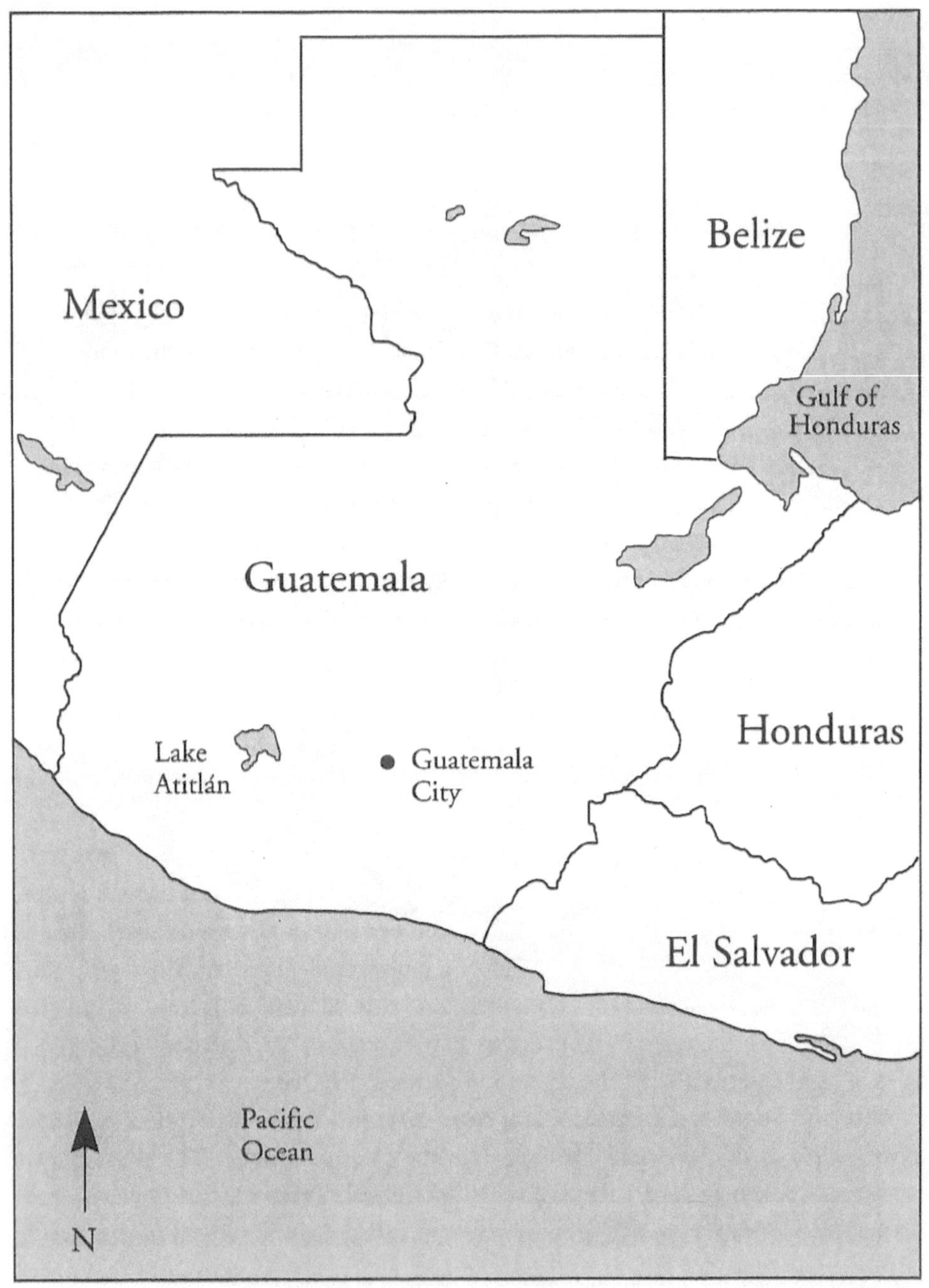


*Map* 1. Guatemala with political boundaries and location of Lake Atitlán / Guatemala con límites politicos y ubicación del lago de Atitlán

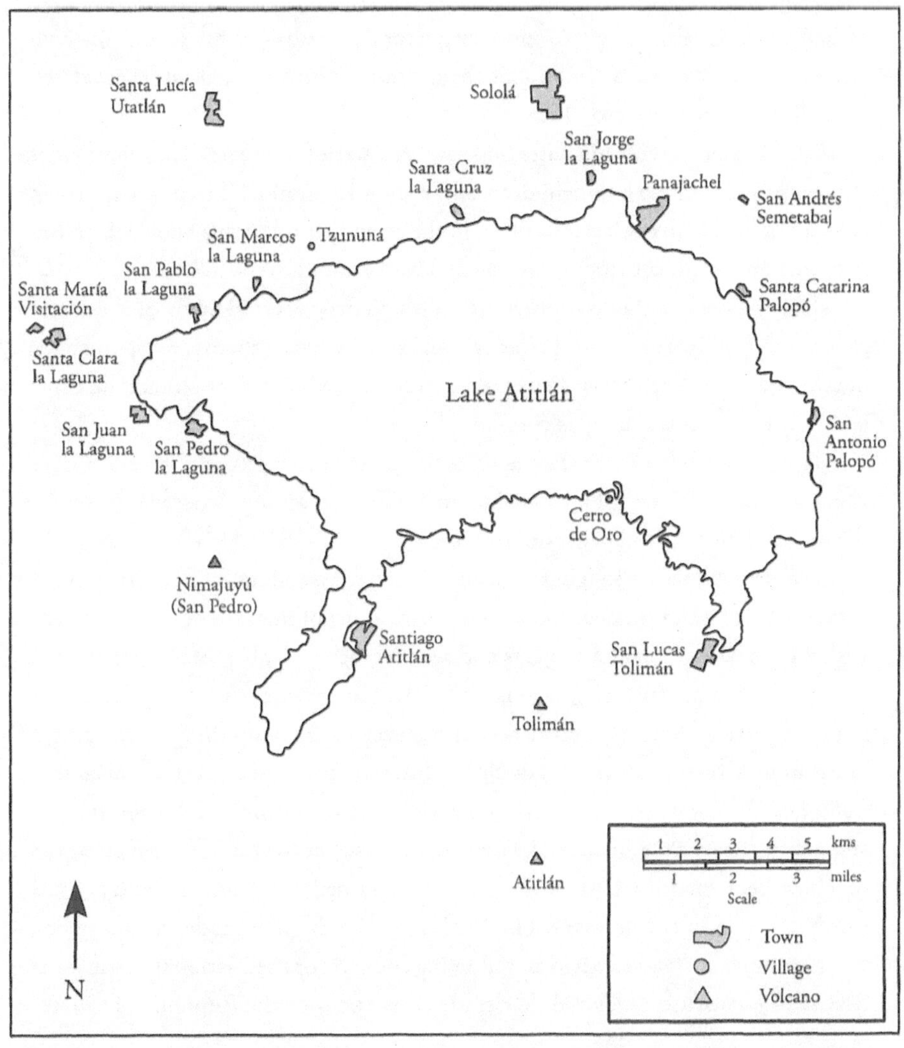


*Map* 2. Lake Atitlán with surrounding towns and aldeas / Lago Atitlán con pueblos y aldeas circundantes

of San Juan Bautista, the two most important cofradías of his town. His civil service includes a year as *síndico*, or town syndic (trustee, legal representative), the second-highest elected office.

Pedro has been with his wife, Nicolasa, for sixty-four years. They have eight children, twenty-three grandchildren, and eight great grandchildren. (Pedro's own account of his life in the community is in the introduction to this book, which follows this preface. It provides more cultural background to the folktales.)

Also, as I have said in our previous books, Pedro was told many of these stories in Tz'utujil by friends and relatives, and he translated them into Spanish for me. At the end of each story, Pedro is careful to say who told it to him, if he alone is the author, or if the story is commonly known.

My goal has been to make the folktales as readable as possible. So, I have checked and rechecked the English translations, retaining, wherever possible, the original diction and syntax of the stories.

In some instances, though, for clarity, I changed a colloquial Spanish expression to a more standard one. Also, I have made most of the verb tenses consistent within each paragraph and subjects and verbs agree in number. Strictly speaking, therefore, these are free translations rather than literal ones. Anything Pedro put in parentheses, I left in parentheses. Whenever I added anything to the text, I put it in brackets. If an Indian or Spanish word appears in *Merriam Webster's Collegiate Dictionary* (eleventh edition) with the same meaning, I did not italicize and define the word. Some readers may be surprised at the number of such words that have been incorporated into English as loan words. All italicized and defined words are also in the glossary. Finally, I used the English model for numbers, using commas instead of periods, following the style of the National Institute of Statistics (Instituto Nacional de Estadisticas 2003) of the Republic of Guatemala.

As I have said in our previous books, I have been working with Pedro since he became my native research assistant in San Juan in 1970 when I was part of Professor Clyde Woods's field school and research team at the University of California, Los Angeles (UCLA), studying modernization and culture change in the fourteen towns surrounding Lake Atitlán. Over the past fifty-five years, my relationship with Pedro has been fruitful. Under his pen name, Ignacio, we published four volumes of his life history—*Son of Tecún Umán* (1981, republished in 1990), *Campesino* (1985), *Ignacio* (1992a), and *Joseño* (2001)—and two volumes of folktales,

*Mayan Folktales* (1992b, republished in 1999) and *Heart of Heaven, Heart of Earth* (1999), the first two books of folktales published in English from the Lake Atitlán region. Under his real name, Pedro (with Fredy Rodríguez-Mejía and Alberto Barreno), we published *The Dog Who Spoke and More Mayan Folktales/ El perro que habló y más cuentos mayas* (2010), a bilingual book in English and Spanish.

Pedro is paid half or all the royalties. Occasionally, I send him additional money. Still, as he indicates within the text, his main goal is to preserve and share this type of cultural material, especially folktales, *costumbres* (rituals, customs), and traditions passed down by his ancestors.

Over the past ten years, Pedro wrote all of the tales in this book by hand and mailed them to me by regular mail or email. Only three stories he wrote down were not used. Pedro's cousin, Juan Upán Ovalle, told him the tale "The Muleteer and Jealous Husband," but Pedro did not send it to me because he thought it was too vulgar. Another story was ethnically insensitive, so I did not use it. Finally, a third folktale was short and not well-developed, so I did not use it.

I moved the tale "*Caso*: Francisco Sojuel Warns of Hurricane Stan" from the last to the first story, right after Pedro's regional account of the impact of Hurricane Stan at the end of the introduction. Doing so better illustrates how a folktale may be linked to a natural, albeit disastrous, event. All the other folktales appear in the order that I received them.

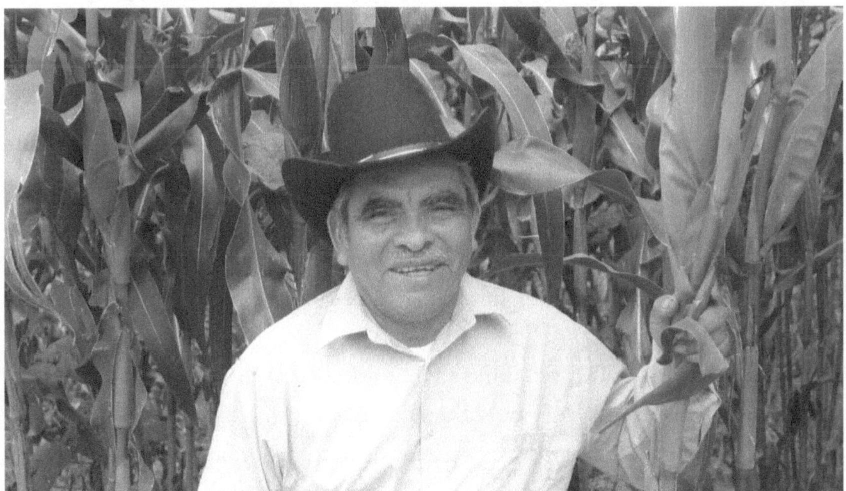

*Figure 2.* Pedro Cholotío Temó standing in a cornfield in San Juan la Laguna / Pedro Cholotío Temó de pie en un campo de maíz en San Juan la Laguna

## Overview of the tales

The tales in the present book are rich in cultural content, and a given tale may contain more than one quality. The stories may reinforce cultural values such as cleverness, as in the case of the clever man who postpones death in "Mayan Folktale: The Man Who Deceived Death." In the *caso* (genre of a folktale based on true events) "*Caso*: The Deer Hunters," hunters must treat the bones of the deer they kill for meat with respect or pay the consequences. Compassion is a virtue in "The Wise and Powerful." Depending on whether he is treated with respect, a traveling old wise man can make things good or bad for the people he meets on his journey.

These folktales also reflect family conflict as in "Story: The King and His Two Daughters," in which a king's eldest daughter runs away from home to rid herself of her angry father. Going against the grain of her husband, the king's wife aids her daughter by bestowing *secretos* (magical objects or acts) to her in hiding.

The stories also advise us to pay attention to our dreams. In "Mayan Folktale: Lady of the Hill That Is Called Chua Suj," an impoverished woman receives a notice in her dream in which Chua Suj, lady of enchantment, tells her what magical act she could do to gain wealth and thus a better way of life; she is also to follow the lady's instructions and not tell anyone how she did it. Likewise, in "Story of The Taltuza" in a dream the *ajau* (also spelled *ajaw* and *aajaaw*, or *dueño* [owner, lord, god]), shows rainmakers how to cure people with *zacate* (grass; *hierba*; herbs).

These stories also reflect a worldview that reinforces traditional beliefs such as *nagualism* (people have a nagual, which is a spirit or animal). In "*Caso*: The Owl-Man: Incredible, but True," church brothers kick an owl to death only to discover it was the *nagual* of a man. In "A Real Story: Strange Things, Unusual Cases, Opossum," after an opossum comes into the room where Rubén is dying and Juan kills it, Rubén dies right afterward because the opossum was Rubén's nagual.

People who visit enchanted hills must be mindful of their deportment or suffer the consequences. In "Mayan Folktale: Lady of the Hill That Is Called Chua Suj," the lady of the enchanted hill is generous to the poor but only if they follow her wish to keep her charity a secret. In "True Visions and Beliefs," Don Juan Televario relates that in San Pedro la Laguna, there are three enchanted places where many strange things have happened to the people of the town. Thus, hunters and foresters should present a Mayan ceremony to prevent suffering, as Francisco did in Pa chojoob'. "A Mysterious Tale of the Matapalo Tree" tells why one should not cut down a *matapalo* tree in an enchanted place.

As in many other folkloric traditions throughout the world, a popular theme in Mayan folktales is transformation. In "The Characotales, a Real Story," a woman turns into a cat and leads a gang of other *characotales* (persons who can transform into her or his nagual and do evil things) who are thieves at night. In "Story: The King and His Two Daughters," the eldest daughter, who ran away from home because of her mean father, shape- shifts her own daughters to three ears of corn to prevent the king's men from finding them. In the "Tz'utujil Story: The Woman Who Buried the Devil," the devil transforms himself into a man with gold teeth to deceive a woman wanting to marry a man with gold teeth, but he also converts into other animals, including serpents when he wishes, and into wood. In "Mayan Folktale: Origin of the Marimba," two princesses convert into trees of different sizes, and in their foliage you may hear the joy of the marimba, the drum, and the *chirimía* (traditional flute). In the "Story of the Taltuza," when a bad person dies, his or her soul reincarnates as a *taltuza* (rodent similar to rats who bores long tunnels in the earth).

As a prelude to "The Man Who Mistreated His Wife," Pedro writes, "Our grandfathers and grandmothers left [bequeathed] us the folktales. For us, it is fascinating, but for them it was a method of [providing] an example to their sons and daughters; they did not use a social worker or psychologist. As part of the Mayan culture, they used stories as a method of orientation for their sons and daughters." Thus, in this story we are told how a husband modifies his behavior for the good.

Proper orientation may reinforce proverbs that contain folk wisdom and may be included in the tale. For instance, at the end of "Tz'utujil Story: The Woman Who Buried the Devil," Pedro, the storyteller, relates that the grandmothers and grandfathers said, "No hay que codiciar cosas porque todos los deseos malos tienen mal fin [Do not covet things because all the bad desires have a bad ending]." However, the storyteller also may leave it up to the reader to come to his or her own conclusion.

Such is the case of the "Old Story: The Enchanted Tiger [Jaguar]," in which a son should mind the wisdom of his mother. In other words, "El que oye consejo de viejo, llega a viejo [He who listens to the advice of the old lives to be old]."Also, "The Tale of Señor Sebastián Ujpán" warns, "Tus mentiras siempre te alcanzarán al final [Your lies will always catch up with you in the end]." In this tale, an extortionist military commissioner suffers the consequences. This tale also demonstrates the saying, "Pagar con la misma moneda [Pay with the same money]." In other words, "To get your just desserts, or taste of your own medicine." "Story: The King and His Two Daughters," because of the king's unreasonable demands, exemplifies the proverb "No mires a los demás; mírate a ti mismo [Don't look at others; look at yourself]."

The stories in this collection relate historical events. For example, "Story of the Taltuza" teaches us about the Mayan calendar. And "The End of the Dance of the Deer" gives an account of what this dance means and how it is disappearing among people under the age of fifty. In a similar manner, "The Witch C'oxol: An Ancient Legend" relates how the early Spaniards deceived the early Mayas out of the gold and silver that the ancient Maya had extracted from Xe K'istalin and in Chua Suj. This story also recounts how when King Tecún Umán was alive, he had a powerful *aj-iitz* (witch) named C'oxol.

These folktales reflect much about the natural habitat, especially its plants and animals. Thus, we learn of plants such as suj (suuj, sare, conacaste) trees, apples, peaches, pears, plums, corn (maize), *tecomates* (gourds), bananas, *injertos, anonas* (graft *anonas* [sugar apples]), cotton, güisquil (a climbing plant whose fruit is the size of an orange), *zacate* (grass or herbs), avocados, *cafetales* (coffee groves), vines, beans, gourds of different sizes, reeds, yuccas, sweet potatoes, lemons, brambles, hormigo trees (not very big [they are] like bushes), and the matapalo tree.

We also find animals such as tigers (jaguars), deer, dogs, pigs, sheep, owls, the short snake (*cuta*), regular sized snakes, chickens, rabbits, fish, crabs, raccoons, opossums, *pizotes* (similar to coatis), tepezcuintle (brown rodent the size of a rabbit with black stripes on its back), the *andasolo* (*pizote* or *coati* of a white nose [species: *Nasua narica*)]) wild pigs, turkeys, coyotes, monkeys, lions (mountain lions), eagle hawks, bees, buzzards, wolves, ants, wild cats, and kinkajous.

In addition to plants and animals in the natural habitat, we discover in these tales supernatural beings. For instance, in "Cuento: The Woman of the Hunter," a magical dwarf-man, who is the lord of the mountain and the animals, magically punishes the hunter's woman. And in the story "Caso: Francisco Sojuel Warns

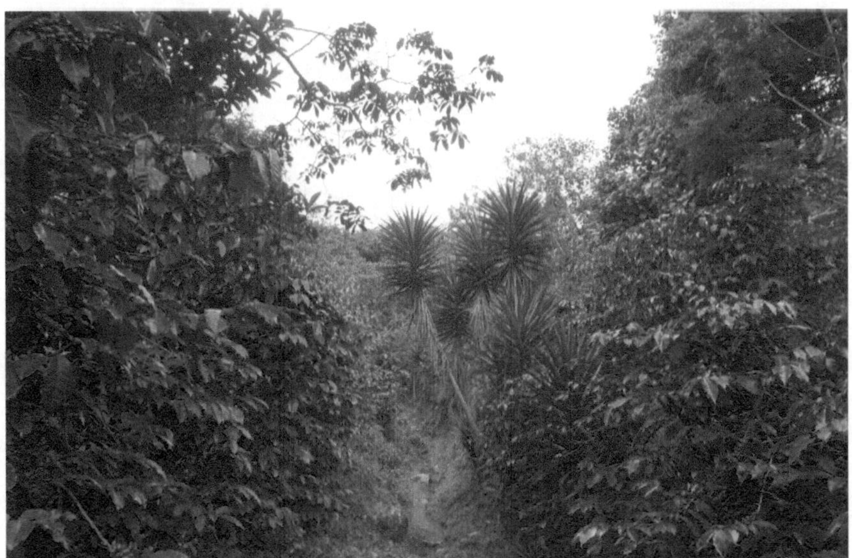

*Figure* 3. A cafetal in the northern foothills above San Juan la Laguna / Un cafetal en las estribaciones del norte arriba de San Juan la Laguna

of Hurricane Stan," an old man, typically dressed, turns out to be Francisco Sojuel, a legendary character, who magically walks the streets of the Panabaj canton warning the inhabitants of the danger of the impending Hurricane Stan.

Finally, many Mayan folktales are simply funny, and the reader may enjoy them in their own right. For instance, there is humor in the "Tz'utujil Story: The Woman Who Buried the Devil," in which the woman who unknowingly marries the devil because he is wearing gold teeth nevertheless gets rid of him. Another comical tale in this collection is "Mayan Folktale: The Man Who Deceived Death." In it, for instance, the man who uses his wits to avoid death still calls her "old bald head."

# Prefacio

Pedro Cholotío Temó es un maya tz'utujil que ha vivido toda su vida de 84 años en San Juan la Laguna, Sololá, Guatemala. Su pueblo está sobre la orilla del lago Atitlán, uno de los lagos más magníficos del mundo.

Pedro es primer principal (primer anciano o dignatario), que es el cargo tradicional más alto en la jerarquía civil-religiosa de San Juan. Aunque el alcalde y el secretario municipal tienen más poder civil, no necesariamente son los más prestigiosos. Como he dicho en *Joseño*, Pedro ha servido en varios cargos civiles y religiosos en su pueblo. Su servicio civil incluye un año como alcalde (jefe) de las cofradías (hermandades religiosas) de María Concepción y de San Juan Bautista, las dos cofradías más importantes de su pueblo. Su servicio civil incluye un año como síndico del pueblo (fideicomisario, represente legal), el segundo cargo electo más alto.

Pedro ha estado con su esposa, Nicolasa, durante 64 años. Tienen ocho hijos, 23 nietos, y ocho bisnietos. (El proprio relato de Pedro sobre su vida en la comunidad se encuentra en la introdució a este libro, que sigue a este prefacio. Proporciona más trasfondo cultural a los cuentos mayas).

También, como he dicho en nuestros libros anteriores, a Pedo le contaron muchas de estas historias en Tz'utujil amigos y familiares, y él me las tradujo al español. A final de cada historia, Pedro tiene cuidado de decir quién se la contó, si solo él es el autor, o si la historia es comúnmente conocida.

Mi objetivo ha sido hacer que los cuentos sean lo más legibles posible. Por lo tanto, he revisado y vuelto a revisar las traducciones al inglés, conservado, siempre que sea posible, la dicción y la sintaxis originales de las historias.

Sin embargo, en algunos casos, para mayor claridad, cambié una expresión coloquial en español por una más estándar. Además, he hecho que la mayoría de los tiempos verbales sean consistentes dentro de cada párrafo y que los sujetos y los verbos concidan en número. Estrictamente hablando, por lo tanto, estas son traducciones libres en lugar de literales. Todo lo que Pedro puso entre paréntesis, yo lo dejé entre paréntesis. Cada vez que agregué algo al texto, lo puse entre corchetes. Si una palabra maya o española aparece en el *Merriam Webster's Collegiate Dictionary* (eleventh edition) con el mismo significado, no puse en curvisa ni definí la palabra en la versión engles. Algunos lectores pueden sorprenderse la cantidad de palabras de este tipo que se han incorporado al inglés. Finalmente, utilicé el modelo inglés para números, usando comas en lugar de puntos, siguiendo el estilo del Instituto Nacional de Estadística (Instituto Nacional de Estadísticas 2003) de República de Guatemala.

También, como he dicho en nuestros libros anteriores, he estado trabajando con Pedro desde que se convirtió en mi asistente de investigación nativo en San Juan en 1970 cuando formaba parte de la escuela del campo y el equipo de investigación del profesor Clyde Woods en la Universidad de California, Los Angeles (UCLA), estudiando la modernización y el cambio cultural en los catorce pueblos que rodean el Lago de Atitlán. Durante los últimos 55 años, mi relación con Pedro ha sido fructífera Bajo su seudónimo, Ignacio, hemos publicado cuatro tomos de su historia de vida—*Son of Tecún Umán* (1981, reeditado en 1990), *Campesino* (1985), *Ignacio* (1992a), y *Joseño* (2001)—y dos tomos de cuentos, *Mayan Folktales* (1992b, reeditado en 1999) y *Heart of Heaven, Heart of Earth* (1999), los dos primeros libros publicados en inglés de cuentos de la región del lago de Atitlán. Bajo su verdadero nombre, Pedro, (con Fredy Rodríguez-Mejía, Alberto Barreno, hemos publicado *The Dog Who Spoke and More Mayan Folktales / El perro que habló y más cuentos mayas* (2010), un libro bilingüe en inglés y español.

A Pedro se le paga la mitad o la totalidad de las regalías. De vez en cuando, además de eso, le envío dinero. Sin embargo, como él mismo indica, su principal objetivo es presevar y compartir este tipo de material cultural, especiamente los cuentos, las costumbres y las tradiciones transmitidas por sus antepsados.

Durante los últimos diez años, Pedro escribío todos los cuentos de este libro a mano y me los envió por correo ordinario o correo electrónico. Solo tres cuentos no se utilizaron. El primo de Pedro, Juan Ujpán Ovalle, le contó el cuento "El arriero y el marido celeso," pero Pedro no me envió porque le pareció demasiado vulgar. Otro cuento era étnicamente insensible, así que no lo usé. Finalmente, un tercer cuento era corto y no estaba bien desarrollado, así que no lo usé.

El cuento, "Caso: Francisco Sojuel advierte sobre el huracán Stan," que pasé de la última a la primera historia para estar justo después del relato regional de

Pedro sobre el impacto del huracán Stan al final de la introducción. Al hacerlo, se ilustra mejor cómo un cuento puede estar vinculado a un evento natural, aunque desastroso. Todos los demás cuentos aparecen en el orden en que los recibí.

## Resumen de los cuentos

Los cuentos del presente libro son ricos en contenido cultural, y un cuento dado puede contener más de una cualidad. Los cuentos pueden reforzar valores culturales como la astucia, como en el caso del hombre listo que pospone la muerte en "Cuento maya: El hombre que engañó a la muerte." En el caso (género de un cuento basado en hechos reales) "Caso: Los cazadores de venados," los cazadores deben tratar con respeto los huesos de los venados que matan para obtener carne o pagar las consecuencias. La compasión es una virtud en "El sabio y poderoso." Dependiendo de si es tratado con respeto, un anciano viajero puede hacer las cosas buenas o malas para las personas que encuentra en su viaje.

Estos cuentos también reflejan conflictos familiares como "Cuento: El rey y sus dos hijas" en la que la hija mayor de un rey se escapa de casa para librarse de su padre enojado. En contra de la corriente de su marido, la esposa del rey ayuda a su hija otorgándole *secretos* (objetos o actos mágicos) a su hija en la clandestinidad.

Los cuentos también nos aconsejan prestar atención a nuestros sueños. En "Cuento maya: Dueña del cerro que se llamada Chua Suj," una mujer empobrecida recibió su sueño un aviso en el que Chua Suj, dueña del encantamiento, le dijo qué acto mágico puede hacer para ganar riqueza y así una mejor manera de vida, sino seguir sus instrucciones de no decirle a nadie cómo lo hizo. Asimismo, en "Historia del mapache," en un sueño el ajau, o dueño (señor, dios), muestra a los hacedores de lluvia cómo curar la gente con zacate (hierba; yerba).

Estas historias también reflejan una cosmovisión que refuerza creencias tradicionales como el *nagualismo* (la gente tiene un *nagual* que es un espíritu o un animal). En "Caso: El hombre búho: Increíble, pero es cierto," los hermanos de la iglesia matan a patadas a lechuza sólo para descubrir que era el *nagual* de un hombre. En "Un cuento real: Cosas extrañas, casos inusuales, tacuazín," después de que un tacuazín entró en la habitación donde Rubén estaba muriendo y Juan la mata, Rubén muere justo después porque el tacuazín era el nagual de Rubén.

Gente que visitan cerros en cantados deben cuidar su comportamiento o sufrir las consecuencias. En "Cuento maya: Dueña del cerro que se llama Chua Suj," la dueña del cerro encantado es generosa con los pobres, pero solo si siguen su deseo de mantener su caridad en secreto. En "Visiones y creencias ciertas," Don Juan Televario cuenta que en San Pedro la Laguna hay tres lugares encantados donde a la gente del pueblo le han pasado muchas cosas raras. Así, Las cazadores y leñadores deben presentar una ceremonia maya para evitar el sufrimiento como lo hizo Francisco en Pa chojoob'. "Un cuento misterioso del árbol matapalo" cuenta por qué no se debe cortar un árbol matapalo en un lugar encantado.

Como en muchas otras tradiciones folclóricas en todo el mundo, un tema popular en los cuentos mayas es la transformación. En la presente colección de cuentos, "Los *characotales*, una historia real," una mujer se convierte en gato y lidera una pandilla de otros *characotales* (una persona que puede transformarse en su nagual y hacer cosas malas) que son ladrones en la noche. In "Cuento: El rey y sus dos hijos," la hija mayor que se escapó de casa porque su padre era malo, transforma a sus propias hijas en tres mazorcas de maíz para evitar que los hombres del rey las encuentren. En "Cuento tz'utujil: La mujer que enterró al diablo," el diablo se transforma en un hombre con dientes de oro para engañar a una mujer que quiere casarse con un hombre con dietes de oro, pero también se convierte en otros animales, incluso en serpientes cuando quiere, y en madera. In "Cuento maya: Origen de la marimba," dos princesas convertían en árboles de diferentes tamaños, y en su follaje se podía puede oír la alegría de la marimba, el tambor, y la chirimía [flauta tradicional]. En "Cuento de la taltuza," cuando una persona mala muere, su alma reencarna en una taltuza (roedores similares a las ratas que perforan largos túneles en la tierra).

Como preludio de "El hombre que maltrató a su esposa," Pedro escribe, "Nuestros abuelos y abuelas nos dejaron [legaron] los cuentos. Para nosotros, es fascinante, pero para ellos era método de [dar] ejemplo a sus hijos e hijas; no utilizaron un trabajador social o un psicólogo. Como parte de la cultura maya, utilizaron los cuentos como método de orientación para sus hijos e hijas." Así, en esta historia se nos cuenta cómo el marido modifica su conducta para bien.

La orientación apropiada puede reforzar los proverbios que contienen sabiduría popular y que pueden incluirse en el cuento. Por ejemplo, al final de "Cuento tz'utujil: La mujer que enterró el diablo," Pedro, el narrador, relata que las abuelas y los abuelos decían "No hay que codiciar cosas porque todos los deseos malos tienen mal fin." Sin embargo, el narrador también puede dejar que el lector llegue a su propia conclusión.

Tal es el caso de "Cuento viejo: El tigre [jaguar] encantado" en que un hijo debe cuidar la sabiduría de su madre. En otras palabras, "El que oye consejo de viejo, llega a viejo [El que escucha el consejo de los viejos, vive para ser viejo]." También, "El cuento del Señor Sebastián Ujpán" advierte "Tus mentiras siempre te alcanzarán al final." En esta historia, un comisionado militar extorsionador sufre las consecuencias. Este cuento también demuestra el dicho: "Pagar con la misma moneda." En otras palabras, "Para conseguir tus postres justos, o para probar tu propia medicina." El "Cuento: El rey y sus dos hijas," debido a las demandas irrazonables del rey, ejemplifica el proverbio "No mires a los demás; mírate a ti mismo."

Los cuentos de esta colección relatan hechos históricos. Por ejemplo, "Cuento de la taltuza" nos enseña sobre el calendario maya. Y "El final del baile del venado" da cuenta de lo que significa este baile y cómo está desapareciendo entre las personas menores de 50 años. De forma similar, "El *aj-iitz* C'oxol: Una leyenda antigua" relata cómo los primeros españoles engañaron a los primeros mayas con su oro y plata que los antiguos mayas extraían de Xe K'istalin y en Chua Suj. Esta historia también cuenta cómo cuando el rey Tecún Umán estaba vivo, tenía un *aj-iitz* (brujo) poderoso llamada C'oxol.

Estes cuentos reflejan mucho sobre el hábitat natural, especialmente sus plantas y animales. Así, aprendemos de plantas como árboles de suj (suuj, sare, conacaste), manzanos, duraznos, perales, ciruelos, maíz, tecomates (guardia), bananas, injertos, anonas (injerto de anonas [manzanas de azúcar]), algodón, güisquil [una planta trepadora cuyo fruto es del tamaño de una naranja], zacate (hierba, yerba), aguacates, cafetales, bejucos, frijoles, calabaza de diferente tamaños, cañas, yucas, patatas dulces, limones, zarzas, hormigo árboles (no muy grande [son como unos arbustos]), y el matapalo árbol.

Nosotros también encontramos animales como tigres (jaguares), venados, perros, cerdos, ovejas, búhos, *cuta* (la culebra corta), culebras de tamaño regular, gallinas, ovejas, conejos, peces, cangrejos, mapaches, zarigüeyas, *pizotes* (parecido a los coatis), tepezcuinte (roedor marrón del tamaño de un conejo con rayas negras en el lomo), el andasolo (pizote *o coatí* de nariz blanca [especie: *Nasua narica*]), jabalíes, pavos, coyotes, monos, leones (leones de montaña), águilas halcón, abejas, zopilotes, lobos, hormigas, gatos de monte, y micoleones.

Además de plantas y animales en el hábitat natural, descubrimos en estos cuentos seres sobrenaturales. Por ejemplo, en "Cuento: La mujer del cazador," un hombre enano mágico, que es el señor de la montaña y los animales, castiga mágicamente a la mujer del cazador. Y en la historia "Caso: Francisco Sojuel avierte sobre huracán Stan," un anciano, vestido típicamente, resulta ser Francisco Sojuel, un personaje legendario, que mágicamente recorre las calles de cantón Panabaj advirtiendo a los habitantes del peligro de próximo huracán Stan.

Finalmente, muchos cuentos mayas son simplemente divertidos, y el lector puede disfrutarlos por derecho propio. Por ejemplo, hay humor en "Cuento tz'utujil: La mujer que enterró el diablo" cuando la mujer que sin saberlo se casa con el diablo porque tiene dientes de oro sin embargo se deshace de él. Otro cuento cómico de esta colección es "Cuento maya: El hombre que engaño la muerte." Por ejemplo, el hombre que usa su ingenio para evitar la muerte sique llamándola "vieja calva."

# Acknowledgments

My wife, Marilyn, has exercised her usual patience when I spent hours at my desk writing and when I sought her opinion on content and wording. Our son, Randall, gave me good legal advice. I should like to thank James Tate for the production of the map of the political boundaries and location of Lake Atitlán and the map of Lake Atitlán with surrounding towns and *aldeas* (villages). Also, I should like to thank the anonymous teacher who helped Pedro with the map of the places at the foot of the San Pedro volcano. For the present book, Pedro's grandson, Francys Cholotío, has been indispensable in my email communications with Pedro.

Also, I should like to thank two anonymous peer reviewers and four known ones—Fredy Rodríguez-Mejía, H. Russell Bernard, Paul Worley, and Liza Grandia—who each read the entire manuscript and gave me invaluable feedback for improving it. The book is much cleaner and readable because of their thoughtful remarks. And special thanks go to Michael Millman, our acquiring editor who kindly guided us through the acquisition process. Equally helpful was our copyeditor, Irina du Quenoy, and University of New Mexico Press editor Anna Pohlod.

Also, I want to thank Professor Clyde M. Woods, my doctoral chairman at UCLA, who inspired me to do my first season of fieldwork in San Juan la Laguna in 1970 and who is coauthor with me of two research articles on demography, development, and modernization in the fourteen Guatemalan towns surrounding Lake Atitlán.

Finally, I want to dedicate this book to the late Elaine Avila Jamison, my first Spanish teacher, who at the beginning of her career taught me three years of Spanish at South High, Bakersfield, California, and who later became the principal of the school for many years. She encouraged me to pursue the language. May she rest in peace.

# Agradecimientos

Mi esposa, Marilyn, ha ejercido su paciencia habitual cuando pasé horas en mi escritorio y cuando lepedí su opinión sobre el contenido y la redacción. Nuestro hijo, Randall, me dio buen asesoramiento legal. Quisiera agradecer a James Tate por la producción del mapa de los limites políticos y la ubicación del lago Atitlán y el mapa del lago Atitlán con los pueblos y aldeas circundantes. También, quiero agradecer al profesor anónimo que ayudó a Pedro con el mapa de los lugares al pié del volcán San Pedro. Para el presente libro, el nieto de Pedro, Francys Cholotío, ha sido indispensable en mis comunicaciones por correo electrónico con Pedro.

Me gustaría agradecer a dos revisores anónimos y a cuatro conocidos—Fredy Rodríguez-Mejía, H. Russell Bernard, Paul Worley y Liza Grandia—que leyeron el manuscrito completo y me brindaron comentarios invaluables para mejorado. El libro será mucho más claro y legible gracias a sus reflexivos comentarios. Y un agradecimiento especial a Michael Millman nuestro editor que amablementes nos guió través del proceso de adquisición. Igualmente servivcial fue nuestra correctora de estilo, Irina du Quenoy y editora Anna Pohlod.

También, quisiera agradecer al catedrático Clyde M. Woods, mi presidente doctoral en UCLA, quien me inspiró a hacer mi primera temporada de trabajo de campo en San Juan la Laguna en 1970 y quien es coautor conmigo de dos artículos de investigación sobre demografía, desarrollo, modernización en los catorce pueblos de Guatemala que rodean el lago Atitlán.

Finalmente, quiero dedicar este libro a la fallecida Elaine Avila Jamison, mi primera maestra de español en South High, Bakersfield, California, y quien luego se convirtió en la directora de la escuela durante muchos años. Ella me animó a seguir el idioma. Que descanse en paz.

# Introduction

*Pedro's Cultural and Historical Background to the Folktales*

## My life in the Community [November 21, 2015]

I am a 100 percent, Indigenous Tz'utujil born in this beautiful Mayan heritage town [of] San Juan la Laguna, situated on the bank of beautiful Lake Atitlán that adorns the beauty of this ancestral corner, a gift from the divine creator of the universe.

I want to recount in these pages and at the same time remember the services and works [that] I have served for free in the services and traditions that still are part of the Mayan culture, the foundation of our grandmothers and grandfathers. They said, "So that it is not forgotten, so that what we leave on earth does not disappear, if you children, grandchildren, and great-grandchildren follow our examples, our customs, our steps, our *costumbres* [rituals], and traditions, [and] put your feet in our footprints, only then will the life of our offspring flourish and we will be asking the Ajau God to take care of you when we are in the afterlife."

It is like this, we, their children, their grandchildren, and their great-grandchildren are fulfilling a duty of those who have already died. Their bodies are already in the ground; they are already dust; they are already ashes. But their teachings, their recommendations, [and] their advice continue. We too are going to die, but our children, our grandchildren, and our great-grandchildren will follow in our footsteps.

That was how I began to serve when I was sixteen years old. In October 1957, they called me at the Catholic church to tell me that I had to serve as third mayordomo [of the cofradía, religious brotherhood] of María Concepción.[1] I had to obediently say, "Yes."

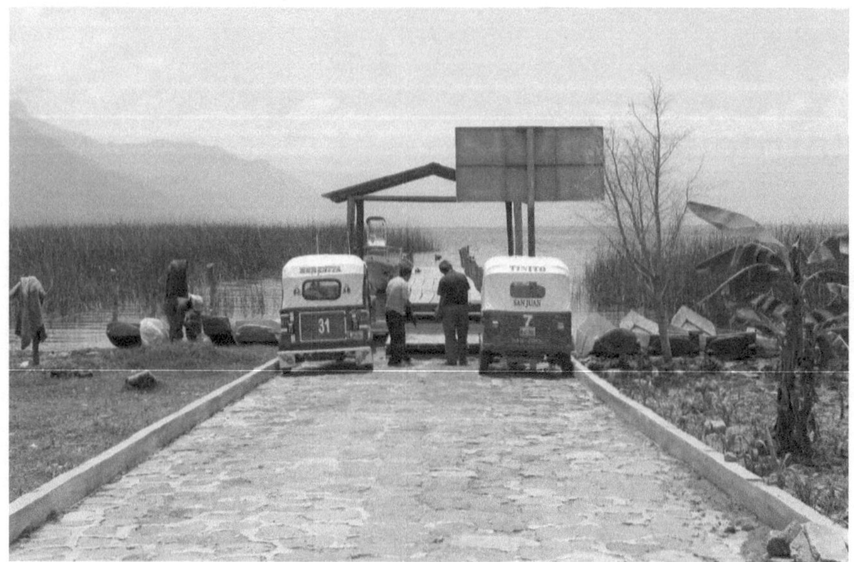


*Figure* 4. The dock in front of the road that leads up the hill to San Juan la Laguna / El muelle frente al camino que sube el cerro a San Juan

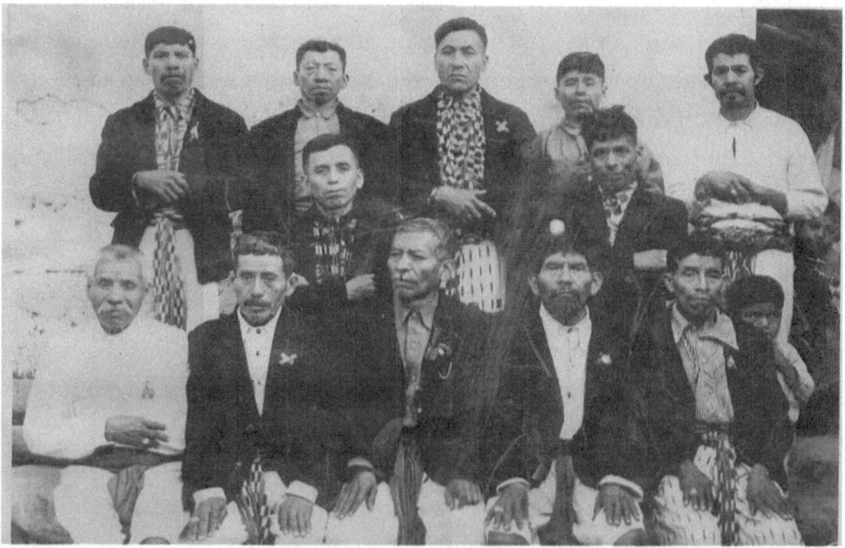

*Figure* 5. The *principales* of San Juan la Laguna in 1953 whom Pedro knew when he was a youngster. Standing in the middle of the top row (the tallest) is the brother of Pedro's grandfather, Pedro Cholotío Pérez. / Los principales de San Juan la Laguna en 1953 a quienes Pedo conoció cuando era joven. De pie en el medio de la fila superior (el más alto) está el hermano del abuelo de Pedro, Pedro Cholotío Pérez.

[In] 1960, the first of February, I was appointed alguacil [bailiff] of the municipality.[2] I was named third mayordomo of the cofradía of San Juan Bautista in 1965. I was named first mayordomo of the cofradía of Santo Domingo Guzmán in 1967. In the year 1982, I was named alcalde of the cofradía of Maria Concepción. In the year 1993, I was elected alcalde of the cofradía of San Juan Bautista.

In November 2000 I was elected as first *fiscal* [person in charge of the local Catholic church where there is no resident priest]. Each fiscal has five *sacristanes* [sacristans]. For the service of the church, the sacristans stay there sleeping to guard against thieves entering. Duties, or rather work of the fiscales [are] to take care of all the assets of the church—the images, ornaments that the priest uses when he celebrates Mass, the candlesticks that leave the interior of the church very clean, [and] to order the pews well.

The two fiscales are in charge of sweeping the site of the church twice a week, Wednesday and Sunday at four in the morning, and sprinkling with water and sweeping the patio and interior of the church. Thursdays of each week, the fiscal on duty prepares the embers for the censer at 12:00 p.m., [and] the exposition of the Blessed Sacrament at five in the afternoon, the Holy Mass. The fiscales are solely responsible for fixing the candlesticks on the altar before and after Masses. [Also] the fiscales are responsible for looking for and buying the pigeon leaves; we also call them flowers of the bouquets, which are used during Holy Week, mainly on Palm Sunday.

## Elected First *Principal*

At Sunday Mass, the parish priest, Bartholomew, published that on Saturday, August 14, 2014, "Pedro Cholotío Temó, was elected First *Principal* of the Catholic community, who will take office on August 30. The entire Catholic community is cordially invited to celebrate a solemn day with a procession in the main streets of the town." Many of the people were surprised when they heard my name because I myself said that I am not religious. Also, my family was surprised when it was announced in the church.

That's how I started to fix up the house, to change the doors and windows because the ones that I had now were rotten or moth-eaten. My family and I had to work a little hard. Before August 30, all was arranged and prepared. I arranged with my wife, Nicolasa, that *atol* [ritual corn drink] would be served to the entire Catholic community on the 30th for the reception.

The insignia of the first principal of the town as a sign of authority is a crucifix; or better said, a cross with the image of Jesus crucified [that] identifies him [the first principal] as an important and reliable person. The crucifix had remained in the house of the deceased, ex-first [principal], Cristóbal Cholotío Sumosa. At eight in the morning of this day, August 30, *principales* [elders], *cofrades* [members of the cofradías], catechists, mothers of families, mothers of the choir, and the Catholic community of the church went to the house of the deceased.

The family became sad. Crying, they gave the image of Jesús Crucificado to the hands of the principal, Pedro Pérez Mendoza. With prayers and songs, we headed toward the church, then the Holy Mass. During a pause, the parish priest called all of us elders for blessing with holy water, saying, "When you were young, you worked for the good of the community. Now that you are seniors, you are an example for the people. Keep going; don't falter."

After the Holy Mass, they gave me the distinguished badge that identifies me as the first principal of the Catholic community; I was praised with applause and hugs. In a solemn procession in the main streets of the town with the recitation of the Holy Rosary [and] religious hymns, all the principales of the town, with me carrying the Crucified Christ, [went] to my house. A block before, my wife went to receive us carrying a censer as a sign of welcome and respect for the Holy Christ.

There was a lot of people; there was not enough room in the house [for all of them]. They stayed in the patio and in the street. I welcomed everyone with pleasant words. Those present were grateful. Then they began to drink atol.

After all, the church board, cofrades, catechists, and principales appointed three, good-aged principales to accompany me to visit the sick and coordinate activities. But our primary duty is to visit Sacred Jesus, exposed in the Blessed Sacrament, three times a week: Monday from five to six in the afternoon; Thursday from seven to eight in the morning; Saturday from twelve to one in the afternoon, assisting in the celebration of Mass.

## The Corner Where I Live

All the Juanera and Pedrana people know and say the "corner of happiness" or "pleasant corner"; thus they call the corner where I live. My house is located on a corner of the canton, Xac'al. Holy Week, Corpus Christi, and the birth of John the Baptist on June 24th have been celebrated. Also, his death is remembered on August 29. And the Day of the Saints on November 1 and the Day of the Dead on November 2 of the same month have been honored, remembering those who were our parents and grandparents from whom we have inherited life.

We are only a few persons that still are conserving the costumbres and traditions. The cofrades are the most helpful in these fiestas. They are the ones who organize the processions. They put together the walks [paths around town], buy the flowers, and they are the ones who carry the images in the processions. They spend money on each fiesta; each cofradía is responsible. The cofradía of Santo Domingo Guzmán is responsible for all the expenses of Holy Week. The cofrades of San Juan Bautista are in charge of all the expenses during June 23–24, and also the 29th of August [the day of beheading of John the Baptist].

For forty years already it has been [that] Holy Wednesday, on the four corners of the town, in each corner an arch on the crossbar will carry fruit to receive the processions on Good Thursday and Friday with the images of Jesus of Nazareth and the Holy Burial; it was very respectful. Some thirty-five years ago, my family and I thought to make small rugs with a little sawdust and flowers. The shabby street we had to fill with dirt to decorate it a little. The people of the town saw that it was good, [and] with the passage of time, they began to form groups.

Thirteen years ago, after the streets were paved, the making of carpets was already a competition. Now in these times, San Juan is one of the towns of the Department of Sololá that follows Antigua in the elaboration of the best, well-designed rugs. We are the ones who started the carpets, very poorly for many years. The friends who helped us a lot were Jerónimo Quiacain, now dead, and Martin Vásquez, who is still alive but who is disabled because of an accident that happened in the capital of Guatemala.

The fiesta of Mary's Conception is celebrated December 8.[3] The procession is at night; [originally] my family and I were the only ones to receive the procession. We bought Chinese rocket bombs in honor of the Virgin Mary. Now in the last ten years, the reception of the image of Mary Conception has competed, as much or even more, with the lighting of color bombs throughout the town.

I don't know why this happens. The fiesta of the town is on June 23 and 24; that is to say, the nativity of Saint John the Baptist is celebrated. [But] the people of the

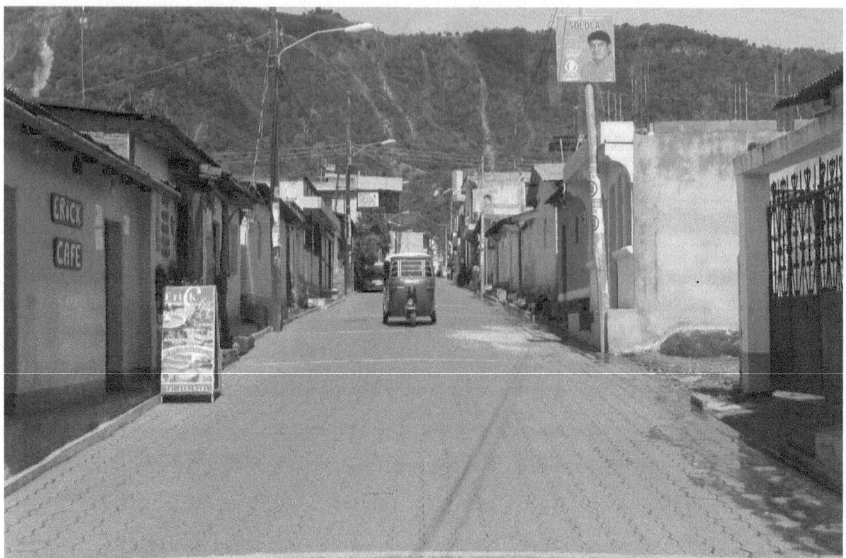


*Figure* 6. A street in San Juan la Laguna through which religious processions pass / Una calle de San Juan por la que pasan las procesiones religiosas

town don't celebrate it. That is to say, they don't want to spend their money—they spend it more on buying clothing and other things. Only my family is the one that gives a little joy [to the people]. We light bombs and rockets; at times we have a marimba play, but only a simple marimba to receive the image of Saint John the Baptist on his birthday. The rest of us present The Dance of the Mexicans [a humorous dance about how cowboys cheat a patron out of his cantina named Resbalón (Swindle) de Mexico and out of his young wife [see Sexton (1992b:151–53)].

I have a group of artists; or better said, a group of dancers. The boys are not all Juaneros; among the twenty-four dancers, three of San Pablo and two from San Pedro participate. I don't pay them. We rent the suits, plus [for] the food, they collaborate. The musicians earn 600 quetzales a day [one queztal was worth $0.13 US as of September 17, 2023]. My family and I spend a little money renting the suits—Q4,000 for five days. The Dance of the Mexicans leads the allegorical parade on June 22. It leaves from the place Xe cak'a; it keeps going around the town, finishing at the municipal football stadium.

But the most traditional and ancestral [practice] of the grandmothers and grandfathers is the bringing of the suits on June 20. The costumes are rented in

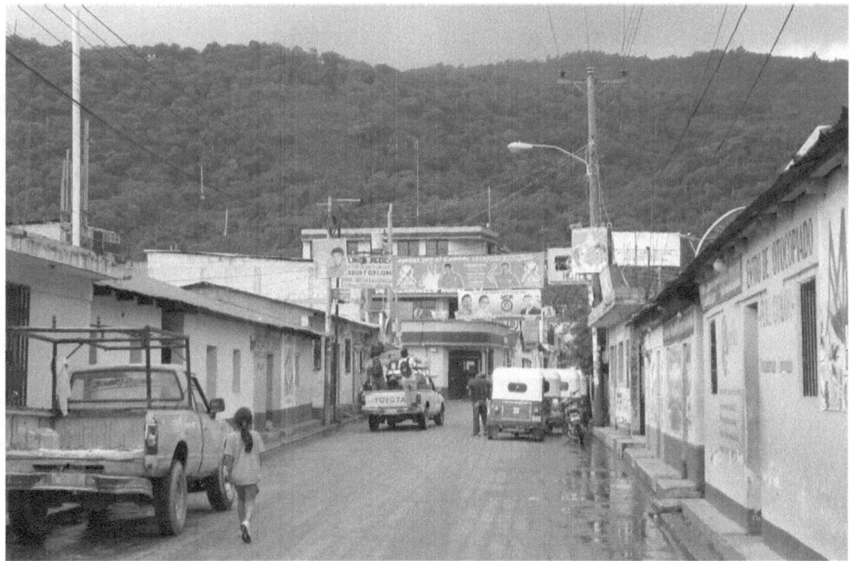

*Figure 7.* Another street scene in San Juan la Laguna / Otra escena callejera en San Juan

Santa Cruz del Quiché or in Chichicastenango; earlier they rented them in San Cristóbal or in Quetzaltenango. Because of custom and respect, they left and returned on foot, in order to go and to bring the suits.

Now, no, we bring it by transport; we hire minibuses. All the dancers go, and when we return in the afternoon of the same day, in Santa Clara all the dancers get off and come by foot down the K'istalin Hill, and when they reach the middle of the hill, there is a place called Chua Cruz. There is where all the dancers rest and begin to ignite bombs and rockets in signal that we are having a fiesta. When the people of the town hear the thunder of the bombs, they rejoice and meditate. [The dancers] begin to descend, and [the people] stand on the small plane to wait for the dancers—very happy. It looks very nice when the boys with their suitcases come down; when they arrive on the plain, many people receive us with applause and a handshake. You see the joy on the people's faces. So, we go around the town until [arriving at] the house where they wait for us.

Eight years ago, they called us to go to dance at the fiesta of San Pedro. The 29th of June, all went well. The people collaborated in paying the musicians and the dancers.

In 2014, they hired us to go to dance in Panajachel on October 3, the eve of the festival of Saint Francis of Assisi. We were hired by the Kaqchiquel Panajachelan Association. It was very crowded.

Also, in the year 2015, we went to present The Dance of the Mexicans. In the first year, they gave us Q6,000. In the second year, they gave Q8,000. With this money, I paid the musicians, transport, renting of suits, and the dancers' pay. We were well received by the foreign people, valuing the traditions of the Mayan people, [expressing] pride for my San Juan la Laguna. My passion is [their] joy, and my family and I want to live in good harmony with others.

It is certain that it is a little tiring, and it takes a little money. I, in the nights, teach the boys how to dance because each dancer has his own way of dancing. In other words, they call me the teacher of The Dance of the Mexicans. Some say that I have money; it is not true. Those who have money are the rich—they don't spend their money; they keep it in the banks [and] monopolize land and homesites. My family and I only have that desire to celebrate the fiestas. No one makes us. It is true that there is a majority of the people of the town who respect and appreciate us. There are people in my town and in San Pedro who tell me, "Don Pedro who will be the person in the town who is going to give us joy when you die," and I tell them, "I don't know."

Now, I am the first principal of the town. I have said many times I am not religious, only a man who does fear God. More for that reason, I respect other persons as equal men, women, and children. I have many young people who are my friends, and I appreciate them as they also appreciate me. We talk; I make certain recommendations to not fall in the vices of alcohol, drugs, and their consequences because they will be the builders of the society and the life of San Juan will depend on them. I have done this personally when there are meetings in the community. Three times on a television channel, Channel 10 of Secovisión, they invited me to talk for an hour, and sometimes they interview me about what life was like, the poverty of fifty, sixty years ago and how people respect each other.

Life is not always rosy and joy—sometimes it ends in sorrows and worries. One time six years ago on November 2 [All Souls' Day and the Day of the Dead], my family and I decided to brighten up the cemetery with five hours of marimba to remember our grandmothers and grandfathers. Then we hired those of the marimba Sonora Pedrana of Don Paulino Cortez Bixcul. After lunch, we went to the cemetery; those of the marimba set up their apparatus. At two in the afternoon, they began to play, finishing at seven in the evening. At three in the afternoon, my wife and children arrived. Not all the things end as one wishes. About ten minutes after my family arrived, one of my daughters began to bleed from the nose—but too much bleeding. The people said that it was a bad hour; others said that it was witchcraft. Well, we took her to Doctor Hernández [but] he could not contain the hemorrhage. The doctor sent us to the clinic. The doctor of the care center said, "It is very delicate; there is danger of death. We have to send her to the hospital of Sololá."

We tried to take her by launch, but very strong [was] the north wind; the boatmen did not dare [to go]. I asked the firemen to do the service for me. They told me the ambulance had malfunctions. Finally, they agreed to transfer Cándida Lesbia to the hospital of Sololá. At five in the afternoon, we left San Juan, leaving from the Hill of Santa Clara. Six kilometers before we arrived at the inter-American route [Pan American Highway], the motor of the ambulance stopped functioning. My situation was critical; the firemen communicated with the firemen of Nahualá. We waited more than an hour; it was the firemen of Nahualá who transported us to the national hospital of Sololá. We arrived at night and entered the emergency room. They told the patient that they had to saturate some of her veins, which became detached inside her nose; she remained in the hands of the doctors.

That day I no longer remembered the party or the marimba. My wife was the one who paid the head of the marimba. That's why I say not all the time it goes as well as one wants.

There is a saying: "Uno comienza cantando, termina llorando" [You begin singing, and end up crying].

In the month of May of the year 2016, my wife and I went to Chichcastenango to see the suits of The Dance of the Mexicans. The owner of the *morería* [workshop in which costumes and implements are made and rented for the "Moorish" and "conquest"[dances (Armas 1971:143)] is Señor Manuel Buchan. We negotiated and agreed that the twenty-four costumes would be given to me for Q4,000 on June 20, to be returned on July 5, with a commitment that the costumes are going to be first class. [During the titular fiesta of San Juan, dancers reenact Pedro Alvarado's slaying of King Tecún Umán (Sexton 1992b:97–115).]

One time I spoke by telephone with Dr. Jaime Sexton, and I asked him for financial help for my fiesta, or better said, the fiesta of San Juan Bautista. The señor sent me electronically $300 to Banco Agro Mercantil en Panajachel. Two Juanero friends offered me financial help; I told them thanks a lot. My friend Bruno Cholotío gave me Q900, and my friend José Vásquez Ujpán gave me Q250.

Monday, June 20 arrived [and] we hired a truck [and] we went to Chichcastenango to get the costumes, but before, we ate breakfast in front of the Clavario. Some did not bring breakfast [but] my wife had a lot of food and tortillas, and everyone ate.

[At] one in the afternoon, we left Chichicastenango; going back, we passed through Santa Clara [and] beyond the town, all the dancers got off the truck. They came on foot down the K'istalin Hill. With my wife and other elders, we came in the truck to meet on the plain. In Chua Cruz, they lit the bombs; the echo of bombs was well heard. On the cab of the truck, we placed a loudspeaker with the music of The Dance of the Mexicans; many people arrived at the foot of the hill to receive the boys, with firemen, civil national police, municipal police, sounding the siren as a sign of joy. We did the turns in the street of the town until arriving at my house, where they were waiting for us.

The 21st of June 2016, during the night of this day, we celebrated a small ceremony [that] the ancestors called Mother Earth. That is done so that when it comes time to present the dance, everyone is out of danger. In this matter, I am in charge of celebrating the ceremony, or custom. Each one brings two or three candles and a little incense. The one who celebrates the ceremony calls them by their names and puts each one on their knees until they are all finished. This job takes three hours. Those who say they are Mayan priests charge Q600 to do this kind of custom. I do not deal with a Mayan priest or shaman; [I am] only a campesino [countryman]. But when I want, I do my costumbres. We all have the mouth [pleasure] to adore God and the Santo Mundo [Holy World]. Because of the great mercy, there has been no problem with the dancers.

The 22nd of June, we presented the dance, leading the allegorical parade, leaving the gas station [and] ending at the municipal soccer stadium.

The 23rd and 24th of June, they danced on the street near my house. And they finished the 1st and 2nd of July. By the way, all is cheerful, but it takes time and money. But when there is a will, everything is possible.

## The Life of Pedro [April 2018]

Grief and sadness even make you want to cry when you remember what the time was like before. Those who were born in the years 1940 through 1960 [remember it as] a time of suffering and extreme poverty, more among us indigenes.

I remember very well, as if it were the present, when I was a child. The worst was that I did not grow up with my parents. My adoptive parents treated me poorly. They hit me a lot; they drank a lot of aguardiente [firewater, cane liquor]; at night they left to drink; I followed them, crying. It was very cold; I couldn't sleep. At times they remained sleeping in the cantina. I was very afraid to go to the house; it was dark; there was no electricity in the town.

[Because] I grew up in extreme poverty, I walked barefoot without *caites* [typical leather sandals]. They ordered me to water a half-cuerda of *tomatal* [tomato plants] on the shore of the lake. They woke me up at five in the morning; it was very cold. My fingers froze and remained motionless; my feet bare. It's a pity that I had no remedy; my toes remained immobile. It's a pity that I had no choice but to keep my toes immobile. For the great cold, I had no more than the shirt I wore; that is to say, I didn't even have a *chumpa* [jacket that covers to the waist] or object to cover me from the cold.

It is certain I am not lying, in the year 1958, when I was mayordomo of the brotherhood of María Concepción, I walked barefoot. At that time, the only person who had caites was the justice of peace. To the last mayordomo, we all walked barefoot. [See note 1.]

In the year 1960, when I was alguacil [bailiff] of the municipality, I walked barefoot. The only persons who used caites were the alcalde and some regidores [councilors]. The guards and alguaciles—all barefoot. The auxiliary mayors and attendants who came from the three aldeas [villages], Pasajquim, Panyebar, and Palestina—all barefoot. At that time, it was not strange to see barefoot persons.

A pair of sandals extracted from old tires that they brought from far away cost Q0.25 [twenty-five centavos]. A pair of sandals with leather straps cost Q0.50 [fifty centavos], and the best ones a quetzal.

One time when I was fourteen years old, my uncle Agustín told me he was going [to] buy me some sandals. I [was] very content when the merchant arrived; he was from Santa Lucía Utatlán. The señor carried a lot of them at different prices. Then I tried on a pair of sandals to see if they fit well. The merchant asked 35 centavos. My uncle offered him only 25 centavos. I was left disappointed. I took off the sandals and had to return them to the seller.

When he sent me to school, he did not give me a single centavo; nothing to buy a fruit. There was no money. Some of my companions had enough to buy some sweets or fruit. Well, I was a very clever child; then I retained what the teacher taught me. My classmates did get it right. I helped them with their homework, and they gave me five centavos. I felt very content [because] then I was able to buy some fruit to eat at recess.

In comparison, now the children do not receive five quetzals. They say with five quetzals, you cannot buy a refreshment. The times have changed a lot. Now, you do not see boys and girls barefoot in the streets. Now, the children [are] well shod.

When I grew up, it was a time of extreme poverty. I used patched shirts and typical pants with many patches. Almost everyone of my age suffered, not because the parents did not want to buy clothing and shoes for their children but because it was a time when there was no money.

It was also the same with the women, the ladies and the girls; they all walked barefoot. Some others used caites. The muchachas and young men of that time went to sell tomatoes and onions in Santa Lucía Utatlán, in Santa Clara la Laguna. They climbed the paths of Cerro K'istalín barefoot, without sandals. Also, they wore patched clothing.

The grandparents explained [that] the poverty of the town was because the dictatorial presidents like Manuel Estrada Cabrera and General Ubico [who] sent many *Juaneros* [people of San Juan] to fulfill the macabre commandment on the coastal farms. The grandparents said that some *Pedranos* [people of San Pedro] usurped the lands of the Juaneros when they fulfilled the commandment to work on the coastal farms. A mayor and a syndic were bribed by the Pedranos. They signed documents in favor of the Pedranos; that is where the natives of the town were dispossessed. The one who was the mayor was Domingo Yojcom and the syndic was Lucas Monroy. The grandparents said that Domingo Yoycom was assassinated on a Saturday of Glory in a place called Xac'al when this man went to San Pedro with his friend Adinerudos. On the road, they killed him. They say that most of the people of San Juan were happy at the death of that man.

It's sad; it [brings up a] lot of feeling to tell my life of before; barefoot, I finished [being] alguacil in 1960. And barefoot, I went to the barracks of the Fourth Military Zone in Mazatenango. There's where they gave me shoes to wear. [Not] until then did my feet feel a little comfortable. After military service, [not] until then was I able to buy plastic shoes because I did not have money to buy leather shoes. Now that I am old, I suffer from calluses on the insoles of my feet. That is to say, since childhood, my feet were cracked; they left me crippled. My defect [is] that I cannot wear socks or tight shoes, but I have been suffering this since I was young. It was due to maltreatment and extreme poverty.

I also want to say a little bit about daily eating when I was a child, suffering a lot. Many times, I ate only twice daily. I remember very well with my Aunt Juana, [with whom] I grew up. She crushed green plantains. She put them to grind with a little nixtamal [corn cooked in lime or ash water] and with that she took out the tortillas, and we ate them with salt. Other times with my Aunt Juana, we went to San Pedro [where] she sold small fish and crabs in the houses of the Pedranos. Often the women did not have money to pay [us]. Instead they gave us tortillas and little tamales. My Aunt Juana carried salt, and we got down to eat where there were not many houses and the people could not see us; that is to say, so that the people did not realize that we went hungry. That is what is called suffering.

At the age of sixteen, I separated from them. My Aunt Juana died on December 16, 1968, fifty years ago. My Uncle Agustín died in the year 1978. With them I grew up.

In the name of God All-powerful with his power, he has created all the things that exist on Earth. The human being was created by God, but first nature was created so that the living being could enjoy the plenitude that existed on Earth. The human being is the addition that beautifies nature with its art, such as painting, music, dance, weaving, games, fishing, [and] stories. As well, the campesino embellishes nature with the greenery of crops, such as corn, beans, coffee, and vegetables, and much more. Being a campesino is to suffer a little because the campesino works under the sun and sometimes under the rain, but he is very happy when he is accustomed to it. In my very personal case, I am not able to work in the shade, but when working under the sun, my body feels very relaxed, working very happily.

Many times, I begin to think and say blessed are those who studied because they were able to learn more and possess a lot of knowledge. But then I step back and say thanks to God for life. While there is life, the human being is able to do or search for how to be able to live even though it be [just] a (small) crumb. I am a man experienced in cultivating corn, beans, and coffee, and vegetables; that you do not learn in school or in the university—you learn [by] working the land. Also, you learn by watching others working [and] cultivating the land. It is more like a legacy of the grandparents to their children and grandchildren.

The same thing happens with my wife Nicolasa. She did not go to school; she does not know letters, nor is she able to speak the Spanish language. She only speaks our native language, which is Tz'utujil. She is a teacher of designs of typical weavings. She possesses much [more] knowledge than the other women. What I am writing is true. Nicolasa, my wife, was working many years in an association, Artisans of San Juan. She is a weaver warper of new designs. But in the association, many women were exploited, [and] my wife had to leave. Now, she works for herself. She sells her waist fabrics [such as fajas, which are cloth belts and sashes] woven in San Juan on backstrap looms and foot looms [(Sexton 1992a:123–37; Sexton 2001:212–23)]. What I am writing are things of life.

## My Life in the Tz'utujil Community

As I always have said and continue saying, I am a poor man, of the poor class. I only have some *cuerdas* [.178 acre each] of coffee. Moreover, I grow corn and beans. I have a small apiary of bees that produces some hundred pounds of honey. With that, my wife and I spend our lives. Extremely poor I am not. I have enough to eat. At times money is scarce, but little by little, we are getting through it. I am a very serene person. I don't like to get angry with anyone. I am sincere and do not like to lie.

I don't have a vice of money; I don't like tobacco. I know I had an alcoholic illness. By the great blessing of God, the hand of Alcoholics Anonymous helped me a lot—it freed me from alcoholism. In the year 1976, I joined Alcoholics Anonymous, which [had] recently arrived in San Juan.

The founders of AA were Señores Lorenzo Pérez Gonzáles, Lorenzo Gonzáles Chavajay, and Juan Gonzáles Matzar, may they rest in peace. They established the group, "Eighth of July," in San Pedro la Laguna, their hometown. And later they founded the group of "Alcoholics Anonymous: San Juan Bautista" in San Juan, my town. I joined with AA after it had been [around for] a few months.

I believe it is the pride that existed in me that made me lose [my way]. I went around with friends who liked to drink, and I went around with them at night. At times, I drank fruit juices or sodas, and carelessly and foolishly I relapsed. When I felt it, I was already drunk. It was a great struggle; in fifteen years I had four relapses. From there, I didn't attend the AA group for nine years. I was not violent or a fighter. From time to time, I lost consciousness; I was a drunk respected by other drunks. My wife told me, "Pedro, have a little shame; you shouldn't get drunk. The people of the town take notice."

Well, I thought a lot about what my wife said. It is true. It is certain I am not a drunk who begs for a drink. No, occasionally, I drank, but it affected my health. I thought a lot about my life. I am already [an] old-timer; my age is going [advancing]. Moreover, the people of the town always have respect for me. I said up to here, [no more liquor]. In the year 2000, I joined Alcoholics Anonymous "Camino a la Felicida" [Road to Happiness]. By the grace of God and my fellow companions of Alcoholics Anonymous, until today, I have not drunk.

I have said many times, we are a pair of poor spouses. The truth is we do not have the means to give a gift to one of our godchildren. The people of the town respect us; they appreciate us; they give us prestige. I have a history and good references in my town.

We have been godparents of the following persons, of baptisms and confirmation, religious acts that are celebrated within the Catholic community: [Here Pedro provides a list of twenty-two people from all walks of life, including a teacher, nurse, student, housewife, accountant, and a police officer.]

With my wife, we have had the greatest gift that Lord Almighty and Mother Earth, or Mother Nature, gave us. We have twenty-two godchildren. In each community, there are different cultures; more than anything, among the Indigenous people, the foundation of the culture of the people is respect.

When a boy or a girl wishes to marry, under the jurisdiction of law, or uniting thus voluntarily, the parents of the couple—that is to say, the father of the man—searches for an honest and respectful godfather of the marriage.

Now when they [the couple] join [marry] this way voluntarily, they always look for a person like a witness and counselor who can help them with ideas and advice, so that that union will be durable until death separates them; so too, with the father of the woman, he has to look for a witness or representative. The two witnesses communicate with the couple; they ask them if they really love each other. The couple answers that they indeed love each other until death. The witnesses, or representatives of the two families, are in charge of giving them useful recommendations in order to have a good life both in poverty, joys, and illnesses. Be careful not to waste money and to work hard, because in time they will be parents of their own children.

I have participated many times in many families, in many homes, in this kind of cultural event, always accompanied by my wife. [Out of] respect and custom, the man has to be accompanied by his wife.

[I have participated] as a witness and honorable representative of the parents of these couples who have united voluntarily: [here, Pedro lists thirty-eight couples.]

## The Coronavirus

I want to tell you something of the Coronavirus in Guatemala. Also, it is called COVID-19.

Before the arrival of the coronavirus in Guatemala, it was heard on the radio and seen on television that in an Asian country, there is serious contagion of a disease that attacks many people around the world. The truth is that we, the Mayas, did not believe it, but in the month of March 2020, the situation became grave.

It is said that the coronavirus arrived in Guatemala. It was [brought to] an international airport, La Aurora, by a person from South America. There appeared the coronavirus in the country.

We suffered a lot; the government declared a curfew throughout the country from Monday to Friday from four in the afternoon until six in the morning the following day. Saturday, two in the afternoon and all day Sunday, no one was able to leave the house until Monday at six in the morning. They closed the schools, put chains on the doors of the churches. The price of products increased. The rich guarded their products, and there was no communication with neighboring ports. They suspended the transport of passengers. [The women were given] two hours to go to the market to shop, and ten had to leave before ten could enter, two times a week.

We have reached a difficult time [July 22, 2020], but that is worldwide; the coronavirus pandemic is raging in many countries, also in Guatemala, thousands of people infected. Many people have died. In San Juan many people have been in quarantine, but none of coronavirus. It is true in San Juan: people have died of common diseases.

We have not been able to leave the municipality since March, nor can we go to the market. [By] order of the president of the Republic: Children and the elderly cannot leave, because it is easier for them to spread the pandemic. If we win the battle against the coronavirus, I will tell you how the Mayas are cured.

I want to tell you [October 1, 2021] that in the town many people got sick in the months of July, August, and September. It was middle of the COVID-19 pandemic. Indeed, Juaneros died, but [there were] many [of] those who won the battle.

Now, my family and I are alive and all vaccinated. I indeed have problems with my health. I suffer from arthritis in my hands. I am not able to sleep peacefully. The truth, I am not bedridden, but my arms and wrists hurt.

My family and I are alive [June 19, 2022] by the great will of God, despite the pandemic. Yes, we have gotten sick with flu, headache, cold and cough, but we have cured ourselves with natural medicine.

The pandemic, or coronavirus, has affected the world; many people in Guatemala have died. In San Juan, only four persons have died; it is certain many Juanero people have become ill, but they have managed to recover through natural remedies both for bathing and for drinking. Indeed, they [the remedies] have worked.

The Mayas do not want to go to the hospital, because they say they isolate and abandon them; it is not the same as being at home. At home, they take care of them; they give them hot things to drink. There is a lot [of] difference—the body of the Indigenous people is a bit resistant. It can be cured with home remedies. Later, I will send you a sheet with the name of the natural remedies, [and] how to do it. We who are not infected are also taking our natural remedy.

# La introducción

*Antecedentes culturales e históricos de Pedro en los cuentos*

## Mi Vida en la comunidad [21 de noviembre de 2022]

Soy un tz'utujil 100/00 indígena nacido en este hermoso pueblo, herencia maya [de] San Juan la Laguna, situado en la orilla del hermoso lago de Atitlán que adorna la belleza de este rincón ancestral, un regalo del divino creador del universo.

Quiero relatar en estas hojas y recodar a la vez los servicios y trabajos [que] sí he servido gratuitamente en los servicios y tradiciones que todavía forma parte de la cultura maya, la fundación de las abuelas y abuelos. Ellos dijeron "Para que no se olvida; para que no se desaparezca lo que nosotros dejamos en la tierra; si ustedes hijos, nietos, y bisnietos sigan nuestros ejemplos, nuestros pasos, nuestras costumbres [rituales], y tradiciones, [y] pongan sus pies en nuestras huellas, solo así florecerá la vida de nuestros retoños [descendencias] y nosotros estaremos pidiendo al Ajau Dios, por ustedes cuando estemos en el más allá."

Es así, nosotros, sus hijos, sus nietos, y sus bisnietos estamos cumpliendo un deber de los que ya han muerto. Sus cuerpos ya están en la tierra; ya son polvo; ya son ceniza. Pero sus enseñanzas, sus recomendaciones, [y] sus consejos siguen. Nosotros también nos vamos a morir, pero se quedarán nuestros hijos, nuestros nietos, y nuestros bisnietos seguirán nuestras huellas.

Era así yo comencé a servir cuando tenía 16 años. En octubre de 1957, me llamaron en la iglesia católica para decirme que yo tenía que servir como tercer mayordomo de [la cofradía] de María Concepción.[1] Yo tuve que aceptar con obediencia decir, "Sí."

[En] 1960 el 1 de enero fui nombrado alguacil de la municipalidad.[2] Fui nombrado tercer mayordomo de la cofradía de San Juan Bautista en 1965. Fui nombrado primer mayordomo de la cofradía de Santo Domingo Guzmán en el año 1967. En el año 1982, fui nombrado alcalde de la cofradía de María Concepción. En el año 1993, fui elegido alcalde de la cofradía de San Juan Bautista.

En noviembre 2.000, fui elegido como fiscal primero [persona a cargado de la iglesia católica local donde no hay sacerdote residente]. Cada fiscal tiene cinco sacristanes. Para el servicio de la iglesia, los sacristanes allá se quedan durmiendo para que no entran los ladrones. Deberes, o vale más decir trabajo de los fiscales, [son] cuidar todos los bienes de la iglesia—las imágenes, ornamentos que usa el sacerdote cuando celebra la misa, las candeleras que dejen bien limpia el interior de la iglesia, [y] ordenar bien las bancas.

Los dos fiscales son los encargados de barrer el sitio de la iglesia dos veces por semana, miércoles y domingo a las cuatro de la mañana, y regar con agua y barrer el patio y el interior de la iglesia. Los días jueves de cada semana, el fiscal de turno prepara las brasas para el incensario las 12 p.m., [y] la exposición del santísimo las cinco de la tarde, la santa misa. Los fiscales son los únicos responsables de arreglar las candeleras en el altar antes y después de las misas. [También] los fiscales son los responsables de comprar y buscar las hojas de paloma; también las llamamos flores de los ramos, que se utiliza en la Semana Santas, principalmente el Domingo de ramos.

## Elegido Primer Principal

En la misa dominical, el párroco Bartolomé publicó que el día sábado 14 de agosto, "Fue elegido Pedo Cholotío Temó Primer Principal de la comunidad católica, el cual tomará posesión el 30 de agosto. Toda la comunidad católica está cordialmente invitada va hacer un día solemne con una procesión en las principales calles de la población." Mucha de la gente se sorprendió cuando oyeron mi nombre porque yo mismo decía que no soy religioso. También, mi familia se sorprendido cuando fue anunciado en la iglesia.

Así fue comencé a arreglar la casa, a cambiar las puertas y ventanas porque las que teníamos ya estaban podridlas o apolilladas. Tuvimos que trabajar un poco fuerte con la familia. Antes del 30 de agosto, todo está arreglado y preparado. Arreglamos con Nicolasa, mi esposa, que *atol* [bebida ritual de maíz] sería servido a toda la comunidad católica el día 30 para el recibimiento.

El insigne del primer principal del pueblo como señal de autoridad es un crucifijo; o vale más decir, una cruz con la imagen de Jesús crucificado [que] lo [el primer principal] identifica como persona importante y confiable. El Crucifico se había quedado en la casa del ex premier [principal] difunto, Cristóbal Cholotío Sumosa. Las ocho de la mañana de este día, 30 agosto, principales, cofrades, catequistas, madres de familia, madres del coro, y la comunidad católica de la iglesia nos dirigimos a la casa del difunto.

La familia se puso triste. Llorando, entregaron la imagen de Jesús Crucificado en manos del principal, Pedro Pérez Mendoza. Con oraciones y cantos, nos dirigimos hacia la iglesia, luego la Santa misa. En una pausa, el párroco nos llamó a todos nosotros los principales para bendición con el agua bendita diciendo: "Cuando eran jóvenes trabajaron en bien de la comunidad. Ahora que eres ancianos, eres un ejemplo para el pueblo. Sigan adelante; no desmayen."

Después de la Santa misa, me entregaron el insigne que me identifica como primer principal de la comunidad católica; fui elogiado con aplausos y abrazos. En una procesión solemne en las principales calles de la población con el rezo del Santo Rosario [y] himnos religiosos, todos los principales del pueblo, conmigo yo llevando a Cristo Crucificado, [fueron] a mi casa. Una cuadra antes, mi esposa nos fue a recibir llevando incensario en señal de bienvenida y respeto al Santo Cristo.

Había mucha gente; no había [bastante] lugar en la casa [para todas]. Se quedaron en el patio y en la calle. Yo les di la bienvenida a todos con palabras agradables. Los presentes quedaron muy agradecidos. Luego ellos comenzaron a tomar atol.

Después de todo, la directiva de la iglesia, cofrades, catequistas y principales nombraron a tres principales de buena edad para que me acompañen a visitar a los enfermos y coordinar las actividades. Pero nuestro deber primordial, es visitar a Jesús Sacramentado, expuesto en el Santísimo Sacramento, 3 veces por semana: lunes 5 a 6 de la tarde, jueves 7 a 8 de la mañana, sábado 12 a 1 de la tarde, asistir en celebración de la misa.

## La esquina donde yo vivo

Toda la gente Juanera y Pedrana, conocen y dice la esquina de la alegría o esquina alegre; así le dicen la calle donde yo vivo; mi casa está ubicado en una esquina del cantón, Xac'al. Se ha celebrado la Semana Santa, el Corpus Christi, y nacimiento de Juan Bautista el 24 de junio. También, se recuerda su muerte el 29 de agosto. Y se ha honrado el Día de los Santos el 1 de noviembre y el Día de los Difuntos el 2 de noviembre, recordando nuestros padres y abuelos de quienes hemos heredado la vida.

Somos pocas las personas que todavía estamos conservando las costumbres y tradiciones. Los cofrades son los más serviciales en estas fiestas. Ellos son los que organizan las procesiones. Arman las andas [caminos alrededor de la ciudad], compran las flores, y ellos son los que llevan las imágenes en las procesiones. Gastan dinero en cada fiesta; cada cofradía es responsable. La cofradía de Santo Domingo de Guzmán es responsable de todos los gastos de la Semana Santa. Los cofrades de San Juan Bautista se encargan de todos los gastos durante los días 23 y 24 de junio, y también el 29 de agosto [el día de la decapitación de Juan el Bautista].

Hace unos cuarenta años pasado, [que] el miércoles Santo en las cuatro esquinas del pueblo, se preparaba en cada esquina un arco en el travesaño se llevara de frutas para recibir las procesiones del jueves y viernes Santo con las imágenes de Jesús Nazareno y el Santo entierro era de mucho respeto. Hace unos 35 años, con mi familia pensamos a formar pequeñas alfombras con poco de serrín y flores. La calle ruin teníamos que rellenar con tierra para adornar un poco la calle. La gente del pueblo vio era bueno [y] con el correr del tiempo comenzaron a formar grupos. Hace 13 años pasado, después que adoquinaron las calles, ya es una competencia la elaboración de alfombras. Ahora en estos tiempos, San Juan es uno de los pueblos del departamento de Sololá que le sigue Antigua Guatemala en la elaboración de las mejores alfombras bien diseñadas. Nosotros son los que comenzamos con las alfombras muy pobremente por muchos años. Los amigos que nos ayudaron mucho fueron Jerónimo Quiacain, ya murió, y Martín Vásquez, que ahora vive todavía, pero con discapacidad por un accidente que tuvo en la capital de Guatemala.

La fiesta de María Concepción se celebra el 8 de diciembre.[3] La procesión es por la noche; nosotros con mi familia éramos los únicos en recibir la procesión. Comprábamos cohetillos bombos chinas en honor a la Virgen María. Ahora, en estos últimos diez años, el recibimiento de la imagen de María Concepción es una competencia, tanto, o mucho, de la iluminación de bombas de colores en toda la población.

No sé porque pasa esto. La fiesta del pueblo es del 23 al 24 de junio; es decir, se celebra la natividad de San Juan Bautista. [Pero] la gente del pueblo no lo celebra. Es decir, no quieren gastar su dinero—lo gastan más en comprar ropa y otras cosas. Solamente mi familia es la que da un poco de alegría o. Quemamos bombas y cohetillos; hay veces ponemos marimba; pero solamente marimba sencilla para recibir la imagen de San Juan Bautista en su día de cumpleaños. Nosotros otros presentamos el Baile de los Mexicanos [un baile humorístico sobre cómo los vaqueros engañan a un patró n de su cantina llamada Resbalón de México y de su joven esposa [vea Sexton (1992b:151–53)].

Tengo un grupo de artistas; o vale más decir, un grupo de bailadores. Los muchachos no todos son Juaneros; entre los 24 bailadores, participaron tres de San Pablo y dos de San Pedro. No les pago. Nosotros alquilamos los trajes, más [para] la alimentación, ellos colaboran. Los músicos cobran 600 quetzales por día [una queztal valía .13 dólares estadounidenses el 17 de septiembre de 2023]. Con mi familia gastamos un poco de dinero el alquiler de los trajes—4,000 quetzales por cinco días. El Baile de los Mexicanos encabeza el desfile alegórico el 22 de junio. Sale del lugar Xe cak'a; sigue dando la vuelta alrededor del pueblo, terminando en el estadio municipal de futbol.

Pero lo más tradicional y ancestral [prática] de las abuelas y abuelos es la traída del traje el 20 de junio. Los trajes se alquilan en Santa Cruz del Quiché o en Chichicastenango; más antes los alquilaban en San Cristóbal o en Quetzaltenango. Por costumbre y respeto se iban y se regresaban a pie, para ir a traer y devolver los trajes.

Ahora, no, ya lo traemos en transporte; contratamos microbuses. Todos los bailadores se van, y cuando regresamos por la tarde de este día, en Santa Clara se bajan todos los bailadores y se vienen a pie bajando el cerro K'istalin, y cuando llegan a media cuesta, hay un lugar que se llama Chua Cruz. Allí, es donde se descansan todos los bailadores y comienzan a quemar bombas y cohetillos en señal que estamos de fiesta. Cuando la gente del pueblo oye los truenos de las bombas se alegran y meditan. [Los bailadores] comienzan a bajar, y [la gente] se pone en la pequeña planicie para esperar a los bailadores—muy alegre. Se ve bien bonito cuando los muchachos con sus maletas vienen bajando; cuando llegan en el plano, mucha gente nos recibe con aplausos y un apretón de mano. Se mira la alegría en el rostro de las personas. Así, damos la vuelta en el pueblo hasta llegar a] la casa donde nos esperan.

Hace ocho años, nos llamaron para ir a bailar en la fiesta de San Pedro

Apostal. El 29 de junio, todo fue bien. La gente colaboró en pagar a los músicos y los bailadores. En el año de 2014, contrataron para ir a bailar en Panajachel el día 3 de octubre, la víspera de la fiesta de San Francisco de Asís. Fuimos contratados por la asociación Kaqchiquel Panajachelense; fue muy concurrida.

También, en el año 2015 fuimos a presentar El baile de los mexicanos. En el primer año nos dieron 6,000 Quetzales. En el segundo año, nos dieron Q8,000. Con ese dinero, pagué a los músicos, transporte, alquiler de traje, y el pago de los bailadores. Fuimos bien recibidos por la gente extranjera, valorando las tradiciones de la gente maya, [expresando] orgullo para mi pueblo San Juan la Laguna. Mi pasión es [sus] alegría; queremos con mi familia vivir con buena armonía con los demás.

Es cierto que es un poco cansado y quiere un poco dinero. Yo por las noches, les enseño a los muchachos como se baila porque cada bailador tiene su forma de bailar. En otras palabras, me dicen el maestro del baile de mexicanos. Algunos dicen que yo tengo dinero; no es cierto. Los que tienen dinero son los ricos—ellos no gastan su dinero; lo guardan en los bancos [y] acaparan terrenos y sitios. Con mi familia, solamente tenemos esa voluntad de celebrar las fiestas. Ninguno nos obliga. Es cierto que hay una mayoría de la gente del pueblo nos respetan y nos aprecian. Hay personas de mi pueblo y de San Pedro me dicen, "Don Pedro quien será la persona que nos va a dar alegría en el pueblo cuando usted se muera," y yo les digo, "No se."

Ahora, yo soy el primer principal del pueblo. He dicho muchas veces yo no soy religioso, solamente un hombre que sí siente temor a Dios. Más por eso, yo respeto a las personas como igual hombres, mujeres, y niños. Tengo muchos jóvenes que son mis amigos, y yo los aprecio como también ellos me aprecian. Conversamos con ellos; les doy ciertas recomendaciones para no caer en los vicios del alcohol, las drogas, y sus consecuencias porque ellos serán los constructores de la sociedad y de ellos dependerá la vida de San Juan. Esto lo he hecho personalmente cuando hay reuniones en la comunidad. Tres veces a través de un canal de televisión, canal 10 de Secovisión, me invitan para hablar por una hora y a veces me entrevista a cerca como era la vida, la pobreza de hace cincuenta, sesenta años y como se respeta la gente.

La vida no todo el tiempo es color de rosas y las alegrías—a veces se termina en penas y preocupaciones. Una vez hace 6 años pasados una fecha 2 de noviembre [Todo el Día de Almas y El Día de los Muertos], con mi familia decidimos alegrar el cementerio con cinco horas de marimba como para recordar a nuestros abuelas y abuelos. Entonces contratamos a los de la marimba Sonora Pedrana de don Paulino Cortez Bixcul. Después del almuerzo, nos fuimos al cementerio; los de la marimba instalaron sus aparatos. A las dos de la tarde, comenzaron a tocar para terminar a las siete de la noche. A las tres de la tarde, llegaron mi esposa y mis hijas. No todas las cosas terminan como uno quiere. Unos diez minutos después de que llegara mi familia, una de mis hijas le comenzó a salir sangre en la nariz—pero demasiado hemorragia. La gente decía que era una mala hora; otros decían que era brujería. Bueno, la llevamos con el doctor Hernández [pero] no pudo contener la hemorragia. El doctor nos mandó al puesto de salud. El doctor del centro de atención dijo, "Es muy delicada, hay peligro de muerte." Hay que mandarla al hospital de Sololá."

Tratamos de llevarla por lancha, pero muy fuerte [era] del viento del norte; los lancheros no se animaron. Pedí favor a los bomberos voluntarios para que me hicieran el servicio. Me dijeron que la ambulancia tenía desperfectos. Al fin, aceptaron de trasladar a Cándida Lesbia al hospital de Sololá. A las cinco de la tarde, salimos de San Juan, saliendo de la cuesta de Santa Clara. Faltando seis kilómetros para llegar a la ruta interamericana, el motor de la ambulancia dejó de funcionar. Mi situación era critica; los bomberos se comunicaron con los bomberos de Nahualá. Esperamos más de una hora; fueron los bomberos de Nahualá los que nos trasladaron al hospital nacional de Sololá. Llegamos de noche y entramos en la emergencia. Le dijeron a la paciente que le tenían que saturar unas venas, que se desligaron a dentro de la nariz; quedó en mano de los médicos.

Ese día ya no me acordé de la fiesta ni la marimba. Mi esposa fue la quien pagó al señor de la marimba. Por eso digo no todo el tiempo sale bien como uno quiere. Hay un dicho: "Uno comienza cantando termina llorando."

En el mes de mayo del año 2016, Con mi esposa, nos fuimos a Chichcastenango para ver los trajes del baile de los mexicanos. El dueño de la *morería* [taller en que se confeccionan y alquilan trajes e implementos para los bailes de "moros" y de la "conquista" (Daniel Armas 1971:143) es el Señor Manuel Buchan. Tratamos y quedamos en el convenio que los 24 trajes me los da para Q4,000 para recoger el 20 de junio y de volverlos el 5 de julio; con un compromiso los trajes van hacer de primera clase. [Durante la fiesta titular de San Juan, los bailarines recrean el asesinato del rey Tecún Umán por parte de Pedro Alvarado (Sexton 1992b: 97–115).]

Una vez habló por teléfono con Dr. Jaime Sexton [y] le pedí me ayudara económicamente para mi fiesta, o vale más decir, la fiesta de San Juan Bautista. El señor mando via electrónica $300 al banco agro Mercantil en Panajachel. Dos amigos Juaneros me ofrecieron ayudarme económicamente; yo les dije muchas gracias. El amigo Bruno Cholotío Cumes me dio Q900, y el amigo José Vásquez Ujpán me dio Q250.

Llegó el día Lunes 20 de junio [y] contratamos un camión [y] nos fuimos a Chicastenango para recoger los trajes, pero antes desayunamos frente la iglesia el Clavario. Algunos no llevaron desayuno, [pero] mi esposa tenía mucha comida y tortillas, y todos comimos.

[A] una de la tarde, salimos de Chichicastenango; de regreso [volver], pasamos por Santa Clara, [y] más acá de la población, todos los bailadores se bajaron del camión. Se vinieron a pié bajando el cerro K'istalín. Con mi esposa y otros ancianos, nos venimos en el camión para encontrarnos en la planicie. En Chua Cruz, quemaron las bombas; se oía bien el eco de las bombas. Sobre la cabina del camión habíamos colocado un altoparlante con la música del baile los mexicanos; mucha gente llegó al pie de cuesta para recibir a los muchachos, bomberos voluntarios, policía nacional civil, policía municipal, sonar la sirena en señal de alegría. Dimos las vueltas en las calles del pueblo hasta llegar a mi casa donde nos estaban esperando.

El 21 de junio 2016, por la noche de este día, celebramos una pequeña ceremonia [que] los abuelos le decían Madre tierra. Este se hace para cuando llega el tiempo de presentar el baile; todos están fuera de peligro. En ese asunto, yo soy el encargado de celebrar la ceremonia, o costumbre. Cada uno trae dos o tres candelas y poco de incienso. El que celebra la ceremonia los llama por sus nombres a cada uno los pone de rodilla hasta terminar con todos. En este trabajo se ocupa tres horas. Los que dicen ser sacerdotes mayas cobran Q600 para hacer esta clase de costumbre. Yo no ocupo con un sacerdote maya o chamán. Yo mismo hago celebrar, [soy] solamente un campesino, pero cuando quiero, hago mis costumbres. Todos tenemos la boca [voluntad] para adorar a Dios y al Santo mundo, por la gran misericordia no ha habido problema con los bailadores.

El 22 de junio, presentamos el baile, encabezando el desfile alegórico, saliendo de la gasolinera [y] concluyendo en el estadio municipal de fútbol.

El 23 y 24 de junio, bailaron en la calle cerca de mi casa. Y terminamos el 1 y 2 de julio. Por cierto, todo es alegre, pero quiere tiempo y dinero. Pero cuando hay una voluntad, todo es posible.

## La vida de Pedro [April 2018]

La pena y tristeza hasta dan ganas de llorar cuando uno recuerda como era el tiempo de antes. Los que hemos nacido de los años 1940 hasta 1960 era tiempo de sufrimiento y extrema pobreza, más en nosotros indígenas.

Recuerdo muy bien, como si fuera el presente, cuando yo era niño. Lo peor es que no crecí con mis padres. Mis padres adoptivos me dieron malos tratos. Me pegaban mucho; tomaban mucho el aguardiente; por las noches salían a tomar; yo atrás de ellos, llorando, era mucho el frio, no aguantaba el sueño. A veces se quedaban dormidos en la cantina. A mí me daba mucho miedo de ir a la casa; era oscuro; no había luz in el pueblo.

[Porque] crecí en extrema pobreza, caminar descalzo sin caites [sandalias típicas de cuerdo]. Me mandaban a regar media cuerda de tomatal (plantas de tomate) en la orilla del lago. Me levantaban a las cinco de la mañana; era mucho el frío. Se congelaban mis dedos de la mano y se quedaban inmóvil, los pies descalzos. Pena que no tenía remedio; se me quedaba inmóvil los dedos de los pies. Es una pena que no tuve más remedio que mantener los dedos de los pies inmóviles. Por el gran frio, no tenía más que la camisa la que tenía puesta; es decir, no tenía ni una chumpa o objeto para cubrirme del frio.

Es cierto no estoy mintiendo, en el año 1958, cuando fui mayordomo de la cofradía de María Concepción, yo caminaba descalzo. En ese tiempo, la única persona que tenía caites era el alcalde de juez. Hasta el último mayordomo, andábamos todos descalzos. [Vea nota uno.]

En el año 1960, cuando fui alguacil [corredor, asistente] de la municipalidad, yo andaba descalzo. Las únicas personas que usaban caites eran el alcalde y algunos regidores [concejales]. Las guardias y alguaciles—todos descalzos. Los alcaldes auxiliarles y alguaciles que venían de las tres aldeas, Pasajguim, Panyevar, y Palestina—todos descalzos. En ese tiempo, no era extra extraño ver personas descalzas.

Un par de caites sacada de llantas viejas que los traían de lejos costaba Q0.25 [veinticinco centavos]. Un par de caites con correas de cuero costaba Q0.50 [fifty centavos], y los más buenos, un quetzal.

Una vez cuando yo tenía catorce años, mi tío Agustín me dijo que me iba a comprar unos caites. Yo [estaba] muy contento cuando el vendedor llegó; era de Santa Lucía Utatlán. El señor llevaba muchos de diferentes precios. Luego me puse un par de caites para aprobar si me quedaban bien. El vendedor pedía Q0.35 [35 centavos]. Mi tío solo Q0.25 ofreció. Me quedé con las ganas. Me quité los caites y tuve que devolver al vendedor.

Cuando me mandaba a la escuela no me daban ni un solo centavo; nada de comprar una fruta. No había dinero. Algunos de mis compañeros tenían como comprar algunos dulces o frutas. Bueno, yo era un niño bien listo; luego se me quedaba lo que el maestro me eseñaba. Mis campañeros no atinaban. Yo les ayudaban con las tareas de la escuela, y me daban cinco centavos. Yo me sentía muy contento [porque] entonces yo podía comprar algunas frutas para comer en el recreo.

A la comparación, ahora los niños no reciben cinco quetzales. Ellos dicen que con cinco quetzales, no se puede comprar una refacción. Los tiempos ha cambiado mucho. Ahora, no se ven los niños ni niñas descalzos por las calles. Ahora, los niños [están] bien calzaditos.

Cuando crecí, fue una época de extrema pobreza. Yo usaba camisas remendadas mi pantalón típico con muchas remiendas. Casi todos los de mi edad sufrían, no porque los padres no quisieran comprar ropa y zapatos para sus hijos sino porque era una época en la que no había dinero.

Así también con las mujeres, las señoritas y las niñas; todos andaban descalzos. Unos que otras usaban caites. Las muchachas y los jóvenes en ese tiempo se iban a vender tomate y cebollas en Santa María Lucía, en santa Clara la Laguna. Subían las veredas de Cerro K'istalín descalzos sin caites. También, ellas usaban la ropa remendada.

Los abuelos justificaban [que] la pobreza del pueblo fue por los presidentes dictadores Ubico [quien] mandaron a mucha gente Juanera cumplir el macabro mandamiento en las fincas de la costa. Los abuelos decían que unos Pedranos usurparon los terrenos de los Juaneros cuando ellos cumplían el mandamiento trabajar en las fincas de la costa. Un alcalde y un sindico fueron sobornados por los Pedranos. Ellos firmaron los documentos a favor de los Pedranos; allí es donde fueron despojados los nativos del pueblo. El que era alcalde se llamaba Domingo Yojcóm y el que era sindico se llamaba Lucas Monrroy. Los abuelos decían que Domingo Yocóm fue asesinado en un sábado de gloria en el lugar llamado Xac'al cuando ese hombre iba a San Pedro con su amigo Adinerudos. En el camino, lo mataron. Se dice que la mayor parte de Juaneros se alegrasen de la muerte de ese hombre.

Da tristeza, me da mucho sentimiento de contar mi vida de antes; descalzo, terminé [de ser] alguacil terminando el 1960. Y descalzo, me fui para el cuartel de la cuarta Zona Militar en Mazatenango. Allí es donde me dieron zapatos para calzarme. Hasta entonces mis pies se sintieron un poco cómodos. Después del servicio militar, hasta entonces pude comprar zapatos de charol (plástico) porque no tenía dinero para comprar zapatos de cuero (piel). Ahora que estoy viejo, sufro de cayos en las plantillas de los pies. Es decir, desde joven, se me rajaron los pies; me quedaron lisiados. Mi defecto [es] no puedo usar calcetines ni zapatos apretados, pero eso venia padeciendo desde niño. Se debía del maltrato y mucha pobreza.

Quiero hablar también un poquito [acerca] el de comer diario cuando yo era niño, sufriendo mucho. Muchas veces, solo comía dos veces al día. Recuerdo muy bien con mi tía Juana, yo crecí. Ella machacaba el plátano verde. Lo ponía a moler con un poco de nixtamal, y con eso sacaba las tortillas, y las comíamos con sal. Otras veces, con mi tía íbamos a San Pedro [donde] ella vendía pescaditos y cangrejos en las casas de los Pedranos. Muchas veces las mujeres no tenían el dinero para pagar[nos]. A cambio, nos daban tortillas y tamalitos. Mi tía Juana llevaba sal, y nos poníamos a comer donde no había muchas casas para que la gente no nos vio; es decir, para que la gente no se diera cuenta que nosotros íbamos con hambre. Esto es lo que se llama sufrimiento.

A los diez y seis años, me separé de ellos. Mi tía Juana murió el 16 de diciembre de 1968. Hace cincuenta años pasados. Mi tío Agustín murió en el año 1978. Con ellos yo crecí.

En nombre de Dios Todopoderoso con su poder, ha creado todas las cosas que existen sobre la tierra. El ser humano era creado por Dios, pero primero fue creada la naturaleza para que el ser viviente pudiera gozar de la plenitud que existe sobre la tierra. El Ser humano es la agregaría que embellece la naturaleza con su arte como la pintura, la música la danza, el tejido, los juegos, la pesca, [y] los cuentos. Como también, el campesino embellece la naturaleza con el verdor de los cultivos como maíz, frijol, café, y las verduras, y mucho más. El ser campesino es un poco sufrido porque el campesino trabaja bajo el sol y a veces bajo la lluvia, pero es muy alegre cuando uno está acostumbrado. En mi caso muy personal, yo no puedo trabajar en la sombra, pero cuando trabajando debajo del sol, mi cuerpo se siente muy relajado trabajando muy contento.

Muchas veces me pongo a pensar y digo dichosos los que estudiaron porque ellos pudieron aprender más y poseen mucho conocimiento. Pero luego, me retrocedo y digo gracias a Dios por la vida. Mientras hay vida, el ser humano puede hacer o buscar como para poder sobre vivir, aunque sea [justo] una migaja (poquito). Soy un hombre experimentado en cultivar el maíz, frijol, café, y las verduras; eso no se aprende la escuela ni en la universidad—se aprende [por] trabajando la tierra. Además, se aprende viendo a otras personas trabajando [y] cultivando la tierra. Más es como una herencia legado de los abuelos a sus hijos; los hijos a los nietos.

Así también pasa con mi esposa, Nicolasa. Ella no estuvo en la escuela; no conoce letras ni puede hablar el idioma español. Únicamente habla nuestra lengua materna que es el idioma tz'utujil. [Ella no aprendió a leer y escribir y en español]. Ella es maestra en diseños en tejidos típicos. Posee mucho [más] conocimiento que las otras mujeres. Lo que estoy escribiendo es cierto. Nicolasa, mi esposa, estuvo trabajando muchos años en una asociación, Artesanos de San Juan. Ella es urdidora tejedora de nuevos diseños. Pero en la asociación, fueron explotadas muchas mujeres, [y] mi esposa tuvo que salir. Ahora, trabaja para ella [sí misma]. Vende sus telas de cintura [como las fajas que son cinturones y fajines, tejidos en San Juan en telares de cintura y de pies (Sexton 1992a:123–37; Sexton 2001:212–23)]. Lo que estoy escribiendo son cosas de la vida.

## Mi vida en la comunidad Tz'utujil

Como lo he dicho siempre lo sigo diciendo, soy un hombre pobre de la clase pobre. Solamente tengo unas cuerdas de café. Además, siembro maíz y frijol. Tengo un pequeño aviario de abejas que me producen unos quintales de miel. Con eso, pasamos la vida con mi esposa. Extremadamente pobre no soy. Tengo suficiente para comer. A veces el dinero es escaso, pero poco a poco la vamos pasando. Soy una persona muy serena; no me gusta enojar con nadie. Soy sincero y no me gusta mentir.

No tengo vicio de dinero; no me gusta el tabaco. Sé que tuve una enfermedad alcohólica. Por la gran bendición de Dios, la mano de alcohólicos anónimos me ayudó mucho–me libró del alcoholismo. En el año 1976 me ingresé con alcohólicos anónimos [que] recién llegado en San Juan.

Los confundidores de AA eran los Señores Lorenzo Pérez Gonzáles, Lorenzo Gonzáles Chavajay, y Juan Gonzáles Matzar, que en paz descansen. Fundaron el grupo "Ocho de julio" en San Pedro la Laguna, su ciudad natal. Y más después, fundaron el grupo de alcohólicos anónimos "San Juan Bautista" in San Juan, mi pueblo. Yo me ingresé con los AA cuando tenía pocos meses de haber fundado.

Pienso que es el orgullo que existía en mí; me hizo perder [mi camino]. Yo salí a andar con mis amigos que les gustaban la bebida, y andaba con ellos por las noches. A veces, yo tomaba jugos de fruto o gaseosas, y por descuido y por tonto, me recaí. Cuando yo [lo] sentí, ya estaba borracho. Fue una gran lucha; en quince años tuve cuarto recaídas. De ahí, me quedé nueve años sin asistir al grupo de AA. No era violente ni peleonero. De vez en cuando, perdía mi conocimiento. Yo era un bolo respetado por otros bolos. Mi esposa me decía "Pedro tenga un poco de vergüenza; no te conviene emborrachar. La gente del pueblo se da cuenta."

Bueno, yo reflexioné mucho de lo que me decía mi esposa. Es cierto no soy un borracho que mendiga el trago. No, de vez en cuando, me tomaba los tragos, pero afectaba mi salud. Pensé mucha por mi vida. Ya soy un hombre veterano; mi edad se está yendo [avanzando]. Además, la gente del pueblo siempre me tiene respeto. Dije hasta aquí, licor ya no. En el año 2000, me uní con los alcohólicos anónimos "Camino a la felicidad." Por la gracias de Dios y a mis compañeros de alcohólicos anónimos, hasta hoy, no he bebido.

He dicho muchas veces, somos una pareja de esposos pobres. De verdad no tenemos como para darle un regalo a uno de nuestros ahijados. La gente del pueblo nos respeta; nos aprecia; nos da prestigio. Tengo una historia y buenas referencias en mi pueblo.

Hemos sido padrinos de las siguientes personas, de bautizos y confirmaciones, actos religiosos que se celebra dentro de la comunidad católica. [Aquí, Pedro proporciona una lista de 22 personas de todos los ámbitos de la vida, incluyendo: profesor, enfermera, estudiante, ama de casa, perito contador, y policía.]

Con mi esposa, hemos tenido el regalo más grande que nos dio el Señor Todopoderoso y la Madre tierra, o Madre de la naturaleza. Tenemos 22 ajeados(as). En cada comunidad hay diferentes culturas; más que todo, entre la gente indígena, el fundamento de la cultura de un pueblo, es respeto.

Cuando un muchacho o una muchacha se quiere casar bajo juramento de ley, o unirse así voluntariamente, los padres de la pareja; es decir, el padre del varón busca una persona honrada y de respecto padrino del matrimonio.

Ahora cuando se juntan [la pareja así voluntariamente, siempre se buscan una persona como testigo y consejero que les puede ayudar con ideas y consejos, para que esa unión sea duradera hasta la muerte los separe; así también, con el padre de la mujer tiene que buscar un testigo o representante. Los dos testigos son ellos los que se comuniquen con la pareja; les preguntan si verdaderamente se quieren por amor. La pareja contesta que sí se aman hasta la muerte. Los testigos o representantes de las dos familias se encargan de darles las recomendaciones útiles para tener una buena vida, tanto en la pobreza, las alegrías, y las enfermedades. Cuidado no malgastar el dinero y trabajar duro, porque con el tiempo serán padres de sus propios hijos.

Yo he participado muchas veces en muchas familias y en muchos hogares en esta clase de evento cultural, siempre acompañado por mi esposa. Como un respeto y costumbre, el hombre tiene que ser acompañado por su esposa.

[Yo he participado] como testigo y representante honorable de los padres de etas parejas de personas que se han unidos voluntariamente: [aquí, Pedro proporciona 38 parejas.]

## El coronavirus

Quiero contarle algo de la pandemia del Coronavirus; también le dicen COVID-19.

Antes de la llegada del Coronavirus en Guatemala; se oía por radio y se miraba por televisión que en un país asiático se está dando contagio grave de una enfermedad que ataca a mucha gente en todo el mundo. De verdad nosotros los mayas no creímos, pero en el mes de marzo 2020, se puso grave la situación.

Se dice que el Coronavirus llegó en Guatemala. Fue llevado a] un aeropuerto internacional, La Aurora, por una persona de Sur América. Allí, apareció el Coronavirus en el país.

Sufrimos mucho; el gobierno declaró toque de queda en todo el país de lunes a viernes de las cuatro de la tarde hasta la seis de la mañana del día siguiente. Sábado, las dos de la tarde y todo el día domingo, nadie podía salir de la casa hasta lunes a las seis de la mañana. Serenaron las escuelas; pusieron cadenas en las puertas de las iglesias. Los productos subieron de precio. Los ricos guardaron sus productos ya no había comunicación con los puertos vecinos; suspendieron los transportes de pasajeros. A las mujeres [se les dio] dos horas para ir al mercado para comprar, y diez tenían que salir antes de que diez pudieran entrar, dos veces por semana.

Hemos alcanzado tiempo difícil [22 julio 2020], pero ese es en todo el mundo. La pandemia del Coronavirus está alocando en muchos países, también en Guatemala, miles de personas contagiados. Han muerto mucha gente. En San Juan muchas personas han estado en cuarentena, pero ninguna de Coronavirus. Es cierto en San Juan han muerto personas de enfermedad común.

Nosotros desde marzo no hemos podido salir del municipio, ni en el mercado podemos ir. [Por] orden del presidente de la república: Los niños y los de la tercera edad no pueden salir, porque para ellos es más fácil el contagio de la pandemia. Si ganamos la batalla contra Coronavirus, le diré como se curan los mayas.

Quiero contarle [1 octubre de 2021] que en el pueblo se enfermaron mucha gente en el mes julio, agosto, y septiembre. Fue el centro de la pandemia COVID-19. Sí, se murieron Juaneros, pero [hubo] muchos [de] los que ganaron la batalla.

Ahora, nosotros con mi familia estamos vivos y todos vacunados. Yo sí tengo problemas con mi salud. Sufro artritis en las manos. No puedo dormir tranquilo. La verdad, no estoy en la cama, pero me duele los brazos y las muñecas de la mano.

Nosotros con mi familia todos estamos [19 de junio de 2022] vivos por la gran voluntad de Dios, a pesar de la pandemia. Sí, nos hemos enfermado de gripe, dolor de cabeza, resfriado y tos, pero nos hemos curado con medicina natural.

La pandemia o Coronavirus ha afectado al mundo, han muerto muchas personas en Guatemala. En San Juan, solamente han muerto 4 personas; es cierto se han enfermado mucha gente Juanero, pero han logrado recuperarse por medio remedios natural tanto para bañarse y para tomar. Sí, han dado resultado.

Los mayas no quieren ir al hospital, porque dicen que los aíslan o los abandonan; no es lo mismo que estar en la casa. En la casa los cuidan; les dan de tomar cosas calientes. Hay mucha diferencia—el cuerpo de la gente indígena es un poco resistente. Se puede curar con remedios caseros. Más adelante, le daré una hoja con el nombre de los remedios natural [y] como se hace. También, nosotros los no contagiados estamos tomando nuestro remedio natural.

# The Impossible Arrives Without We People Who Live in This World Realizing It

WE ARE OF MANY qualities, angry, envious, greedy, arrogant, vicious, liars, and little good. Thus is humanity. Without realizing it, we are only like a shadow when the clarity of the light disappears. Many things happen in our lives from night to morning.

I want to write a little, better said, record the past when Hurricane Stan happened. In my old notebook, there is a little of what happened nine years ago—we suffered the consequences of the times.

The first of October 2005 was a Saturday, [we were] thinking that winter had ended its phase, but all was to the contrary. In the afternoon of this day, the rain began, not strong, but all night. It dawned Sunday, October 2, 2005, all the hills and mountains covered with a gray cloud. One could not see the sky. The small hills that were near the town were covered with [a] cloud. After midday, a light rain began, but with [a] menacing wind from north to south from south to north, [I] thinking that it would end like this. Thus, it passed all night, without us realizing what was going to happen later.

It dawned Monday, October 3, with a stronger wind. No one was able to leave to work. Eleven in the morning, the rain held on stronger; it turned into a shower with a strong wind. In the afternoon of this day, Monday, we remained without electricity. This became a sadness; now, there was no communication. There was no television, radio, or telephone signal; we remained in obscurity [about] the towns [of] Santa María, Santa Clara, San Pablo, San Marcos, San Pedro, and San Juan. Even with the family, one could not communicate; we stayed locked in the house.

Tuesday dawned, October 4, the day that in Panajachel the fiesta of San Francisco de Asís, patron of this town, is celebrated. It could not be celebrated because of the intense rain and hurricane. The strongest was coming; you could no longer look at the hills or the towns. All were covered with rain, and [the] storm had turned into a calamity—there was neither signal nor light.

Night falling on this day Tuesday, October 4, a fear was felt—something bad was going to happen. A candle was not sufficient to illuminate the house. What I did, I lay down on my bed; my wife Nicolasa did not want to go to sleep. She told me that she had a presentiment that a bad thing was going to happen. I told her to stop thinking about things, but she insisted on telling me that indeed something bad was going to happen.

Nine at night, the storm grips more strongly, [with] an unbearable rain. You could hear the hills thundering; the restlessness began. You could hear every moment the roars of K'istalín Hill and other hills. No one was able to sleep tranquilly, nor could you communicate with neighbors or with family a little away—all was an immense darkness; [the] rain with hurricane winds was a scourge of nature.

At two in the morning, Wednesday, October 5, 2005, the landslides that fell from the Hills began, dragging thousands of tons of rocks and mud; it was a pity to be incommunicado. We who live in the town suffered, but those of the Colony of 5 January suffered more. They were the victims of Hurricane Stan. They lost their homes and all their belongings. There are families who were left with only the clothes they were wearing. In that colony, it is not so grand.

Three o'clock in the morning, the streets of the town filled with water. One could not pass. At this same hour, when the great currents came down [with] rocks and mud, as well as the trees dragged by the river, caused by Hurricane Stan, many houses that were constructed very near where the Panatzán River flows disappeared. There pass all the currents that come from the hills when it rains.

The most affected families—that is to say, those who lost their homes and all their belongings—[were] Pedro Mendoza Bizarro, Candelaria Méndez, Gabriel Pantzay, Domingo Mendoza, Susana Ujpán, Felix Yoycom, Abel Pérez, [and] Juan Toc. But there are many houses, the names of whose owners I do not know, that remained half-buried with rocks and mud and entirety unusable. They say of those of the colony, that since three in the morning they began to abandon their homes, but because of all the current of rocks, mud, and trees, they were unable to go to the Colony of San Juanerita to take refuge; they were unable to cross the river.

Sunrise of this day was a great suffering of all the persons of the Colony of 5 January. They remained isolated inside the coffee groves, without obtaining help from anyone because we who live in the town were not able to leave because the situation was serious. They said that they began to shout and ask for help since three in the morning, but no one helped them until eight in the morning [when] it became known that the people of 5 January were in a critical situation.

The rain continued, but indeed now one could walk; I arrived a little late. Men, women, and children spent the rest of the night under the rain.

The muchachos of good age laid large cables for rescuing. Yes, the people of the colony could be saved; none died. They were left with only the clothes they were wearing. They lost all their things. The important thing is that nobody died.

Señor Agustín Gonzáles told me, "Pedro, where are the religious people? I do not see anyone; only I am seeing young people who are not religious rendering assistance, helping our people." There are nineteen families most affected by the hurricane, but it left the whole colony with fear that it will happen again, even worse. More for that reason, no one remained; everyone went to the town to lodge. It was sad to see how the poor women came carrying their babies in their hands with wet clothes.

The affected families remained housed at two points, in the municipal hall and in the Evangelical church, Bethel, better known [as] the Central American Church. There, in those places they received attention and help. The Catholic Church turned deaf and blind. It did not show its face in presenting help to the people in need. The children are the ones who suffered most. It is true that food, clothing, and sleeping clothing arrived; [but] being in your house is not the same as being in the municipal hall.

The rich benefit the most in the adversity of the poor. They say now indeed, we are going to make more money until finishing with the poor. The rich monopolized all the basic necessities and raised the prices. A pound of sugar reached Q3.00 a pound; at that time, it was worth Q2.00. A candle that was worth Q0.50 reached a price of Q1.50. A pound of corn at that time that was valued Q1.25 reached Q2.00 a pound. An egg that cost Q0.60 reached Q1.50. The rich, shop owners, raised the prices every day.

It is very difficult to get from one day to another—there are people who live in extreme poverty. They live with what they earn daily.

The only ones that thought to maintain the prices were the owners of the super market named Super Quic. They kept their prices normal, and they said that after the merchandise is exhausted, they could not help more.

This happened because there now was no communication with the neighboring towns. From San Juan to San Pedro, one could pass, but on foot, only two kilometers. The road of San Juan, San Pablo, Santa Clara, Santa María Visitación until kilometer 148, the Inter-American route, [there were] countless landslides that fell on the road. The roads in the villages Panyebar and Pasajquim [had] parts that were no longer visible.

The worst that happened in San Juan was that the thousands of tons of rocks that fell from the hills disfigured the plains that were cultivated with coffee. [The] places Pachicoc, Xe K'istalín, Pa-Tza'lú, Xek'ac'abaj, and Xe cajnom were a great loss in the economy of the town because hundreds of acres of coffee plantations were buried under the rocks, not only of Juaneros, including myself, but also the Pedranos. I also lost my corn field; I was left with nothing.

Señor Pedro Mendoza and his wife, Candelaria Méndez, said that they were not able to take out their things because there was no light [electricity]. That family is very big; they had four houses. They were unable to do anything. They saw when the flow of water carried away the bed and closet where they had all their clothes and the deeds of their land and homesites, moreover [where] they say they had a little money.

Pedro Mendoza said even the animals wanted help—three serpents that were dragged by the current wanted to climb on the body of a lady [who was] screaming a lot. There was no one able to help her; with a flashlight she was defending herself [by] running under the coffee plantations. It was a torment; what happened to the people of the colony was suffering.

To finish, I want to write about what happened to the affected persons. There is a saying that says "Rio revuelto es ganancia de pescadores [A raging river is profit for fishermen]." After the storm, some days later, the mayor and his councilors left to see all the damage Hurricane Stan caused. They took photos of the coffee groves [that had] disappeared from there.

They put out a notice throughout the town so that each person would come and report the cuerdas [0.178 acre each] of coffee or milpa [cornfield] lost, to get help from the international organizations and from the central government, which would send economic support to each campesino [farmer]. That was [how] people from San Juan and San Pedro reported what they had lost. I am mentioning San Pedro because there are many Pedranos who have land in the jurisdiction of San Juan; they also lost their coffee groves.

The saddest thing that happened was that when the organizations and the government of Guatemala agreed to help the affected persons, but this was done through the municipalities. To make it clearer, the money came to the municipality to be delivered by the mayor to each one according to the losses suffered. This kind of help came to fall into the pocket of Mayor Mario Tuc Soto [a pseudonym] and his three companions. We found out that there indeed [was] money, but they didn't give it to us. The truth is that due to lack of money, it was not possible to hire a lawyer. Thus, we left it.

Here [is] a little history of Hurricane Stan.

# Llega lo imposible sin darnos cuento nosotros las personas que vivimos en este mundo

SOMOS DE MUCHAS CUALIDADES, enojados, envidiosos, avaros, prepotentes, viciosos, mentirosos, y pocos buenos. Así es la humanidad, sin darnos cuenta, solamente somos como una sombra cuando la claridad de la luz se desaparece. De la noche a la mañana transcurre muchas cosas en nuestras vidas.

Quiero escribir un poco, vale más decir, recordar el pasado cuando ocurrió Huracán Stan. En mi cuaderno viejo, hay un poco de lo que sucedió hace nueve años pasados—sufrimos las consecuencias del tiempo.

El 1 de octubre del año 2005 fue un día sábado, pensando que el invierno había terminado su fase, pero todo fue, al contrario. Por la tarde de este día, comenzó con lluvia, no fuerte, pero toda la noche. Amaneció el día Domingo, 2 de octubre 2005, todos los cerros y montañas cubierta de una nube gris. El cielo no se podía ver. Los pequeños cerros que están cerca de la población están cubiertos de [un] nube. Después del mediodía, comienza una lluvia lento, pero con [un] viento amenazante de norte a sur de sur a norte, [yo] pensando que se terminaba así. Así pasó toda la noche, sin darnos cuenta lo que iba suceder más después.

Amaneció el día Lunes, 3 de octubre con una lluvia más fuerte. Nadie podía salir a trabajar. Once de la mañana, la lluvia agarró más fuerte; se volvió un chubasco con fuerte viento. Por la tarde de este día, lunes, nos quedamos sin luz. Este se volvió una tristeza; ya no había comunicación. No había señal de televisión, radio, y teléfono; nos quedamos en la oscuridad [acerca] los pueblos Santa María, Santa Clara, San Pablo, San Marcos, San Pedro, y San Juan. Hasta con la familia, no se podía comunicar; nos quedamos encerrados en la casa.

Amaneció el día martes, 4 de octubre, el día que se celebra en Panajachel la fiesta de San Francisco de asís, patrono de ese pueblo. No se pudo celebrar por la fuerte lluvia y huracán. Venía el más fuerte, ya no se miraban los cerros ni los pueblos. Todo era cubierto de lluvia, y [la] tormenta se volvió una calamidad—no hay señal ni luz.

Entrando la noche de ese día martes, 4 de octubre, se sienta un miedo—un mal va a suceder. Una candela no era suficiente para alumbrar la casa. Lo que yo hice, me acosté en mi cama; mi esposa Nicolasa no quería dormir. Me dijo que ella presentía que un mal va a pasar. Yo le dije que deje de estar pensando cosas, pero ella insistía de decirme que sí que un mal va suceder.

Las nueve de la noche, agarra más fuerza la tormenta una insoportable lluvia. Se oía que los cerros tronaban; comenzaba la intranquilidad; se oía cada momento los bramidos del cerro K'istalín y de otros cerros. Nadie podía dormir tranquilo, ni se podía comunicar con los vecinos ni con familiares poco lejos—todo era una inmensa oscuridad; lluvia con vientos huracanada era un azote de la naturaleza.

Las 2 de la mañana del día miércoles, 5 octubre 2005, comenzaba a los derrumbes o deslaves que caían de los cerros arrastrando miles toneladas de rocas y lodo; era una pena estar incomunicados. Nosotros los que vivimos en el pueblo sufrimos, pero más sufrieron los de la Colonia 5 de enero. Fueron ellos las victimas de huracán Stan. Perdieron sus viviendas y todas sus pertenencias.

Hay familias que se quedaron únicamente con ropa que tenían puesta. En esa colonia, no es tan grande.

Las tres de la mañana, las calles de la población se llenaron de agua. No se podía pasar. En esa misma hora, cuando bajaron las grandes correntadas [con] rocas y lodo, así como los árboles arrastrados por los ríos provocados por Huricán Stan, muchas casas que estaban construidos muy cerca donde paso el Río Panatzán, desaparecieron. Allí, pasa todas las correntadas que viene de los cerros cuando llueve.

Las familias más afectadas; es decir, los que perdieron sus viviendas y todos sus enseres [fueron]: Pedro Mendoza Bizarro, Candelaria Méndez, Gabriel Pantzay, Domingo Mendoza, Susana Ujpán, Felix Yoycom, Abel Pérez, [y] Juan Toc. Pero hay muchas casas que no sé los nombres de los dueños, que también quedaron semi- enterrados con rocas y lodo en su totalidad quedaron inservibles. Dicen ellos, los de la colonia, que desde las 3 de la mañana comenzaron abandonar sus viviendas, pero por toda la correntada de rocas, lodo, y árboles. No podían pasar para refugiarse a la Colonia San Juanerita; no podían atravesar el río.

Amanecer de este día de la colonia era un gran sufrimiento de todas las personas de la Colonia 5 de enero. Quedaron aislados adentro de los cafetales, sin obtener ayuda de nadie porque nosotros los que vivimos en el pueblo no podíamos salir porque era grave la situación. Ellos decían que comenzaron a gritar y pedir ayuda desde 3 de la mañana, pero nadie los ayudaba hasta las ocho de la mañana [hasta] se llegó a saber que la gente de la Colonia 5 de enero estaba en una situación crítica.

Seguía la lluvia, pero sí ya se podía caminar; yo llegué un poco tarde. Hombres, mujeres, y niños pasaron el resto de la noche debajo de la lluvia.

Los muchachos de buena edad colocaron cables grandes para rescatar. Sí se pudo salvar a la gente de la colonia; ninguno murió. Solamente quedaron con la ropa que tenían puesta. Perdieron todas sus cosas. Lo importante es que nadie murió.

El Señor Agustín Gonzáles me dijo "Pedro donde están los religiosos? No veo ninguno; solo estoy viendo jóvenes que no son religiosos prestando auxilio, ayudando a nuestra gente." Son 19 familias las más afectadas por el huracán, pero dejó a toda la colonia con miedo de que vuelva a suceder, aún peor. Más por eso, nadie se quedó; todos fueron al pueblo a alojarse. Daba tristeza viendo como venÍan las pobres mujeres llevando sus bebes en las manos con las ropas mojadas.

Las familias damnificadas quedaron albergadas en dos puntos, en el Salón municipal y en la iglesia evangélica Bethel, más conocido [como] la Iglesia centroamericana. Allí, en esos lugares [eran] donde recibieron atención y ayuda. La Iglesia Católica se hizo el sordo y siego. No dio la cara en prestar auxilio a la gente necesitada. Los niños son los que más sufrieron. Es cierto llegó comida, ropo, y ropo de dormir; [pero] no es igual estar in la casa a que estar en salón [municipal].

Los ricos son los que más se alegan en la adversidad de los pobres. Ellos dicen ahora sí, vamos a ganar más dinero hasta terminar con el pobre. Los ricos acapararon todos los productos de primera necesidad y lo subieron de precio. Una libra de azúcar llegó a Q3.00 la libra; en ese tiempo, valía Q2.00. Una candela que valía Q0.50 llegó un precio a Q1.50. Una libra de maíz que en ese tiempo valía Q1.25 llegó a Q2.00 la libra. Un huevo que costaba Q0.60 llegó Q1.50. Los ricos, dueño de tiendas, cada día subían los precios.

Cuesta mucho pasar un día a otro—hay gente que viven en extrema pobreza. Viven con lo que ganan diario.

Los únicos que pensaran en mantener los precios fueron los dueños del supermercado que lleva el nombre Super Quic. Mantuvieron los precios normales, y dijeron que después de se agota la mercadería, no podrían ayudar más.

Esto pasó porque ya no había comunicación con los pueblos vecinos. De San Juan a San Pedro se podía pasar, pero a píe, solamente dos kilómetros. La carretera de San Juan, San Pablo, Santa Clara, Santa María Visitación hasta al Kilometro 148, ruta interamericana [había] incontable los derrumbes que callaron sobre la carretera. Los caminos en las aldeas Panyebar, y Pasajquim [tenía] partes que ya no se miraba.

Lo peor que pasó en San Juan, los miles de toneladas de rocas que cayeron de los cerros desfiguraron las planicies que estaban cultivadas de café. [Los] lugares, Pachicoc, Xe k'stalín, Pa-Tza'lú, Xek'ac'abaj, y Xe cajnom, fueron una gran perdida en la economía del pueblo porque debajo de las rocas quedaron enterrados cientos de cuerda de cafetales, no solamente de Juaneros, incluyéndome, también los Pedranos. También perdí la milpa; me quedé sin nada.

El Señor Pedro Mendoza y su esposa, Candelaria Méndez, decían que no pudieron sacar sus cosas porque no había luz [electricidad]. Esa familia es bien grande; tenía cuatro casas. No pudo hacer nada. Venía cuando la corriente de agua llevó arrastrada de la cama y el ropero donde tenían toda su ropa y las escrituras de sus terrenos y sitios, además [donde] dicen que ellos tenían un poco de dinero.

Pedro Mendoza decía hasta los animales querían ayuda—tres serpientes que venían arrastradas por la corriente querrían trepar sobre el cuerpo de la señora [quien era] dando muchos gritos. No hay quien podía ayudarla; con una linterna estuvo defendiéndose [por] corriendo debajo los cafetales. Fue un tormento; lo que pasó con la gente de la colonia fue sufrimiento.

Para terminar, quiero escribir lo que pasó con las personas damnificados. Hay un dicho que dice "Rio revuelto es ganancia de pescadores." Después del temporal, unos días después, el alcalde y sus concejales salieron a ver todo el daño causó el huracán Stan. Tomaron fotos de los cafetales [que había] desparecido de ahí.

Sacaron un aviso en toda la población para que cada persona llegaría y reportaría las cuerdas de café o milpa que se perdió, para obtener ayuda de las organizaciones internacionales y del gobierno central para que envíen apoyo económico a cada campesino. Así fue [como] gente de San Juan y de San Pedro reportaran lo que habían perdido. Estoy mencionando San Pedro es porque hay muchos Pedranos que tienen terreno en la jurisdicción de San Juan; también perdieron sus cafetales.

Lo más triste que pasó era que cuando las organizaciones y gobierno de Guatemala concedieron de ayudar a los campesinos damnificados, pero esto se hiciera a través de la municipalidad. Para [hacer] más claro, el dinero llegó a la municipalidad para entregue el alcalde entre que a cada uno de acuerdo con las perdidas sufrido. Esta clase de ayuda vino a caer a la bolsa del alcalde Mario Tuc Soto [un seudónimo]y sus tres compañeros. Supimos que sí había dinero, pero no lo nos dieron. La verdad [es que] por falta de dinero, no fue posible pagar un abogado. Así lo dejamos.

Aquí [es] un poco la historia de Huricán Stan.

# FOLKTALES / CUENTOS

CASO

# Francisco Sojuel Warns of Hurricane Stan

A YEAR AFTER HURRICANE STAN, my wife and I went to Santiago Atitlán. When we arrived, leaving the boat, passing in front of the typical shops [selling Mayan goods], Diego Mendoza recognized me and told me, "Pedro, now you do not remember me, I am your friend; I am Diego Mendoza, the oldest son of Pascual Mendoza, [who] also was your friend."

I had to ask him for forgiveness because truly I had forgotten him, because it had been a long time since we had talked. Diego Mendoza had a store on the shore of the lake. I saw him as being a little sick and I asked him what was the matter, and he told me that he suffered from the liver. He told me that he had changed his religion; he moved to the Protestant church after they killed his father in the cemetery.

I asked him the reason that they killed his father in the cemetery. Diego told me that his father was a shaman, or *ajkuum*. He learned how to divine, to do costumbres in the home of the sick persons, and he healed with grass [herbs]. But he told me that his father did not obtain this from birth, to do these things. Only he learned with other shamans. Diego told me, "In Santiago there are two strong groups—group one is the group of witches who are dedicated to witchcraft, to look for the death of persons they consider their enemies."

Group two, [he told me], is the one of the ajkuuumes, shamans, and healers. Diego said that these groups lend themselves to do costumbres of the sick persons, and then heal them with herbs, and if it is necessary, they go to the cemetery to bring the spirits of the sick persons to obtain their cure. This is the problem that exists among those two groups, causing rivalries. The witches are in charge of bewitching the curers, and if they can't do it with witchcraft, they look for thugs. This was the case of his father; they killed him for hire in the cemetery when he was doing costumbres. He was alone and they killed him with a machete.

Diego told me that his father had served in the Catholic church for thirty years as Nicodemus in accordance with the Bible. Nicodemus was the person who lowered the body of Lord Jesus off the cross after the crucifixion. Pascual Mendoza was one of the Nicodemus group who are in charge of crucifying and lowering the image of Lord Jesus off the cross on Holy Fridays, imitating Nicodemus for thirty years. Francisco Sojuel lives, Diego told me.

I told Diego that his father had told me the story of don Francisco Sojuel and of General Ubico.[4] Diego Mendoza surprised me when he said Francisco Sojuel continues living; he appears and disappears. He is always taking care of the people. What happens is that the people have lost respect and belief in everything that nature has given us. "Francisco Sojuel lives," Diego told me.

Days before Hurricane Stan, an old man typically [traditionally] dressed was walking by the houses of the canton, Panabaj, to tell the people that a rain with a storm was approaching. Many people are going to die, and the canton, Panabaj, is going to disappear. They say that the old man went by saying at many houses, "Better to leave and look for shelter in the town." They say that the old man carried a sack, acting as if he were carrying his suitcase to go to town to ask for shelter. He says that they asked the old man where his house was; he said that he was from the same canton, Panabaj.

The people did not believe what the old man said because they never had seen him in that canton and they took him for an indigent.

Diego told me, "One day when it already was raining, when the storm was approaching, they saw the old man crying there by the Park of Peace where people of Santiago were massacred by the military." He says they asked him why he was crying, and he says he told them, "In my town, Santiago, a misfortune is going to happen, an evil, many people are going to die. Misfortune is close, but the people do not pay any attention to me. I told them to leave the canton and to look for [a] place in the town."

No one knew what was going to happen in this canton; the calamity happened during the night of the fourth, dawning the fifth of October. Some of the people were saved from the great wash that came off the slopes of the volcano that completely buried the canton, Panabaj. Many people were submerged, or buried, by the force of nature. Diego says that also many cadavers were recovered.

[Not] until after the storm did those who were left alive believe in the old man dressed as an *Atiteco* [male inhabitant of Santiago Atitlán], who was saying that it is better to abandon the canton because something bad was going to happen. Now, it was late when they thought that Señor Francisco Sojuel was the one who was walking around warning the people and it was Sojuel himself who was crying for his people because of the bad that befell the town, Santiago Atitlían. More for that reason, the people say that don Francisco Sojuel is a Tz'utujil prophet.

Still, I asked Diego Mendoza why he changed his religion, and he told me, "For the death of my father, because he got involved in evil things. More for that reason, I belong to a Protestant Church, but indeed I believe in the *naguales* [spirits] of don Francisco Sojuel." That was what Diego Mendoza told me. Regrettably, Diego died two years ago.

—Diego Mendoza

CASO

# Francisco Sojuel advierte sobre huracán Stan

UN AÑO DESPUÉS DE Huracán Stan, fuimos con mi esposa a Santiago Atitlán. Cuando llegamos, saliendo de la lancha, pasando en frente de las tiendas típicas [vendiendo productos mayas], Diego Mendoza me reconoció y me dijo: "Pedro ya no te recuerdas de mí, eres mi amigo; yo soy Diego Mendoza, el hijo mayor de Pascual Mendoza [quien] también fue tu amigo," me dijo.

Yo tuve que pedirle disculpas porque de verdad se me había olvidado de él, porque por mucho tiempo que no nos hemos hablado. Diego Mendoza tenía una tienda en la orilla del lago. Le vi como un poco enfermo, y le pregunté ¿qué es lo tiene? Él me dijo que padece del hígado. Me dijo que él cambió de religión; se paso a la iglesia protestante después lo mataron a su padre en el cementerio.

Yo le pregunté la razón porque le mataron a su padre en el cementerio. Diego me dijo que su papá era un chamán, o akuum. Aprendió como a divinar, hacer costumbres en la casa de los enfermos, y curaba con zacate. Pero me dijo que su padre no traía de nacimiento, para hacer estas cosas. Solamente aprendió con otros chamanes. Diego me dijo, "En Santiago hay dos grupos fuertes—grupo 1 [uno] es el grupo de los brujos que se dedican a la hechicería, para buscar la muerte de las personas que consideran ser sus enemigos."

Grupo 2 [dos] es el de los ajkuumes, chamanes y curanderos. Diego decía que estos grupos se prestan para hace costumbres de las personas enfermas, y las curan con zacate [hierbas], y si es necesario, van al cementerio a traer los espíritus de las personas enfermas para obtener su curación.

Este es el problema que exista entre estos dos grupos, traen rivalidades. Los brujos se encargan de hechizar a los ajkuumes, y si no pueden con la brujería, buscan matones. Así fue el caso de su padre; le dieron muerte por encargo en el cementerio. Cuando estaba haciendo costumbres, andaba solo, y le dieron muerte con machete.

Diego me dijo que su padre estuvo sirviendo en la iglesia católica por 30 años como Nicodemo de acuerdo con la Biblia. Nicodemo era a la persona que se bajó el cuerpo del Señor Jesús de la cruz después de la crucifixión. Pascual Mendoza era uno del grupo de Nicodemo quienes se encargan de crucificar y bajar de la cruz la imagen del Señor Jesús los Viernes Santo; imitando a Nicodemo durante 30 años.

Yo le dijo a Diego que su papá me había contado la historia de don Francisco Sojuel y del General Ubico.[4] Diego Mendoza me sorprendió cuando me dijo Francisco Sojuel sigue viviendo; aparece y se desparece. Él siempre está al cuidado del pueblo. Lo que pasa que la gente ha perdido el respeto y la creencia de todo lo que la naturaleza nos ha regalado.

"Francisco Sojuel vive," me dijo Diego. Días antes de la tormenta, un viejito vestido de típico estuvo andando por las casas del cantón, Panabaj, a decirle a la genta que se está acercando una lluvi con una tormenta. Se va a morir mucha gente, y se va a desparecer el cantón, Panabaj. Dice que el viejito pasó diciendo en muchas casas "mejor salir y buscar posada en el pueblo." Dice que el viejito lleva un costal, haciendo como que estuviera llevando su maleta para ir al pueblo a pedir posada. Dice que le preguntaron al viejo donde quedaba su casa; él decía que era del mismo cantón, Panabaj.

La gente no creía lo que decía el viejito porque nunca la habían visto en ese cantón, y lo tomaron como un indigente.

Diego me dijo, "Un día cuando ya estaba lloviendo cuando la tormenta se está aproximando lo vieron al viejito llorando por allí por el parque de la paz donde fueron masacrado gente de Santiago por los militares. Dice que le preguntaron porque él está llorando, dice que les dijo, "En mi pueblo Santiago va a pasar una desgracia, un mal; mucha gente va a morir. La desgracia está cerca, pero la gente no me hace caso. Yo les dije que salieran del cantón y buscar [un] lugar en el pueblo."

Nadie sabía lo que iba a suceder en ese cantón; la calamidad pasó durante la noche del 4 amanecer el 5 de octubre. Una parte de la gente se salvaron del gran lavado que se desprendió de las faldas del volcán que enterró por completo el cantón, Panabaj. Mucha gente quedó soterrada, o enterrados, por la fuerza de la naturaleza. Diego dice que también fueron recatados muchos cadáveres.

[No] hasta después de la tormenta, los que quedaron vivos creyeron en el viejito vestido de atiteco que quien les estuvo diciendo que mejor abandonar el canton porque un mal va a pasar. Ya era tarde cuando pensaron que el Señor Francisco Sojuel el que estuvo andando avisando a la gente; y era el mismo Sojuel el que estuvo llorando por su pueblo por el mal que cayó sobre el pueblo, Santiago Atitlán. Más por eso, la gente dice que don Francisco Sojuel es un profeta tz'utujil.

Todavía, yo le pregunté a Diego Mendoza porque cambió su religión, y me dijo: "Por la muerte de mi padre, porque él se involucró en cosas del mal. Más por eso [razón], pertenezco en una iglesia protestante, pero sí creo en los nahuales de don Francisco Sojuel. Esto fue lo que me dijo, Diego Mendoza. Lamentamente, Diego hace dos años que murió.

—Diego Mendoza

# Old Story

## *The Enchanted Tiger [Jaguar]*

IT IS SAID [THAT] the people from before; that is to say, speaking of our grandfathers and grandmothers, they said that the body of a person speaks when it is sleeping.

The story says that three brothers were hunters. Their job was to hunt small and large animals. They stayed in the mountains for two or three nights. They carried their tortillas and little tamales, not much food because in the mountains they did not lack animal meat. They carried their blankets in order to sleep in the mountains.

Their mom told them it is better to perform a costumbre [ritual] to the *dueño* [lord, owner] of the world so that nothing bad would happen to them, her three sons. But the muchachos did not give any importance to what their mother was telling them.

Their mom said that she dreamed that one of her three sons was eaten by *tigres* and mountain lions in the mountains. The lady insisted on telling her three sons to do something as a present in order to ask forgiveness of the Señor of the Holy World. It is said that the three sons continued with a hard heart—they did not do a thing that their mother told them.

Thus it was with them; the three brothers continued with their hunt. They remained sleeping under the big trees in the mountain. One time they made a big fire for the night so that they would not feel so cold. The three lay down; about midnight two of the three brothers slept. The other could not get to sleep; he felt that something bad was going to happen to them. The two continued sleeping very soundly, but the one who was awake felt bothered. He did not feel calm.

Suddenly, he saw coming a big tiger, wagging his tail. He sat down at the feet of the three boys. The brother who was awake [was] trembling, very cold and afraid of the moment the tiger was going to eat him. The other two were sleeping tranquilly. The tiger grabbed the left foot of the one who was not sleeping, and he asked the last toe, "Are you for me? I am going to eat you!" But the toe did not answer because its owner was awake. The tiger left his foot lying.

The tiger was seated near the feet of the three men who were lying down. Then, he grabbed the toe of the other who was sleeping, and he asked the last toe, "Are you for me? I'm going to eat you!"

The story says the toe answered, "No, no you cannot eat me; I am not yours. I have to die *embarrancado*" [inside a ravine; in other words, sensing how he was going to die by falling accidentally inside an abyss]. Thus said the toe of the left foot of the second brother.

The story says that the tiger grabbed the foot of the other who was sleeping and asked the last toe, "Are you for me? I am going to eat you!"

And the toe answered the tiger, "Yes, you may eat me, but not right now. It will be not until tomorrow because I want to spend this night sleeping with my brothers."

Thus said the last toe, but the story says that these two were fast asleep. They did not know that their bodies had talked with a tiger. But the brother who had heard these things was shivering with great fear from everything he had heard the toes of his brother say to the tiger.

When it dawned, he told his two brothers what he had seen and heard. But his two brothers did not believe that a tiger was able to speak, nor did they believe that their toes were able to answer a tiger. But their brother did not feel well because something bad was going to happen on the road.

Then, they left the mountain back for their home. The brother who feared being in danger of being the tiger's meal, they told him to walk ahead, and the two others behind in protection. Thus, they went walking because it was far when they were leaving the mountain.

The boy told his brothers that he had to go into the bush to relieve himself. But his brothers told him not to go into the bush because the tiger could be there. They told him that he could relieve himself behind a rock that was on the side of the road, without thinking if the tiger had converted into a rock.

When the man was relieving himself on the other side of the rock, in a blink of an eye, the rock transformed into a tiger and carried off the muchacho.

Roaring, he entered the mountain. The two brothers arrived [home] crying to tell what had happened to their brother, who was eaten by an enchanted tiger.

—This story was related by Señor Deigo Pérez Có,
dad of Nicolasa, my wife. He did not tell me the name of the story.
I gave it the name, "The Enchanted Tiger [Jaguar]."

# Cuento viejo

## *El tigre [jaguar] encantado*

[SE] DICE [QUE] LA gente de antes, es decir, hablando de nuestros abuelos y abuelas, contaban que el cuerpo de una persona habla cuando está durmiendo.

El cuento dice que tres hermanos eran cazadores. El trabajo de ellos era cazar animales grandes y pequeños. Se quedaban por las montañas por dos o tres noches. Llevaban sus tortillas y tamalitos, menos comida porque en la montaña no les faltaba la carne de animal. Llevaban sus chamarras para dormir en la montaña.

Su mamá les decía es mejor hacer costumbre al dueño del mundo, para que nada mal va a pasar con ellos, sus tres hijos. Pero los muchachos no le dieron importancia lo que les decía su mamá.

La mamá de ellos decía que soñó que uno de sus tres hijos fue comido por tigres y leones en la montaña. La señora insistía de decirles a sus tres hijos que hicieran algo como un presente para pedir perdón al Señor del Santo Mundo. Se dice que sus tres hijos siguieron con el corazón duro—no hicieron una cosa que les dijo su madre.

Así fue con ellos; los tres hermanos siguieron con la cacería. Se quedaban durmiendo debajo de los grandes árboles en la montaña. Una vez juntaron mucho fuego por la noche para no sentir tanto el frio. Ellos tres se acostaron; como a media noche, dos de los tres hermanos se durmieron. El otro no le entraba el sueño; sentía que algo mal va a pasar con ellos. Los dos siguieron durmiendo muy profundo, pero dice el que estaba despierto se sentía molesto. No se sentía tranquilo.

De repente, vio venir un gran tigre meneando la cola. Se sentó donde estaba los pies de los tres muchachos. El hermano que estaba despierto [estaba] temblando de mucho frio y miedo del momento en que el tigre se le iba a comer. Los dos [otros] estaban durmiendo tranquilamente. El tigre agarró el pie izquierdo del que no estaba durmiendo y le preguntó al último dedo del pie, "¿Eres tu para mí? ¡Te lo voy a comer!" Pero el dedo no contestaba porque el dueño estaba despierto. El tigre dejó tirado el pie.

El tigre estaba sentado cerca de los pies de los tres hombres que estaban acostados. Luego, agarró el dedo del otro que estaba durmiendo, y le pregunta al último dedo del pie, "¿Eres para mí? ¡Te lo voy a comer." Pero el dedo no contestó porque su dueño estaba despierto. El tigre dejó tirado el pie.

Luego, agarro el dedo del otro que estaba durmiendo, y le pregunta al último dedo del pie, "¿Eres tú para mí? ¡Te lo voy a comer!"

El cuento dice que el dedo contestó, "No, no me puedes comer; no soy tuyo. Yo tengo que morir embarrancado [dentro de un barranco; en otras palabras, sintiendo cómo iba a morir al caer accidentalmente dentro de un abismo]. Así habló el dedo del pie izquierdo del segundo hermano.

El cuento dice que el tigre agarró el pie del otro que estaba durmiendo, y le pregunta al último dedo del pie diciendo, "¿Eres tú para mí? ¡Te lo voy a comer!"

Y el dedo del pie contestó al tigre, "Sí me puedes comer, pero no ahorita. Será hasta mañana porque quiero pasar esta noche durmiendo con mis hermanos."

Así habló el ultimo dedo del pie, pero el cuento dice que estos dos estaban muy dormidos. No sintieron que sus cuerpos habían hablado con un tigre. Pero el hermano que había oído estas cosas estaba temblando de frio del gran miedo de todo lo que había y oído que los dedos de los pies de sus hermanos habían hablado con el tigre.

Cuando amaneció, les contó a sus dos hermanos lo que había visto y oído. Pero sus dos hermanos no lo creían que un tigre podía hablar ni creían que sus dedos de sus pies podrían contestar a un tigre. Pero su hermano no se sentía bien porque algo mal va a pasar en el camino.

Entonces, salieron de la montaña del regreso para su casa. El hermano que temía estar en peligro de hacer una comida para el tigre, le dijeron que se adelantara, y los dos otras detrás en protección. Así fueron caminando porque estaba lejos cuando salían de la montaña.

El muchacho les dijo a sus hermanos que él tenía que entrar en el monte para hacer sus necesidades. Pero sus hermanos le decían que no entrara en el monte porque allí puede estar el tigre. Le dijeron que se quedara haciendo sus necesidades detrás de una piedra que estaba a la orilla del camino sin pensar si el tigre se había convertido en piedra.

Cuando el hombre estaba haciendo sus necesidades por detrás de la piedra, en un abrir y cerrar de ojos, la piedra se convirtió en tigre y se llevó al muchacho. Rugiendo, entró en la montaña. Los dos hermanos llegaron llorando a contarlo lo que le había pasado a su hermano que fue comido por un tigre encantado.

—Este cuento era de Señor Diego Pérez Có,
papá de Nicolasa, mi esposa. Él no me dijo el nombre del cuento.
Yo puse el nombre "El Tigre [Jaguar] encantado."

# Mayan Folktale

## *The Man Who Deceived Death*

DEATH, THE STORY GOES, has controlled the lives of people—the day, the hour, where and when they are going to die. Death happens, sending them to the grave.

One day, Death examined [her] list in her notebook [and] she saw that now was the day for don Francisco to die. Don Francisco had told his family and his friends if someone asked for him, to tell her that he was not there. Don Francisco was very liked in the town for being a hardworking man, but he also had enemies.

Then so it was; death was bald, with a sunken nose, and green eyes. One day, she covered her head with a black cloth, and she headed to don Francisco's house to carry him to his grave. When Death arrived at the house, she gave him a greeting, saying, "Good day, good day, I need don Francisco."

Then the gardener spoke, saying, "Here, Francisco does not live; I am called Paco," said the gardener.

"But I need Francisco," said Death.

"Here, Francisco does not live," Paco said again. "Here, Francisco does not live. It is that he has four parcels, and he always is taking care of them, cleaning his cultivations."

But Francisco at each plot is known as don Paco, don Chico, don Francisco, and also, they say, don Pancho. He is the same person.

Death says to don Paco, "I need Francisco!"

Paco tells her, "Perhaps you can find him at the other parcels, but it will [not] be until tomorrow."

But he was the same Francisco. Death, scratching her head, [said], "Damn,

I'm late, and I cannot find the hapless Francisco. Where are the other plots?" she asked don Paco.

He answered her, "Walk from here six *potreros* [wide open spaces between the houses where children play and where the people keep chickens and large animals], and around the corner is the house of Francisco."

"It would [not] be until tomorrow. I am late. I have to go to cook," said Death.

The next day, Death arose very hastily. She dressed in her black robe and smock and went walking in search of don Francisco. She walked the six potreros as she had been told. She arrived at the house saying, "Good day, good day, is this the house of Francisco?"

No one answered.

"I need Francisco," she said.

Don Chico left the house, and he said, "Good day, bald señora, with whom do you wish to speak?"

Death tells him, "You are Francisco. I come to bring you. For a long time, I have been looking for you; the day has passed. Come on!" said Death.

Don Chico says to her, "You are very mistaken, bald old woman. Here is not the house of Francisco. I am called Chico," said the señor.

Death again, scratching her head, did not find the hapless one that she went looking for. "Damn, and now what am I going to do, I am already wasting a lot of time," she said.

Don Chico tells Death, "Bald Lady, I know such a Francisco, but he lives a little distantly. You need to climb this hill; the house is on the plain. More or less in four hours you will arrive at the house of Francisco."

"The distance does not matter; I'm able to get [there]. Can you give me [some of Francisco's] characteristics?"

"Very well," said don Chico, "He is tall, fat, mustached, dark brown, crippled, has ten wives, huffy, laughs alone, and he is a little crazy."

"Thanks," said Death. She went running, climbing the hill, sweating a lot under the hot son. She arrived suffocating, but seeing the garden with a lot of *Flor de muerto* [wild plant whose yellow flowers the people use to adorn the tombs on the Day of the Saints (Armas 1991:98)], Death forgot for a moment the search for don Francisco and began to smell the flowers of death. She began to meditate, saying, "Oh, how my flor de muerto smells, my favorite flower. Each day that people die, they always bring the flower of my liking to the cemetery," she said.

Then, she remembered that she walking in search of don Francisco, always with the salutation, "Buenas tardes" [Good afternoon]. But no one answered back.

She says again, "Buenas tardes."

Don Pancho comes out of the house, and he says to her, "Buenas tardes, bald old lady; you don't have any meat [to sell]. What do you want? With whom do you wish to speak?"

Death says to him, "You are Francisco; now I am taking you. I have been looking for you for days. Well, let's go!"

Don Pancho tells her, "You are very crazy, old bald woman. Here is not the house of Francisco. I am called Pancho."

Death, frightened, did not know what to do. She became furious, ripped her dress, and you could see all bone.

[She exclaimed], "Now, what am I going to do! I have lost a lot of time looking for this ingrate. I am going to return without taking anything with me, and my husband is going to scold me." Crying and crying, she now did not want to return to the cemetery.

The woman of the ranch came out to ask Death, "Why are you crying? Here is the house of Francisco. He is also known as Paco. At work they call him Chico, and all of his godchildren call him Pancho."

"Oh, what a disgrace! I have no luck! Well, I have talked with Chico, with Pancho, and with Paco. What I do not know is whether he is the same Francisco, but now I'm going to take him," said Death. She says again, "Pancho, out, out; let's go! I need to take you right now!"

The family tells her, "Francisco left; he's not coming until noon tomorrow."

"Then I will come tomorrow after midday." And Death went back distressed.

Don Francisco told his family, "Death is walking around looking for me. But I do not want to die. I have a lot of work [to do]. The children are in school; there is no one who cares for the crops. I need to marry; there is no money. And for that [reason], I do not want to die yet. I know I'm going to conquer death."

He and his family prepared the house. In the middle they placed a mortuary box [casket without a cadaver]. Around it, they placed a lot of candles and flowers, the whole house with the scent of incense, pretending that inside the box was the dead man.

Death arrived again, as she had said she would arrive, to take poor don Francisco, saying, "Buenas tardes."

Then, the family came out to ask her what she wanted.

Death said, "I am coming for don Pancho. Today, I have to take him. I have waited a long time."

The woman of don Chico told her, "Francisco died yesterday in an accident. They brought him here dead. Now we are waiting for the kin and friends for the burial," said the señora of don Chico.

Death, surprised, said, "It is strange that I knew nothing of the death of this man. Not even did they advise me when the accident was. Now, I have to return without anything; I have lost a lot of time." Death went away crying.

Don Francisco was the one who defeated Death when Death disappeared. Don Francisco and his family threw away the flowers, the candles, and the coffin, and they began to celebrate because Francisco had conquered death.

In the towns of Guatemala, Francisco is called Chico, Pancho, [and] Paco, [and] it refers to the same person.

—Pedro Cholotío Temó, 100 [percent] indigenous

# Cuento maya

*El hombre que engañó la muerte*

LA MUERTE, DICE EL cuento, tiene controlada la vida de las personas—el día, la hora, donde y cuando van a morir. La muerte pasa, llevándolos a la tumba.

Un día, la muerte examinó [su] lista en su cuaderno, donde vio, que don Francisco ya le llegó el día para morir. Don Francisco le había dicho a su familia y a sus amigos, si alguien preguntara por él, que le dijeron que no está. Don Francisco era muy querido en el pueblo por ser un hombre muy trabajador, pero también tenía enemigos.

Entonces así fue; la muerte era pelona, con la nariz hundida, y ojos verdes. Un día se amarró la cabeza con tela negra, y se dirijo a la casa de don Francisco para llevarse a la tumba. Cuando la muerte llegó a la casa, dando el saludo, diciendo, "Buenos días, buenos días, necesito a don Francisco."

Luego habló el señor del jardín, diciendo "Aquí, no vive Francisco; yo me llamo Paco" dijo el jardinero.

"Pero yo necesito a Francisco," decía le muerte.

"Aquí, no vive Francisco," Paco le vuelve a decir; aquí no vive Francisco. Es que él tiene cuatro parcelas, y él siempre se mantiene, limpiando sus cultivos."

Pero Francisco en cada parcela lo conocen como don Paco, don Chico, don Francisco, y también le dicen don Pancho. Es la misma persona.

La muerte le dice a don Paco, "Yo necesito a Francisco."

Paco le dice, "Tal vez lo puede encontrar en las otras parcelas, pero [no] sería hasta mañana."

Pero era el mismo Francisco.

La muerte, rascando la cabeza, [dijo] "Maldición, se me hace tarde, y no encuentro al desventurado Francisco. ¿Dónde queda las otras parcelas?" le preguntó a don Paco.

Él le contestó, "Camine de aquí seis *potreros* [amplios espacios abiertos entre las casas donde juegan los niños y donde la gente tienen gallinas y animales grandes], y a la vuelta está la casa de Francisco."

"[No] sería hasta mañana. Se me hace tarde. Tengo que ir a cocinar," dijo la muerte.

Al día siguiente la muerte se levantó muy apresurada [precipitadamente]. Se visitó con su túnica negra y su delantal y se fue caminando en busca de don Francisco. Caminó los seis potreros tal como le habían dicho. Llegó hasta la casa diciendo, "Buenos días, buenos días, ¿aquí es la casa de Francisco?"

Nadie le contestaba.

"Necesito a Francisco," decía.

De la casa, sale don Chico y le dice, "Buenos días, señora pelona, ¿con quién quieres hablar?"

La muerte le dice, "Tu eres Francisco. Te vengo a traerlo. Desde hacía, te venía buscando; ya pasó el día. ¡Vamos!," dijo la muerte.

Don Chico le dice, "Estas muy equivocada, vieja pelona. Aquí, no es la casa de Francisco. Yo me llamo Chico," dijo el señor.

La muerte otra vez rascándose la cabeza, no encuentro al desventurado que ando buscan. "Maldición, y ahora que voy hacer; ya voy perdiendo mucho tiempo," decía.

Don Chico le dice a la muerte, "Señora pelona, yo conozco un tal Francisco, pero vive un poco lejos. Tienes que caminar subiendo este cerro; la casa la tiene en la planicie. Más o menos en cuatro horas puedes llegar hasta la casa de Francisco."

"No importa la distancia; yo puedo llegar [allá.] ¿Puede usted darme algunas características [de Francisco]?"

"Muy bien," dijo don Chico, "Es alto, gordo, con bigotes, moreno oscuro, lisiado, tiene diez mujeres, enojado, se ríe solo, y es un poco loco."

"Gracias," dijo la muerte. Se fue corriendo, subiendo el cerro, sudando mucho debajo el fuerte sol. Llegó sofocando, pero viendo el jardín con mucha *flor de muerto* [planta silvestre cuyas amarillas flores usa el pueblo para adornar las tumbas de sus difuntos en el Día de los Santos (Armas 1991:98)]; marigold la muerte se le olvidó por un momento la búsqueda de don Francisco; comenzó a oler las flores de muertes. Comenzó a meditar, diciendo "¡Ay, como huele mi *flor de muerto*, mi flor favorita! Cada día que mueran las personas, siempre llevan al cementerio la flor de mi agrado," dijo.

Luego, recordó que anda en busca de don Francisco, siempre con el saludo, diciendo, "Buenas tardes." Pero nadie le contestaba.

Vuelve a decir "Buenas tardes."

De la casa, sale don Pancho, y le dice, "Buenas tardes, viejita pelona; ni carne tienes [que vender]. ¿Qué quieres? ¿Con a quién quieres hablar?"

La muerte le dice, "Tu eres Francisco; ahorita te llevo. Hace días te venía buscando. ¡Pues, vamos!"

Don Pancho le dice, "Estas muy loca, vieja pelona. Aquí no es la casa de Francisco. Yo me llamo Pancho."

La muerte, asustada, no sabía que hacer. Se puso rabiosa, rasgó su vestido, y se veía todo hueso.

[Ella exclamó] "¡Ahora, que voy hacer! He perdido mucho tiempo de buscar a este ingrato. Voy a regresar sin llevarme nada, y mi marido me va a regañar." Llorando y llorando, ya no quería regresar al cementerio.

Sale la mujer del rancho a decirle a la muerte "¿Te porqué lloras? Aquí es la casa de Francisco; también lo conocen como Paco; en el trabajo lo llaman Chico, y todos sus ahijados lo llaman Pancho."

¡Ay, que desgracia! ¡No tengo fortuna! Pues, yo he hablado, con Chico, con Pancho, y con Paco. Lo que no sé es si es el mismo Francisco, pero ahorita me lo llevo," dijo la muerte. Y vuelve a decir, "Pancho, salga, salga; vamos. Te necesito te llevo ahorita mismo."

La familia le dice," Francisco salió; él no viene hasta mañana a medio día.

"Entonces vendré mañana después del mediodía." Y la muerte regresó apenada.

Don Francisco le dijo a la familia, "La muerta me anda buscando. Pero yo no me quiero morir. Tengo mucho trabajo [que hacer]. Los hijos están en la escuela; los cultivos no hay quien lo cuida. Falta el matrimonia; no hay dinero. Y por eso razón, no quiero morir todavía. Yo sé voy vencer la muerte," dijo don Francisco.

Él y la familia prepararon la casa. En el medio pusieron una caja mortuoria [ataúd sin cadáver]. En su alrededor, pusieron muchas velas y flores, toda la casa con olor a incienso, haciendo [como] que dentro la caja estaba el muerto.

Llegó de nuevo la muerte, como había dicho que tendría que llegaría, para llevarse al pobre don Francisco para llevárselo, diciendo "Buenas tardes."

Luego, sale la familia a preguntarle qué es lo que quería.

La muerta dijo: "Vengo por don Pancho. Hoy, me lo tengo que llevar. He esperado mucho tiempo."

La mujer de don Chico le decía, "Francisco murió ayer en un accidente. Lo trajeron aquí muerto. Ahora estamos esperando a los familiares y amigos para el entierro," dijo la señora de don Chico.

La muerte, sorprendida, dijo "Es raro que yo no supe nada la muerte de este hombre. Ni siquiera me avisaron donde fue el accidente. Ahora, tengo que regresar sin nada; he perdido mucho tiempo." La muerte se regresó llorando.

Don Francisco fue el que venció la muerte cuando la muerte se desapareció. Don Francisco y su familia botaron las flores, las velas, y la caja, y comenzaron a celebrar porque Francisco había vencido la muerte.

En los pueblos de Guatemala, Francisco le dicen Chico, Pancho, [y] Paco, [y] se refiere a la misma persona.

—Pedro Cholotío Temó, cien [por ciento] indígena

CASO

# The Deer Hunters

WHEN I WAS A child, I remember that in my town, San Juan la Laguna, a group of Juaneros was leaving on the weekends to hunt deer. They used the words, "Let's run the deer."

And thus, they went to the mountains of the villages Panyevar, Pasajquim, [and] Palestina. They finished in parts of San Juan. It was very fun and cheerful to walk with the hunters. I remember the year of 1952 when I was eleven years old, the runners of the deer were Señores Agustín Chavajay Cox, my great uncle; Gaspar Cholotío Có Pérez; [and] Simón Có Pérez. Those three sirs had shotguns; they were the ones in charge of shooting the deer. Their assistants, José Cholotío Pérez and Manuel Menodoza, were in charge of the dogs. When the dogs began to bark, it was because they already got the deer out from where he was sleeping.

The three who had shotguns placed themselves in high places to be able to see and hear where the dogs were barking in order to see if the deer passed by to kill it. But the deer is very fast and runs a lot.

At times, they [the hunters] came upon the mountains of Suchitepéquez. There, the dogs were lost, and they went back. Thus, the hunters did not achieve anything, [and] they returned a little sad to their houses.

I remember well the names of the dogs: Otelo, Parri, Carrlesio; they were the dogs of Great Uncle Gaspar. The dogs of Señor Agustín were called by their names Popí, Cusca, and Lili. The dogs that I am mentioning were deer hunters, and [they hunted] no other animals.

When I was thirteen, fourteen, [and] fifteen years of age, I managed to leave with them on the deer hunt. I managed to go with them as the one in charge of putting the dogs where the deer tracks occur. [While] hunting, I only saw four deer: one at Patz'unuj, another at Chua Wonon, the third at Chuí Caynom, and the last on the shore of the lake. This last deer [that I saw] was on June 22, two days before the town festival [of John the Baptist]. About one in the afternoon of that day, the deer without doubt certainly got out of control; he did not continue for the mountains. He went down by the hill and plunged into the lake, but the dogs cornered him and made him return to the shore of the lake. There, Gaspar shot him. But there is a *secreto* [magical act or ritual] when the deer falls dead—the shooter then takes out a scarf from his pack [and] blindfolds the eyes of the dead deer. The belief says that the open eyes asks for justice from the Santo Mundo for being an animal that has no sins; it is bad for the shooter if the dead animal's eyes are open.

The last time that we tried to hunt a deer was in San Marcos la Laguna. We went into the mountains [and] found the deer tracks there. Then we released the dogs. In less than a half hour, the dogs chased the animal from its den. But the place is very sloping, [and] the shooters did not realize when the animal passed near where they were. The deer and the dogs entered the town. It became comical because all the dogs in the town were running after the deer. We went running down the hill, but the shooters were not able to discharge their arms because in the town there were many people.

The strangest thing for us [was that] the deer lost us near the town in the place called Cua Sacab, [an] enchanted place according to the locals. Men and women tried to help us find it, but it was futile. The dogs lost the scent. The dogs and we were like fools. The people told us that the deer threw itself in the lake and drowned; we went down to the shore [but] we could see nothing. We concluded [that] the Santa Mundo hid it from us so that we could not kill him.

## The Most Beautiful [Thing]

Before, when the hunters hunted a deer, they assembled in the place where the animal was lying [after he was shot]. Everyone in the group used to meet there. The shooter began to play a horn of bronze or bone as a signal that the dead deer was there. Then, they blindfolded it, tied it with a lance and leather strap, and, taking turns, carried it on their backs until they arrived at the place Paru-chi Abaj [also spelled Paruchi Abaj]. Our grandfathers and grandmothers who have departed said that in this holy place, the hunters always rested when they carried [back] a dead deer or other animals. That is to say, at this place, the shooter pauses, taking a little rest, and asks his companions to say a brief prayer for forgiveness to the Santo Mundo.

Then they send ahead a companion to advise the wife of don Gaspar, named Concepción Pérez Ujpán, to prepare the clay censer with incense. She prepares the bath [purification or cleansing] censer, and with incense she goes out to meet the group of hunters, one of whom carries the deer on his back. When they enter the *sitio* [homeplace], they have to walk around in front of the house forming a circle. He who carries the deer on his back remains in the middle, covered with the smoke of the incense—it is a *secreto* of the hunters. After everything, they rest a moment. Then, they begin to take off the hide, or skin, and they give the hide to the marksman as a reward for his good aim. Then, they chop it up and divide the meat.

Then, don Gaspar recommends that no one lose a piece of bone. When he calls them, they have to deliver the bones to go and deposit them in the place called Paru-chi Abaj. The most sacred days to deposit the bones of the deer are

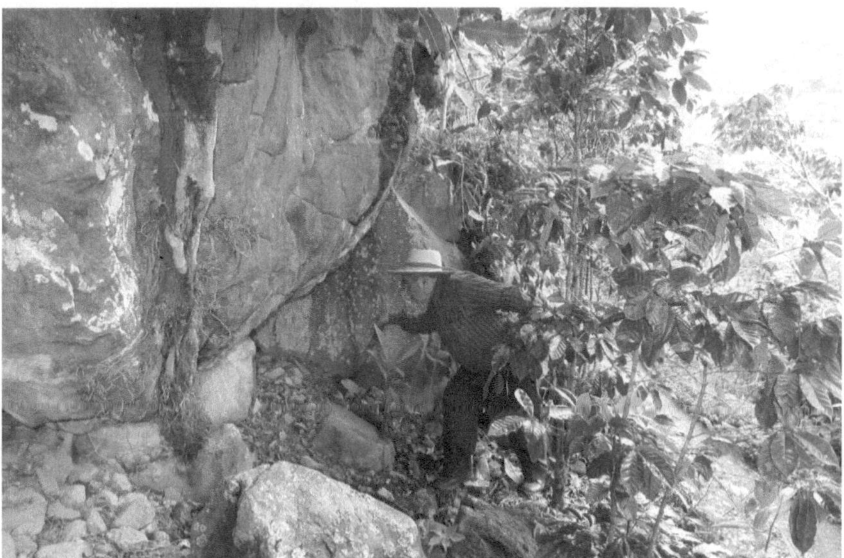

*Figure* 8. Paru-chi Abaj / Paru-chi Abaj

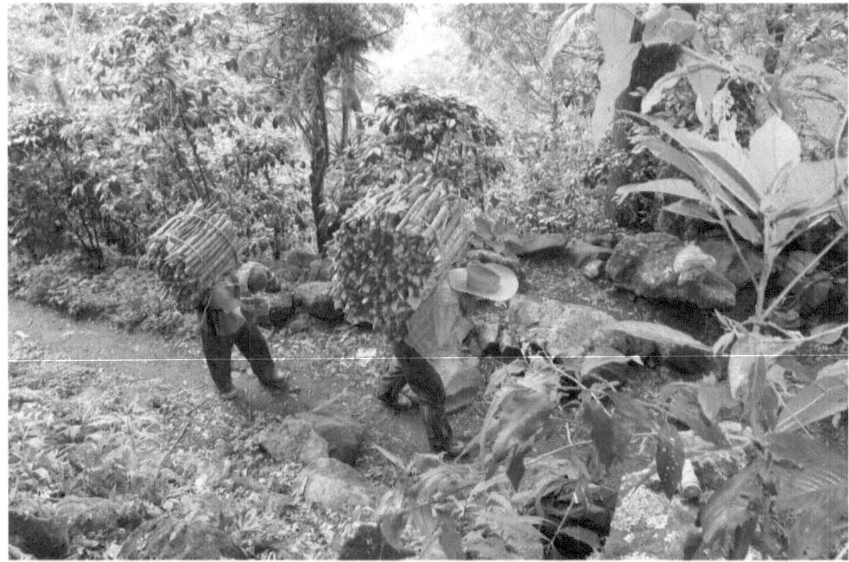

*Figure* 9. Men carrying firewood on the path near Paru-chi abaj / Hombres cargando leña en el camino cerca de Paru-chi abaja

5 Ajpú—7 Ajpú—13 Ajpú, days of the Mayan ritual, the same as the Mayan calendar.[5]

Our grandparents (ancestors) said that "ajpub" is the day of the nagual of the hunters. More for that reason, those days they looked to do costumbres. Then, in this manner, the bones of the deer were laid below the stone, at Paru-chi Abaj with costumbres, or ceremonies.

The grandfathers and grandmothers said that it is very delicate if they do not return the bones of the deer. When the hunter dies, his spirit goes to the enchanted hill. There, the dueño of the hill orders him to form [or reconstruct] the skeleton of the deer, and if he does not manage to do it exactly, it is said that the spirit of the hunter is thrown into the fire.[6]

—Pedro Cholotió Temó

CASO

# Los cazadores de venados

CUANDO YO ERA NIÑO, recuerdo que en mi pueblo, San Juan la Laguna, había un grupo de Juaneros salía los fines de semana a cazar el venado. Ellos usaban la[s] palabra[s], "Vamos a correr al venado."

Y así, se iban en las montañas de las aldeas, Panyebar, Pasajquim, [y] Palestina. Venían a terminar hasta en las partes de San Juan. Era muy divertido y alegre andar con los cazadores. Yo recuerdo del año 1952 cuando tenía 11 años, los corredores de venado eran los Señores Agustín Chavajay Cox, mi tío abuelo; Gaspar Cholotío Có Pérez; [y] Simón Có Pérez. Esos tres señores tenían escopetas; eran los encargados de fusilar el venado. Sus ayudantes, José Cholotío Pérez y Manuel Mendoza, eran encargados de los peros. Cuando los perros comenzaban a ladrar, es porque ya sacaron el venado de donde estaban durmiendo.

Los tres que tenían escopetas se ponían en lugares altos para poder ver y oír donde ladraban los perros para ver si el venado pasaba cerca para matarlo. Pero el venado es muy veloz [y] corre mucho.

A veces, agarraban las montañas de la costa de Suchitepéquez. Allí los perros se quedaban perdidos; y se regresaban. Así, los cazadores no lograban nada, [y] se regresaban poco triste a sus casas.

Yo recuerdo bien al nombre [los nombres] de los perros: Otelo, Parri, Carrlesio; eran los perros de Tío abuelo Gaspar. Los perros del Señor Agustín los llamaban por sus nombres Popí, Cusca, y Lili. Los perros que estoy mencionado eran cazadores de venado y no [cazaban] otros animales.

Cuando yo tenía 13, 14, [y] 15 años, logré salir con ellos a la cacería de venados. Logré irme con ellos como encargado de poner los perros donde pasan las huellas del venado. Solamente vi, [mientras] cazar, cuatro venados: uno en Patz'unuj, otro en Chua Wonon, la tercera en Chuí Caynom, y la última en la orilla del lago. Este último venado [que yo vi] fue el 22 junio, dos días antes de la fiesta del pueblo [de Juan el bautista]. Como la una de la tarde de ese día, el venado sin duda se descontroló; no agarró por la montaña. Bajó por el cerro y se tiró al lago, pero los perros lo encorralaron le hicieron regresar a la orilla. Allí, Gaspar le baleó. Pero hay secreto cuando el venado cae muerto—el tirador luego saca un pañuelo de su morral [y] venda los ojos del venado muerto. La creencia dice que los ojos abiertos piden justicia al Santo mundo por ser un animal que no tiene nada de pecado; es malo para el tirador si los ojos del animal muerto están abiertos.

La última vez que tratamos de cazar un venado fue en San Marcos la Laguna. Nos metimos en la montaña [y] allí encontramos las huellas del venado. Luego soltamos los perros. En menos de media hora, los perros sacaron el animal de su guarido. Pero el lugar es muy pendiente, [y] los tiradores no se dieron cuenta cuando el animal pasó cerca de donde estaban. El venado y los perros entraron en la población. Se volvió cómico porque todos los perros de la población corrían tras del venado. Del cerro nos bajamos corriendo, pero los tiradores no pudieron disparar sus armas porque en el pueblo había mucha gente.

Lo más extraño fue para nosotros [era que] el venado nos perdió cerca de la población en el lugar llamado Cua Sajcab, [un] lugar encantado asegún los lugareños. Hombres y mujeres intentaron nos ayudaron a encontrarlo, pero no fue posible; los perros perdieron el olfato. Los perros y nosotros nos quedamos como tontos. La gente nos decía que el venado se tiro a lago y ahogó; bajamos a la orilla [pero] nada logramos ver. Llegamos a la conclusión [que] el Santo mundo lo escondió de nosotros para no podríamos matarlo.

## Lo más bonito [cosa]

Antes, cuando los cazadores cazaban un venado, se reunían en ese lugar donde quedaba tendido el animal [después de que le dispararan]. Allí se juntaban todos los del grupo. El tirador comenzó a tocar una de bronce o cuerno como señal de que el venado muerto estaba allí. Luego, le vendaron los ojos, lo ataron con lanza y correa de cuero, y por turnos lo cargaron a la espalda hasta llegar a lugar Paruchi Abaj [también deletreado Paruchi Abaj]. Nuestros abuelos y abuelas que se han ido dijeron que en este lugar sagrado, los cazadores siempre descansaban allí cuando llevaban [de regreso] un venado muerto u otros animales. Es decir, en este lugar, el tirador se detiene, descansan un poco, y pide a sus compañeros que digan una breve oración de perdón al Santo Mundo.

Luego envían por delante a un compañero para avisar la esposa de don Gaspar, llamaba Concepción Pérez Ujpán, a preparar el incensario de barro con incienso. Ella prepara el incensario de baño [purificación o limpieza], y con incienso sale a encontrar o a recibir al grupo de cazadores con el venado cargado. Cuando entran en el sitio, tienen que dar una vuelta en frente de la casa formando un circulo. El que lleva el venado en la espalda queda en el medio, cubierto por el humo del incienso—es un *secreto* [ritual] de los cazadores. Después de todo, descansan un momento. Luego, comienzan a quitarle el cuero, o piel, y dan el cuero al tirador como recompensa por su buena puntería. Luego, lo destazan y se reparten la carne.

Luego, don Gaspar recomienda que nadie pierde un pedazo de hueso. Cuando él los llama, tienen que entregar los huesos para ir a depositarlos en el lugar llamado Paru-chi Abaj. Los días más sagrado para depositar los huesos del venado son 5 Ajpú—7 Ajpú—13 Ajpú, días del Ritual maya, lo mismo que el calendario maya.[5]

Nuestros abuelos (antepasados) decían que "ajpub" es el día del nagual de los cazadores. Más por eso, esos días buscaban hacer costumbres. Luego, de esta manera, se colocaron los huesos del venado debajo de la piedra, Paru-chi-Abaj, con costumbres, o ceremonia.

Los abuelos y abuelas decían es muy delicado si no devuelvan los huesos del venado. Cuando el cazador se muere, su espíritu va al cerro encantado. Allí es donde el dueño [señor, dios] del cerro lo mande que formar [o reconstruir] el esqueleto del venado, y si no llega a hacerlo cabal [exactamente], se dice que el espíritu del cazador es arrojado al fuego.[6]

—Pedro Cholotío Temó

# The Man Who Mistreated His Wife

OUR GRANDFATHERS AND GRANDMOTHERS bequeathed us the folktales; for us, it is fascinating, but for them it was a method of [providing] an example to their sons and daughters; they did not use a social worker or psychologist. As part of the Mayan culture, they used stories as a method of orientation for their sons and daughters.

A story that says: There was a man who was very bad, but very bad, disobedient, [and] restless. From his mouth came very bad words. They say from childhood, he was disobedient. He did not respect his parents, and so it was.

When he became a man, he looked for a muchacha to be his woman, and they united. The girl was from a good, God-fearing family, and a very hard worker. But her husband was a pretentious man, lazy, drunk. For whatever thing, he beat his wife. That's the way it was—every little bit, he hit his woman. The poor woman felt very sad.

She cried and asked God, "Better to meet with death than to have this life full of pain."

[The story] says that one night the woman went to bed crying because of the blows and the mistreatment that she suffered. When she was sleeping, in a dream a young boy appeared to her and said, "I also am sad for you; it is a pity that your husband is a person of bad character. But, now, when it dawns, go to the priest in the convent. Tell him all your suffering, and truly he has a solution to your problem." Thus, the woman dreamed.

The following day, she went to the convent to tell the father what she suffers in life. The father was surprised when he heard [of] all the evil that had happened to the woman.

The father tells the woman, "Dear girl, your problem has a solution. Go call your husband so I can talk to him, and you will see that your husband will change from bad to good."

The woman ran to call her husband. Then, the two arrived to see the father. The father said, "Is she your woman?"

"Yes father, she is my woman."

"So that you do not give a bad life to this poor woman, I am going to give you an assignment that will serve you well in the future. When you have sold this pig, bring me the money. But you have to go to a distant town to handle this business and get to know how the people live and how they are behaving in their homes. This will help you a lot."

The man left the town and took the road to other towns offering the pig to sell. The animal became tired and did not want to go (walk) [any farther]. And no one wanted to buy it. The man began to cry; he felt hungry [and] thirsty. Night came, and he did not have a place to sleep; [he was] convinced that he was going to remain in the street with the animal.

But a charitable family spoke to the man so that he could eat and drink a little. Also, they gave him lodging to sleep inside the house. Before going to sleep, the owners of the house invoked the name of the heart of heaven and heart of earth, giving thanks for the life of each one.

The man lay down on the floor of the house. He saw the couple sleeping and at midnight something like a light appeared near the bed, but it was not a natural light. It was a divine light that was shining on the sleeping couple. Then, the man lying down and watching said to himself, "The life of this couple is full of joy—even a divine light guards them through the night."

The next day, the man arose and took the road again, offering the pig. He went to other towns, [but] no one wanted to buy the animal because the people were poor. By late afternoon, again [there was] the same problem—he had no water, no food, and no place to sleep. In many houses he asked [for] lodging, but no one allowed him to enter for being a stranger. Without a blessed remedy, he remained sleeping in the street together with the swine, thinking, "My wife must be fast asleep in bed, and [I am] suffering with a pig."

Dawn came the third day; he took the road to other towns, offering the pig, but no one wanted to buy it. Now three days went by, [and] the man had not been able to sell the pig. He said, "The priest sent me to do this business, but now I am in hell at nightfall the third day."

He asked [for] lodging at a house, but the owners were angry. They told the man that they would give him lodging and food, but with the condition that the hog had to stay far from the house because of its bad odor. The man went to steer the hog near the forest.

The man remained sleeping inside the house. Also, the owners of the house slept. About midnight, the man could not sleep because it was very cold. Thus, he saw a dwarf dressed in black, who had a tail, jumping over the bed where the owners were sleeping. He grabbed the tip of his tail and put it in the man's nose. The man, crazy from his sleep, began to hit his wife, thinking that she was bothering him. At midnight, it caused a feud between the couple; they woke up fighting. The man was surprised and said, "This dwarf inserts his tail in my nose when I fight with my woman."

At dawn, he [the bad man] left the house to see the pig in order to continue offering it for sale. But due to his bad luck, coyotes had devoured the pig during the night. The man had to return to the padre's convent to tell him that he was unable to sell a pig in three days.

The padre asked him, "What was your story in the last three days?"

"The first day, I was offering the pig; no one wanted to buy it. They gave me food and lodging. I was trying to sleep on the floor when over the bed of the owners of the house [I saw] a divine light that glowed, not a natural light. I asked if they saw it, and they told me that they saw nothing. That was the first day.

"The second day, I went to the other towns offering the pig. But I was unable to sell it. I had to remain on the street because no one gave me food or lodging.

"The third day I went to other towns offering the pig; no one bought it. At night, they gave me food and lodging. There, I slept, but in the night, I saw a black dwarf with a tail. At night when the owners were sleeping, the dwarf grabbed his tail and put it in the nose of the husband. That is where the problem arose, with the husband thinking his wife was bothering him. They began taking offense. They woke up fighting. In the morning, I realized I could not sell the pig [because] the coyotes ate it and I had to come here to tell you."

The father gave him the answer to all that had happened to him. He said, "Dear boy, you have not been able to sell the pig in three days, nor have you been able to return the pig to me. I am giving you the answer to the last three days and nights. This will serve you well.

"The divine light that shone over the bed of the couple is the [light] of peace, the tranquility, the good harmony between the husband and his wife—that is what you lack. The second night when you were sleeping on the street with the pig, thus will be your life, to remain on the street or in jail because of so much evil that you are causing your poor wife.

"The third night when you saw the dwarf stick his tail up [the man's] nose, it is the devil who gets into the man's thoughts. So it is with you. The devil tickles your nose when you begin to mistreat you wife. Every time you want to quarrel, remember the dwarf so that you will change your attitude."

Thus ends this story.

—Señora Rosario Ujpán, the mother of Nicolasa, my wife, died twenty years ago. She told us this story so that we could turn out well.

# El hombre que maltrató a su esposa

NUESTROS ABUELOS Y ABUELAS nos legaron los cuentos; para nosotros, es fascinante, pero para ellos era un medio para [proporcionar] un ejemplar a sus hijos e hijas; ellos no usaron un consejero social ni psicólogo. Como parte de la cultura maya, usaban los cuentos como un medio de orientación a sus hijos e hijas.

Un cuento que dice: Había un hombre que era muy malo, pero muy malo, desobediente, [e] inquieto. De su boca salían malas palabras. Dicen desde pequeño, fue desobediente. No respetaba a sus padres, y así fue.

Cuando llegó a ser hombre, buscó a una su muchacha para que fuera su mujer, y se juntaron. La muchacha era de buena familia temerosa de Dios, y muy trabajadora. Pero su marido era un hombre pretencioso, haraganes, borracho. Por cualquier cosa, golpeaba su esposa. Así fue—a cada poco, le pegaba a su mujer. La pobre mujer se siente muy triste.

Lloraba y le pedía a Dios, "Mejor hallar la muerte que tener esta vida llena de dolor."

[El cuento] dice que una noche la mujer llorando se acostó por los golpes y los maltratos que se la daban. Cuando estaba durmiendo, en el sueño se le apareció un muchachito que le decía: "Yo también estoy triste por ti; te tengo lastima tu marido es una persona de mal carácter. Pero, ahora, cuando amanece, vaya con el sacerdote en convento. Cuéntele todo tu sufrimiento, y [de] veras tiene la solución de tu problema." Así, soñó la mujer.

Al día siguiente, se fue al convento a contarle al padre lo que ella padece en la vida. El padre se sorprendió cuando oyó [de] todos los males que la mujer la pasa en su vida.

El padre le dice a la mujer. "Hijita, tu problema tiene solución. Anda a llamar a tu marido para yo platique con él, y verás que tu marido cambiará de malo a bueno."

La mujer corrió a llamar a su marido. Luego, los dos llegaron con el padre. El padre dice al hombre, "¿Es ella tu mujer?

"Sí padre, ella es mi mujer."

"Para que no le des mala vida a esta pobre mujer, te voy una tarea que te servirá mucho en el futuro. Cuando hayas vendido este cerdo, me traer el dinero. Pero tienes que ir en pueblo lejos para puedes hacer este negocio y conocerás como viven la gente y como se están portando en sus hogares. Este le ayudará mucho."

El hombre salió del pueblo agarro camino a otros pueblos ofreciendo el cerdo para venderlo. El animal se cansó ya no quería andar (caminar) [más lejos]. Y nadie quería comprarlo. El hombre se puso a llorar; sentía hombre [y] sed. Entrando la noche, no tenía donde dormir; [estaba] convencido que se iba a quedar en la calle junto con el animal.

Pero una familia caritativa le habló al hombre para que pudiera comer y tomar un poco. También, le dieron posada para quedar durmiendo adentro de la casa. Los dueños de la casa antes de dormir invocaron el nombre del corazón del cielo y al corazón de la tierra, dando gracias por la vida de cada uno.

El hombre acostaba en el piso de la casa. Viendo la pareja durmiendo, a media noche cerca de la cama apareció como una luz, pero no era luz natural. Era una luz divina que brillaba sobre la pareja durmiendo. Entones, el hombre, acostado y viendo y diciendo a sí mismo, "La vida de esta pareja está llena de alegría—hasta una luz divina [que] los cuida por la noche."

Al otro día, el hombre se levantó y agarró el camino otra vez, ofreciendo el cerdo. Se fue a otros pueblos, [pero] nadie quería comprar el animal porque la gente era pobre. Al caer la tarde, otra vez [había] el mismo problema—no tenía agua, no comida, y no lugar dónde dormir. En muchas casas, pedía por posada, pero no le dejaban entrar por ser un desconocido. Sin santo remedio, se quedó durmiendo en la calle junto al cerdo, pensando, "Mi mujer ha de estar bien dormida en la cama, y yo [estoy] sufriendo con un cerdo."

Amaneció el tercer día; agarró camino a otros pueblos, ofreciendo el cero, pero ninguna persona quería comprarlo. Ya van tres días, [y] el hombre no había podido vender el cerdo. Él decía, "El sacerdote me mandó a hacer este negocio, pero ahora estoy en el infierno al anochecer el tercer día."

Pidió [para] posada en una casa, pero los dueños eran enojados. Le dijeron al hombre que sí le daban posada y comida, pero con la condición de que el cerdo tiene que estar lejos de la casa porque por el mal olor que tenía el animal. El hombre fue a manejar el cerdo cerca del bosque.

El hombre se quedó durmiendo dentro de la casa. También, se durmieron los dueños de la casa. Como a medianoche, el hombre no le entraba el sueño porque había mucho frio. Así, el vio un enano vestido de negro, quien tenía cola, brincando sobre la cama donde estaban durmiendo los dueños. Él agarró la punta de la cola y se la mete en la nariz del hombre. El hombre, alocado por el sueño, comenzó a pegarle a su mujer, pensando que ella lo estaba molestando. A medianoche, se armó un pleito entre la pareja, amanecieron peleando. El hombre se extrañaba y decía, "Este enano mete su cola en mi nariz cuando peleo con mi mujer."

Al amanecer, se fue [el hombre malo] a ver el cerdo para seguirlo ofreciendo. Pero [por] su mala suerte, los coyotes devoraron al cerdo durante la noche. El hombre tuvo que regresar al convento del padre para decirle que no pudo vender un cerdo en tres días.

El padre le preguntó, "¿Cuál fue su historia en los tres días?"

"El primer día, estuve ofreciendo el cerdo, ninguno no quiere compralo. Me dieron pasada y comida. Estaba tratando de dormir en el piso cuando sobre la cama de los dueños de la casa [vi] una luz divina que brillaba, no una luz natural. Yo les pregunté ellos si lo vieron, y me dijeron que no vieron nada. Esto fue el primer día.

"El segundo día, fui a otros pueblos ofreciendo el cerdo. Tampoco pude venderlo. Tuve que quedarme en la calle durmiendo porque ninguno me dio posada ni comida.

"El tercer día, fui a otros pueblos ofreciendo el cerdo; nadie lo compró. Por la noche, me dieron comida y posada. Allí, me quedé dormido, pero por la noche, vi un enano negro con una cola. Por la noche cuando los dueños estaban durmiendo, el enano agarró la cola y se la metió en la nariz del marido. Ahí, surgió el problema con el esposo pensando que su mujer lo estaba molestando. Comenzaron ofenderse. Amanecieron peleando. Por la mañana, me di cuenta de que no podía vender el cerdo [porque] los coyotes se lo comieron y tuve que venirme aquí decírtelo."

El padre le dio la repuesta de todo lo que había pasado con ese hombre. Le dijo, "Hijito, no has podido vender un cerdo en tres días, ni me has podido devolver el cerdo. Te estoy dando la respuesta a los últimos tres días y tres noches. Esto te servirá bien.

"La luz divina que resplandecía sobre la cama de la pareja es la [luz] de paz, la tranquilidad, y la buena armonía entre el marido y mujer—eso es lo que te falta a ti. La segunda noche cuando te quedaste durmiendo en la calle junto el cerdo, así será tu vida, te quedar en la calle o en la cárcel por tanto maldad que le estas causando a tu pobre mujer.

"La tercera noche cuando viste el enano meter la cola en la nariz [del hombre], es el diablo que se mete en los pensamientos del hombre. Así pasa contigo. El diablo te hace cosquillas en la nariz cuando comienzas a dar maltrato a tu mujer. Cada vez que quieras pelear, acuérdate del enano así te cambiarás de actitud."

Así finaliza este cuento.

—Señora Rosario Ujpán, madre de Nicolasa, mi esposa, murió hace 20 años. Nos contaba para que nosotros nos cortaramos bien.

CASO

# The Owl-Man

*Incredible but True*

[THIS IS] A REAL story. Many times, we people don't believe in the naguales of others, but indeed naguales exist, or [that is,] that people turn into animals. It is difficult to ascertain what the *suerte* [fate], or destiny, of a person is.

In San Marcos la Laguna lived a señor who was called Francisco San Coy; he was a *jornalero* [day-worker who] worked a lot of time in San Juan, but the family fell into alcoholism. His wife they killed in Tzununá. The news was only that she was brutally assassinated with sticks and stones. Her body was left on the road that goes to San Marcos. Who knows who killed her? There was no investigation. Because she was an alcoholic, no one asked for justice.

Her son, Miguel, died drunk. That is why Francisco remained alone; he spent more time in San Pablo because in that town they sold a lot of *cusha* [abbreviation for cushusha, clandestine aguardiente]. An *octavo* [eighth of a liter] cost one quetzal.

Well, the people of San Marcos said Francisco should not drink because he had a bad nagual, but we did not believe it because Francisco was a humble man. He came to work with me, but after the illness, he was worse. He threw himself into the vice of alcoholism.

The strangest thing is what an evangelical brother of a church in San Pablo said. When the one in charge of opening the church arrived and opened its doors over the pulpit was a big *búho* [owl, tecolote]. The frightened man called the rest of the brothers to see what he could do to extract that owl. Many thought that this thing was bad for the church, or all its members said that no one should touch it. One of them ran to fetch a *brujo* [witch] to say what this animal was about—inside the church.

The brujo told them, "This owl is the nagual of a drunk, but the drunk now is an old person. Go buy two octavos of aguardiente." The brothers ran to buy the *guaro* [home-brewed aguardiente].

Then, the brujo opened the beak of the owl [and] gave him an eighth. The animal swallowed it. The witch asked, "Do you want another?" The animal was not able to speak; but they say with his head he signaled that indeed he would like another.

The witch gave him another drink; he drank two complete octavos. It looked as if the animal now felt drunk. He remained bent over where he was. Then the witch told all those who were there to kick it until it died. Thus, they all did; they all kicked that owl to death. Now [that it was] dead, the shaman told two of them to go with him to put that animal in a deep ditch. The three, the shaman and his two companions, went to throw that dead animal in a ditch a little below the town. They carried it in a sack to the ditch, and there in the ditch they left that owl. The shaman and his two companions returned.

The following day, out of curiosity the same persons very early went to the place where they had dropped that dead owl. To their surprise, they got a big scare. In that place, they found not the owl but the body of a dead man. It was the lifeless body of Francisco San Coy. His body was lying down over the sack where they had put the dead animal. That is where the news spread that a dead owl had been left lying in the ditch, and that in that place was found the corpse of a man from San Marcos who died drunk.

Many people of San Pablo and San Marcos commented that that owl was the man who died in that ditch. And they say that when they opened the eyes of the cadaver, they looked like the eyes of the owl. [That is] where it was said that that man was the owl.

This is a real story [*caso*].

—Pedro Cholotío Temó

CASO

# El hombre búho

*Increíble, pero es cierto*

[ESTE ES] UN CUENTO real. Muchas veces, nosotros las personas no creemos en las naguales de otros, pero sí existen los naguales, o [es decir,] que las personas se conviertan animales. Es difícil averiguar cual es la suerte o el destino de una persona.

En San Marcos la Laguna, vivía un señor que se llamaba Francisco San Coy; era jornalero [quien] trabajó mucho tiempo en San Juan, pero la familia cayo en el alcoholismo. Su esposa la mataron en Tzununá. Solamente se oyó la noticia que fue brutalmente asesinada con piedras y con palos. Su cuerpo fue dejado en el camino que conduce a San Marcos. ¿Quién sabe quien la mató? No hubo averiguación. Por ser una mujer alcohólica, no hay que pidió justicia.

Su hijo, Miguel, se murió bolo. Es así Francisco se quedó solito; más pasaba el tiempo en San Pablo porque en ese pueblo venden mucha *cusha* [abreviatura de cushusha, (aguardiente clandestino). Un octavo [de un litro] cuesta un quetzal.

Pues, decía la gente de San Marcos Francisco no dejaba de tomar porque tiene un nagual malo, pero nosotros no creíamos porque Francisco era un hombre humilde. Llegaba a trabajar conmigo, pero después la enfermedad, fue peor. [Él] se tiró al vicio el alcoholismo.

Lo más extraño es lo que cuenta un hermano evangélico de una iglesia de San Pablo. Cuando él en cargado de abrir la iglesia llegó [y] abrió las puertas de la misma iglesia, sobre el pulpito estaba un gran búho (tecolote). El hombre asustado llamó a los demás hermanos para ver que es lo se va hacer para sacar ese búho. Muchos pensaron que esta cosa era mal para la iglesia, o sus miembros entre todo, dijeron que nadie lo toque. Uno de ellos corrió a traer un brujo para que diga de qué se trata este animal—adentro la iglesia.

El brujo les dijo, "Este tecolote es el nagual de un bolo, pero el bolo ya es una persona vieja. Vayan a comprar dos octavos de aguardiente." Los hermanos corrieron a comprar el guaro.

Luego el brujo abrió el pico del búho [y] le da un octavo. El animal se lo tragó. El brujo le preguntaba "¿Quieres otro?" El animal no podía hablar, pero dicen que con la cabeza hacía señas que sí quería otro.

El brujo le dio otro trago; cabal se tomó los dos octavos. Se miraba que el animal ya se sentía bolo. Quedo agachado de donde estaba. Entonces, el brujo les dijo a entre todos los que allí estaban que patearlo hasta que se muere. Así, lo hicieron; entre todos patearon ese búho hasta matado. Ya muerto, el chamán les dijo a dos de ellos que le acompañaran a meter ese animal en una zanja profunda. Entre los tres, el chamán y sus dos compañeros, se fueron a botar el búho muerto en un zanjón un poco abajito del pueblo. Se lo llevaron en un costal, y allí en el zanjón dejaron ese búho. El brujo y sus compañeros se regresaron.

Al día siguiente, por curiosidad de las mismas personas, muy temprano fueron al lugar donde habían dejado ese búho muerto. Para su sorpresa, se llevaron el gran susto. En ese lugar, ya no estaba el tecolote, pero [había] el cuerpo de un hombre muerto. Se trataba del cuerpo sin vida de Francisco San Coy. Su cuerpo estaba recostado sobre el costal donde habían dejado el animal muerto. Allí es donde corrió la noticia que en el zanjón habían dejado tirado un tecolote muerto y que en ese lugar se encontraba el cadáver de un hombre de San Marcos que se murió bolo.

Mucha de la gente de San Pablo y de San Marcos comentaban que ese búho era el hombre que se murió en ese zanjón. Y dicen que cuando le abrieron los ojos del cadáver se parecían los ojos del tecolote. [Ahí es] donde se dijo que ese hombre era el tecolote. Este es un cuento real.

—Pedro Cholotío Temó

# Mayan Folktale

*Lady of the Hill That Is Called Chua Suj*

[THE CUENTO] SAYS THAT [in] this town lived a señora who was sick all the time. Some days she was able to walk; other days [she was] sick. Thus, she spent her life. Her husband was a very poor fisherman, looking for crabs under the rocks on the shore of the lake. The lady was the one in charge of selling the fish and crabs. With that, they earned a daily living.

The señora meditated and meditated about her illness; she wanted an improvement of health and of the poverty that tormented them. Well, her meditation was heard by the *dueña* [owner lady, goddess] of enchantment.

One night, the señora received a notice in her dream—a señora spoke to her in a dream, saying, "It gives me great sorrow to see an illness that you have been suffering for a long time and the poverty that is happening to you. You and your husband are very poor. I am the charmed woman, dueña of the hill called Chua Suj. I have gold and silver, and I will give you a little of my fortune so that you will have a little happiness with your husband."

In the dream, the woman answered the enchanted woman, saying, "What is it that I need to do to find what you are offering me?"

The enchanted señora told her, "You need to go three times to the place of Chua Suj. There, in that place you will find a young woman. With her, you are going to chat, and she will tell you everything that you will have to do."

When it dawned, the woman got up from her bed a little sad and a little content because of all that she had dreamed. Then, she told her husband everything that she had dreamed during the night.

It is said that her husband encouraged her to go to that place, Chua Suj, at twelve midday. There, they were two hours, but they did not see anything, and they returned home. Her husband told her that her dream had been [the] madness of a nightmare.

Again, the following night when the woman was sleeping, she began to dream the same, speaking again with the lady of enchantment who said again she better go to the hill, Chua Suj. In the dream, the woman answered the enchanted lady, saying, "Yesterday, together with my husband, we went to the hill, Chua Suj. You told me a young woman [there would] tell me all I would have to do. We had to return because we did not see anything."

The enchanted woman said again, "Yes, but you have to go alone, without your husband. You can go again tomorrow and meet a young woman. She is going to say all you have to do." Thus, was the second dream.

At dawn, she told her husband all that she had dreamed for the second time. But her husband took her for a fool or crazy person. The poor sick woman, between her pains, went again to the place called Chua Suj at noon [where] she saw a young woman seated over the same rock (stone) beneath the suj tree. She was combing her beautiful hair.

The poor woman felt a great fear, as [if] ice fell over her body. Then the young woman who was combing her hair spoke to the poor woman, saying, "Do not be afraid. Here, I am seated over this stone, combing my hair. I am waiting for you. I am the errand girl; I am the one who takes care of the dueña of enchantment. Come again tomorrow, and tomorrow I will give you the result of your three visits." So she told the woman.

The next day, at midday, the poor sick woman went again to the hill, Chua Suj. Again, the young woman was seated over the same stone, combing her hair. She spoke to her, saying, "Don't be afraid; I am called Alaxik. I want to say I am your sister." And she began to say to the woman, "I am the messenger; I am the one who cares for the lady, owner of enchantment, lady and owner of this hill. She appeared in your dream; she is aware of your illness and of your poverty, but you should make three visits. Now is the second, and tomorrow will be the third visit. I will not wait for you tomorrow; you have to come alone. Bring your *perraje* [blanket of cotton or wool] or shawl that you are going to spread under that suj tree.

"Over your blanket or shawl, thirteen snakes will pass by. First, six big snakes will pass by. [After that will come] a *cuta* snake (a short snake), thicker than other snakes, but short in length—like the arm [pestle] of a grinding stone [*metate*]. It is the cuta that brings the fortune, leaving over your blanket a little piece of stone with gold.[7]

"After the short snake passes by, six more snakes will go by. Then they will disappear from there, and you will be able to wrap the fortune in the shawl. And you have to walk a certain distance backward so that the fortune remains with you. (If not), on the contrary, it will return to its owner [of the hill of Chua Suj]. When you arrive at your house, place it in the door of your house and pass by it four times. Then, you are going to put it in a clay jar and change the place every twenty days. You will see that your illness will disappear and [that] money will come very easily." So she said to that woman.

Thus, the poor and sick woman went for the third time on Chua Suj Hill, worried and thinking about what was going to happen to her because that woman was very afraid of snakes. She arrived again at the place called Chua Suj with the horrifying creatures. Very afraid, she spread out her shawl under the tree at twelve noon. The cave opened, and from there, the first six snakes came out that passed over the shawl. From there, came a short snake. It is said that when the short snake was passing over the blanket, it vomited and hurled a piece of jade with gold. After vomiting, it continued after the six snakes that were going ahead, and after it came the other six snakes. In all, there were thirteen snakes that passed over the lady's shawl.

The thirteen snakes returned to meet in the cave from where they had come. The hill, it is said, swallowed them. The woman picked up and wrapped up her shawl, and she walked backward, just as she had been told. When she arrived home, she did the secreto, [putting it in her door and passing by it four times]. Then, she grabbed the clay jar and put it under her bed. This was the fortune that the dueña of enchantment of the hill, Chua Suj, gave the woman.

It is said that this was how, little by little, [she and her husband] realized the change. They began raising chickens, pigs, bees, and rabbits. With the money that they earned from the sale of the animals, they bought land and built their little houses. They had a better life; now, they did not suffer as before.

But the story says that the woman told her husband all that had happened to her—the fortune that she had received from the enchanted lady of the hill, Chua Suj. But they say in time the lady died, and the husband told the rest of the people that [the house held the fortune of] his deceased wife. The neighbors gave *guarro* [plain distilled liquor] to the man, and when he was drunk, stole the fortune. And so he lost everything he had. Again, the husband remained in a poverty worse than before.

The hill Chua Suj is about three kilometers from the town. The people of earlier times always said that from this place came out chickens, pigs, and many rabbits, but [only] once in a while; that is to say, when the exact day [of the dueña] of the [enchanted] hill comes.[8] The suj tree in Spanish is the conacaste tree [also known as the Guanacaste tree].

—This is the story of Señor Francisco, who has been dead for about twenty-five years. He left this tale to his son Diego Toc. Diego told it to me. We were good friends since we were young; we played on the soccer team. Diego died two years ago; he was seventy-three years old.

# Cuento maya

*Dueña del cerro que se llama Chua Suj*

[EL CUENTO] DICE QUE [en] este pueblo vivía una señora que solo enferma se mantenía. Unos días se ponía a caminar; otros días [estaba] enferma. Así, pasaba la vida. Su marido era un pescador muy pobre, buscando cangrejos debajo de las piedras en la orilla del lago. La señora era la que se encargada de vender los pescados y los cangrejos. Con eso, se ganaban la vida diaria.

La señora meditó y meditó por su enfermedad; quería una mejoría de su salud y de la pobreza que les atormentaba. Pues, su meditación fue oída por la dueña del encanto.

Una noche, la señora recibió una noticia en el sueño—una señora le habló en un sueño diciendo, "Me da mucha pena de ver con una enfermedad que vienes padeciendo por mucho tiempo y la pobreza que vienen pasando. Tú y tu marido son muy pobres. Yo soy la mujer encanto, dueña del cerro llamado Chua Suj. Tengo oro y plata, y te daré un poco de mi fortuna para que tengas un poco felicidad con tu marido.

En el sueño la mujer le contestó a la mujer encantada, diciendo "¿Que es lo que debo de hacer para hallar lo que me estas ofreciendo?"

La señora encantada dice que le dijo, "Tienes que ir tres veces en el lugar Chua Suj. Allí, en ese lugar encuentres a una mujer joven. Con ella, vas a platicar, y ella te dirá todo lo que tienes que hacer."

Cuando amaneció, la mujer se levantó de su cama un poco triste y un poco contento por todo lo que había soñado. Luego, le contó a su marido todo lo que había soñado durante la noche.

Se dice que su marido le dio ánimo para que se fueran a ese lugar, Chua Suj [a] las 12 del medio día. Allí, estuvieron dos horas, pero no vieron nada, y se regresaron para su casa. Su marido dijo era que era [la] locura o una pesadilla lo que había tenido en el sueño.

Otra vez, la noche siguiente cuando la mujer estaba durmiendo, volvió a soñar lo mismo, otra vez hablando con la señora dueña del encanto, y le volvió a decir mejor que se fuera al cerro Chua-Suj. En el sueño, la mujer le contestó a la señora encantada, diciendo, "Ayer, junto con mi marido, fuimos al cerro Chua Suj. Usted me dijo una mujer joven me tendría que decir todo lo que yo tengo que hacer. Tuvimos que regresar porque no vimos nada.

La mujer encantada le volvió a decir, "Sí, pero tienes que ir sola, sin tu marido. Puedes ir otra vez mañana y encuentras una mujer joven. Ella te va a decir todo lo que tienes que hacer." Así fue el segundo sueño.

Al amanecer, dice que le contó a su marido todo lo que había soñado por segunda vez. Pero su marido la tomó por tonta o loca. La pobre mujer enferma, entre sus dolores, se fue otra vez al lugar llamado Chua-Suj las 12 del medio día [donde] vio una mujer joven sentado sobre una roca (piedra) debajo del árbo suj.[5] Estaba peinando su hermoso cabello.

La mujer pobre sintió un gran temor como [si] hielo le cayeron sobre el cuerpo. Luego la mujer joven que se peinaba le habló a la mujer pobre, diciendo, "No tengas miedo. Aquí, estoy sentada sobre esta piedra, peinándome mi cabello. Te estoy esperando. Yo soy la mandadera; yo soy la que cuido la señora dueña del encanto. Venga otra vez mañana, y mañana mismo te daré el resultado de las tres visitas." Así, le dijo a la mujer.

Al otro día, al mediodía, la mujer enferma y pobre se fue otra vez al cerro Chua Suj. De nuevo, la mujer joven estaba sentada sobre la misma piedra, peinando su pelo. Le habló, diciendo, "No tengas miedo; me llamó Alaxik. Quiere decir soy tu hermana." Y comenzó a decirle a la mujer, "Yo soy la mensajera; yo soy la cuido a la señora dueña del encanto, señora y dueña de este cerro. Ella apareció en tu sueño; se dio cuenta de tu enfermedad y de tu pobreza, pero tendrías que hacer las tres visitas. Ahora es la segunda y mañana será la tercera visita. Yo no te espero mañana; tendrás que venir sola. Traes tu perraje [manta de algodón] o rebozo que lo vas a poner tendida debajo de este árbol *suj*.

Sobre tu perraje o rebozo pasarán treces culebras. Primero, pasarán seis culebras grandes. De ahí, viene una culebra cuta (tiene más grosor que las otras culebras, pero corto de longitud—como ver el brazo de una piedra de moler). Es la cuta que trae la fortuna, dejando sobre tu perraje un pedacito de piedra con oro.[7]

Después de pasar la culebra cuta, seis culebras más pasarán. Luego se desaparecen de ahí, y puedes envolver la fortuna entre rebozo. Y tienes que caminar una cierta distancia hacia para atrás para que la fortuna se queda contigo. (Si no,) al contrario, se va a regresar con su dueña [del cerro de Chua-Suj]. Cuando llegas a tu casa, la colocas en la puerta de tu casa y te pasas cuatro veces. Luego, la vas a poner[la] en una olla de barro y le cambias el lugar a cada veinte días. Verás que tu enfermedad se desaparece y [que] dinero te llega muy fácilmente." Así, le dijo a esa mujer.

Así, la mujer pobre y enferma por tercera vez se fue en el cerro Chua Suj, preocupada y pensando que era a pasar con ella porque esa mujer tenía mucho miedo a las culebras. Llegó otra vez al lugar llamado Chua-Suj con los cuerpos espeluznante. Con mucho miedo, tendió su rebozo debajo del árbol, las 12 del medio día. Se abrió la cueva, y de ahí, salieron las primeras seis culebras que pasaron sobre el rebozo. De allí, venía una culebra cuta [corta]. Se dice que cuando la culebra cuta estaba pasando sobre el perraje, se vomitó y dejó arrojado un pedazo de jade con oro. Después de vomitar, siguió a las seis culebras que van adelante, y de allí venían las otras 6 culebras. En total eran 13 las culebras que pasaron sobre el rebozo de la señora.

Las trece culebras se volvieron a meterse en la cueva de donde habían salido. El cerro, se dice, las trago. La señora recogió y envolvió su rebozo, y caminó hacia para atrás, tal como le habían dicho. Cuando llegó a su casa, hizo el secreto, [ponerlo en su puerta y pasarlo cuatro veces]. Luego, la guardó en olla de barro y lo puso por debajo de su cama. Este era la fortuna que la dueña del encanto del cerro Chua Suj le dio a la señora.

Se dice que así fue poco a poco [ella y su esposo] sintieron el cambio. Comenzaron con la crianza de pollos, cerdos, ovejas, y conejos. Con el dinero que ganaban con la venta de los animales, compraron sus terrenos e hicieron sus casitas. Tuvieron una vida mejor; ya, no sufrieron como antes.

Pero el cuento dice que la señora le contó a su marido todo lo que pasó con ella —la fortuna que había recibido de la señora encantada del cerro, Chua Suj. Pero dicen con el tiempo la señora se murió, ye el marido le contó a la demás gente que en la casa había quedado una fortuna de su fallecida esposa. Los vecinos le dieron guarro [licor destilado simple] al hombre, y cuando estaba muy bolo, le robaron la fortuna. Y así perdió todo lo que tenían. Otra vez, el marido quedó en una pobreza peor que antes.

El cero Chua Suj está como a tres kilómetros del pueblo. La gente de antes siempre contaba que en ese lugar salían pollos, cerdos, y muchos conejos, pero [solamente] de vez en cuando; es decir, cuando llega el mero día [de la dueña] del cerro [encantado].[8] El árbol suj en español es el árbol conacaste [también conocido como el árbol guanacaste].

—Esta es el cuento del Señor Francisco que hace más o menos 25 años que murió. Él le dejó este cuento a su hijo Diego Toc. Diego me lo contó a mí. Éramos muy amigo desde jóvenes; jugamos en el equipo de fútbol. Diego murió hace dos años. Tenía 73 años.

# Story of the Taltuza

THE OLD FOLKS TELL very beautiful stories, and, little by little, it [story telling] is ending because the elders of eighty to ninety years [of age] are few. And those who are forty to fifty years old now do not have these tales.

Don Juan Juárez narrated [the tale] like this: He says that formerly there was not so much sin in the world because also there were not as many people as now. Accordingly, it [culpability] was increasing [with] the [number of] people in the world. That is, evil was increasing with the greater number of people than before.

In the winter time, God sent rain over the land, but very slowly and controlled by persons that had been born with much power. Don Juan says that they were called rainmakers. These men are said to have been born on the day of Oxlajuuj' Ik' (13 Ik' [wind] of the Mayan calendar).[9] It speaks of thirteen winds, thirteen hurricanes, thirteen storms, [and] thirteen clouds loaded with water to execute rain over the earth. It is said that these men controlled the rain, controlled the hurricanes, controlled the winds. They disappeared in the clouds; they went in the air and in the storms. It is said that these men did not smoke or drink aguardiente, nor did they get together with women; they lived alone in their houses and came to be like orphans.

He says that in the dream, they were told how long winter lasts and when summer begins. They also can divine whether there will be a good or bad harvest for the year. He says that also in this way they [by means of dreams] can cure sicknesses. In the dream, the ajau, or dueño [owner, god, lord], shows them what kind of zacate [generic name for several species of grass that serve as pasture and forage; herbs] to use to cure the sick. He says that there is grass to cure every ailment. Don Juan said that his grandparents did not know medicine, much less a doctor.

It is said that the rainmakers dream the punishment that comes over the earth. They come together to offer sacrifice to the ajau, lord of heaven and of earth. In other words, they ask for forgiveness.

But as evil was increasing in the land, so too the rainmakers were dying. Little by little they disappeared, and now they did not return to be born again. For the great evil on earth, men and women now did not honor the ajau, lord of nature. It was for that reason that men like rainmakers were no longer born.

He says that was when men and women began to be born with naguales of animals like pigs, coyotes, donkeys, goats, and other ugly animals, and it was those who converted into their naguales, into *characoteles*, brujos, and *malignos* [devils] that only seek to cause damage to the rest [of people]. But he says, "When the characoteles, brujos, and malignant people; that is to say, all the bad people, die, their spirits convert into *taltuzas* [rodents similar to rats who bore long tunnels in the earth; gophers], and they go to live below the earth to cause damage to the crops of the people, eating the roots of the cultivations like corn, beans, flowers, vegetables, and bananas."

Don Juan says, more for that reason, the taltuzas are the souls of the people who live badly in this life, and they continue causing evil. For that reason, the ajau sends them to live below the earth in order not to see the light of day; by day and by night they are in obscurity.

—This tale is of a principal [elder], Juan Juárez; a few years ago, he died. He came to my house and loved me like a brother. He had no family; he was seventy-five years old when he told me this story. I, Pedro, gave this story a name [title]; it was not Don Juan.

# Cuento de la taltuza

LOS VIEJITOS CONTABAN CUENTOS muy bonitos, y, poco a poco se está terminado [la narración de cuentos] porque los ancianos de 80–90 años quedan poco. Y los que tienen 40–50 años ya no tienen estos cuentos.

Don Juan Juárez contaba así: Dice que antes no era tanto el pecado en el mundo porque también no era mucha gente como ahora. En consecuencia, [la culpabilidad] estaba aumentando [con] el [número de] las personas en el mundo. Es decir, el mal estaba aumentando con el mayor número de personas que antes.

En el tiempo del invierno, Dios mandaba la lluvia sobre la tierra, pero muy lento y controlado por unas personas que habían nacido con mucho poder. Don Juan dice que se les llamaba hacedores de lluvia. Se dice que estos hombres han nacido en el día Oxlajuuj' Ik' (13 Ik' [viento] del calendario maya).[9] Se habla de los 13 vientos, 13 huracanes, 13 tempestades, 13 nubes cargados con agua para ejecutar la lluvia sobre la tierra. Se dice que estos hombres que controlaban la lluvia, controlaban los huracanes, contralaban los vientos. Se desaparecían en las nubes, se iban en el aire y en las tempestades. Se dice que estos hombres no fumaban ni tomaban aguardiente ni juntaban con mujeres; vivían solitos en sus casas y vino a ser como huérfanos.

Dice que en el sueño se les manifestaba cuanto tiempo dura el invierno y cuando comienza el verano. También, pueden adivinar si habrá una buena o mala cosecha para el año. Dice que también de esta manera [por medio de los sueños] pueden curar las enfermedades. En el sueño, el ajau, or dueño [dios, señor], les manifestaba que clase de zacate usar para curar a los enfermos. Dice que hay *zacate* [nombre genérico de varias especies de gramíneas que sirven como pasto y forraje; herbia] para curar cada dolencia. Don Juan decía que sus abuelos no conocieron medicina, mucho menos un doctor.

Se dice que los hacedores de lluvia soñan el castigo que viene sobre la tierra.

Ellos se juntan para ofrecerle sacrificio al ajau, dueño del cielo y del mundo. Vale más decir, piden perdón.

Pero conforme fue creciendo la maldad en la tierra, así también los hacedores de lluvia se murieron. Poco a poco se desaparecieron, y ya no volvieron a nacer más. Por la mucha maldad en la tierra, hombres y mujeres ya no repelaban al ajau, dueño de la naturaleza. Fue por eso, que ya no nacieron hombres como los hacedores de lluvia.

Dice que así era cuando comenzaron a nacer los hombres y mujeres con naguales de animales como cerdos, coyotes, burros, abras y otros animales feos, y esos eran los que se convierten sus naguales en characoteles, brujos, hechiceros, *malignos* [diablos] que solo buscan para causar daño a los demás. Pero dice, "cuando mueren los characoteles, brujos y malignos; es decir, todas las personas malas, mueren, sus espíritus se convierten en *taltuzas* [ardillas terrestres], y se van a vivir abajo de la tierra a causar daño a los cultivos de las personas, comiendo las raíces de los cultivos, como el maíz, frijol, flore, verduras, bananos."

Don Juan dice, más por eso, que las taltuzas son el alma de las personas que vivieron mal en esta vida, y siguen causando el mal. Por eso, el ajau las mando a vivir abajó de la tierra para no ver la luz del día; de día y noche están en la oscuridad.

—Este cuento es de un principal, Juan Juárez; hace unos años que murió.
Él llegaba a mi casa y me quería como hermano. No tuvo familia;
tenía 75 años cuando me canto este cuento. Yo, Pedro puse
el nombre [título] de este cuento; no fue don Juan.

# A Real Story

*Strange Things, Unusual Cases, Opossum*

THINGS AND CASES SEEM to be an invention, but no, there are strange things, unusual cases. Many times, I ask myself, and, in the end, I conclude that it is true; it is not a lie. What I do not know is whether it happens only among the Mayan people, or perhaps it also happens with the Ladino people.

There are persons who are born with a natural power. Also, it is said persons are born with [a] nagual that converts into an animal. In other words, they are called characoteles, or beings of the night.

In this month of January of the year 2015, an accident happened at the place called Chua Bolab in the jurisdiction of San Juan la Laguna, less than two kilometers from the town. The owner of the land, Señor Nicolás, contracted a señor, Señor Alberto, who works with a chainsaw, to cut some trees for firewood. With them went a friend, Rubén, as an assistant to cut the branches. As it was not far, at three in the afternoon, they arrived to do the work.

[The story] says that they began the work, but the one that had the chainsaw lacked knowledge. He could not fell the tree; it leaned on another. In other words, it got stuck on another tree.

Then, the owner [Señor Nicolás] and man with the chainsaw told Rubén to cut off the branches to see how to cut it [the tree trunk] up. Then Rubén was cutting the branches when the tree dropped, and it fell on the boy and broke his spine, [leaving him] screaming and screaming, but between the two, they were not able rescue him. They had to call the volunteer firemen. Not until then were they able to remove the tree from the injured man. But they say that he was not able to move his lower half body—from his belt to his feet.

The firemen sent him to the hospital in Sololá, and from Sololá they sent him to the hospital in Guatemala [City], where they [declared] that there was no cure because the spine and the ribs were broken in two parts. From Guatemala [City] they transferred him to the western hospital in Quetzaltenango. There, they told the kin that there was nothing that could be done; they would just have to wait for his death. Thus, they brought him [back] to San Juan.

The truth is I heard the news that indeed there had been an accident, but I did not believe it. I thought it had been a simple accident. Rubén was my friend. I was not concerned; I thought he was going to recuperate from this accident.

The concern [came] when he left the hospital in Quetzaltenango, they told him his life was over. My friend Rubén was about forty-five years old. From childhood, he was abandoned by his father. His mother married another man. That was [when] Rubén grew up with his stepfather. He went to work for many years in San Lucas Sacatepéquez; he did not have a family. He liked to drink and he liked politics.

[As I said] Rubén was a friend; I never imagined what he was. His nagual was seen some thirty minutes after he died.

[It is the] custom among us Tz'utujiles to help the family when someone is sick, especially when someone dies; it is customary among the population.

This case took place a hundred meters from the municipal soccer stadium, when night was falling on Wednesday, February 28, 2015. When the accident victim, Rubén, was fighting between life and death, the kin and neighbors gathered, waiting for the final resting of the one in agony. I did not see it; those who saw it were my son-in-law, Juan Francisco, my daughter, Lesbia, and my two granddaughters, Elena and Oneida.

Juan Francisco was kin to the patient. He says that they were there with the rest of the relatives, waiting the repose of Rubén's soul. [Then] the strangest thing happened between 8:00 and 8:30 at night. Rubén fought with death—crying, shouting, and asking that they help him. There were those who were taking care of him, some inside the house, others outside, because not all could fit inside. Those who saw it said that [an opossum appeared in the alley], not very big nor very small. It passed over the feet of those who were on the corridor [porch]. The animal got inside. He got below a small altar that the family had prepared near the bed of the sick person.

The people were more frightened when the opossum got below the altar. He [Juan] says they wanted to get him out with a stick, but they were unable [to do so]. The animal did not want to leave. Finally, they were able to extract him, but he says that it jumped and put itself on the awning of the house looking over the bed of the dying man. He says that there was another person called Juan who was not afraid. Then, Juan lowered the opossum with a pole. Now it was not able to run. It remained near the bed of the sick one. From there, he [Juan] killed it with a machete. He quartered it; the blood of the animal spilled near the bed of the dying man.

When Juan was killing the animal with a machete, the sick one asked what it was that they were killing, and they told him they were killing an opossum that had entered the house.

Then, he says he said, "Now, I have no life; now I am going to die; take care." Fifteen or twenty minutes after they had killed the animal was when Rubén ceased to exist.

Many of those who witnessed this case were frightened and believed that the opossum was the nagual of the dead person. The 29th of January 2015, there was a lot of commentary among the kin, friends, visitors, and the whole town. The opossum that they killed near the bed of the dead person was his nagual. They went to bury the ripped-to-pieces animal in the place where the accident took place, at the foot of the trunk of a tree.

Well, I did not very much believe in what the people said about the nagual. I thought they were lies or some joke. But Sunday, February 1, my daughter, Candida Lesbia, and her daughters, Elena and Oneida, came to visit me. Then, I wanted to eliminate the doubt, and then we began to comment about what happened with the death of Rubén. They assured me everything that happened and what they saw that night; all that the people said was certain. They assured me that the opossum passed over their feet looking for the bed where the dying man was. This was a strange or rare case.

—Pedro Cholotío Temó and Juan Francisco

# Un cuento real

*Cosas extrañas, casos inusuales, tacuazín*

CASOS Y COSAS PARECE ser un invento, pero no, hay cosas extrañas, casos insólitos. Muchas veces, me pregunto yo mismo, y, al final, concluyo que es cierto; no es una mentira. Lo que no sé es si pasa solamente entre la gente maya, o tal vez pasa con la gente ladina.

Hay personas que nacen con un poder natural. También, se dice nacen personas con [un] nagual que se convierte en un animal. En otras palabras, se le llaman characoteles, o seres de la noche.

En este mes de enero del año 2015, un accidente sucedió en el lugar llamado Chua Bolab en jurisdicción de San Juan la Laguna, menos de dos kilómetros de la población. El dueño del terreno, Señor Nicolás, contrató a un Señor Alberto que trabaja con motosierra para cortar unos árboles para la leña. Con ellos se fue el amigo Rubén como mozo para cortar las ramas. Como no estaba lejos, a las tres de la tarde llegaron a hacer el trabajo.

[El cuento] dice que comenzaron el trabajo, pero el que tenía la motosierra carecía de conocimiento. No pudo botar el árbol; se recostó sobre [otro]. En otras palabras, quedó trabado sobre otro árbol.

Entonces, el dueño [Señor Nicolás] y él hombre de la motosierra le dijeron a Rubén cortara las ramas para ver que hacer para trocearlo [el tronco del árbol]. Entonces Rubén estaba cortando las ramas cuando se dejó caer el palo y cayó sobre el muchacho y quebró la columna vertebral, gritando y gritando, pero entre los dos no lo pudieron rescatar. Tuvieron que llamar a los bomberos voluntarios; hasta entonces pudieron sacar el palo sobre el accidentado, pero dicen que no podía mover su medio cuerpo inferior—de la cintura hasta los pies.

Los bomberos lo mandaron al hospital de Sololá, y de Sololá lo mandaron al hospital de Guatemala [ciudad] donde detectaron que no tiene curación porque se quebró en dos partes la columna y las costillas. De Guatemala [lo] trasladaron al hospital de occidente en Quetzaltenango. Allí, les dijeron a los familiares que no se puede hacer nada, solo hay que esperar su muerte. Así, lo trajeron [de vuelta] para San Juan.

La verdad es que escuché la noticia de que efectivamente había habido un accidente, pero no me lo creí. Pensé que fue un accidente simple. Rubén era mi amigo. No tuve preocupación; pensé que se iba recuperar de ese accidente.

La preocupación fue cuando salió del hospital de Quetzaltenago le dijeron que ya no tenía más vida. El amigo Rubén tenía más o menos 45 años. Desde pequeño, fue abandonado por su padre. Su mamá se casó con otro hombre. Eso fue [cuando] Rubén creció con su padrastro. Fue a trabajar por muchos años en San Lucas Sacatepéquez; no tuvo familia. Le gustaba los tragos y le gustaba la política.

[Como dije] Rubén era un amigo; nunca me imaginé lo que era. Su nagual se vio unos 30 minutos de morir.

[Es la] costumbre entre nosotros Tzutujiles compartir con la familia donde hay enfermos, más cuando la persona muere; es costumbre entre la población.

Este caso sucedió a 100 metros del estadio municipal de fútbol, al entrar la noche del día miércoles 28 de enero 2015. Cuando el accidentado, Rubén, estaba luchando entre la vida y la muerte, los familiares y vecinos reunidos, esperando el descanso final del hombre agonizante. Yo no lo vi; los que lo vieron fueron mi yerno, Juan Francisco, mi hija Lesbia, y mis dos nietas, Elena y Oneida.

Juan Francisco era familiar del paciente. Dice que allí estaban con los demás familiares esperando el descanso del alma de Rubén. [Luego] lo más extraño paso dentro las ocho y ocho y treinta de la noche. Rubén luchó con la muerte—llorando, gritando, y pidiendo que le ayudaron. Allí estaban los que lo estaban cuidando, unos adentro de la casa, otros afuera porque adentro no cabían todos. Los que lo vieron decían que en el callejón iba un *tacuazín* [zarigüeya], no muy grande ni muy chiquito. Pasó sobre los pies de los que estaban en el corredor. El animal se metió para adentro. Se metió debajo de un pequeño altar que la familia tenía preparado cerca de la cama del enfermo.

Más se asustaron la gente cuando el tacuazín se metió debajo del altar. Dice [Juan] que lo querían sacar con un palo, [pero] no podían. El animal no quería salir. Al fin, lo pudieron sacarlo, pero dice que saltó y se puso sobre el tendal [toldo] de la casa viendo sobre la cama del hombre agonizante. Dice que allí estaba una otra persona que no tenía miedo se llama Juan. Entonces, Juan lo bajo con un palo el tacuazín. Ya no pudo correr. Se quedó cerca de la cama del enfermo. De ahí, [Juan] lo mató con machete. Lo descuartizó; la sangre del animal quedó derramada cerca la cama del hombre agonizante.

Cuando Juan estaba matando el animal con el machete, el enfermo preguntó qué es lo que están matando, y le dijeron que lo están matando un tacuazín que había entrado en la casa.

Entonces, dice que el dijo, "Ya no tengo vida, me voy a morir cuídense," dijo. Quince o veinte minutos después que lo habían matado el animal fue cuando Rubén dejó de existir.

Muchos de ellos que vieron este caso se asustaron y creyeron que el tacuazín era el nagual del muerto. El 29 de enero 2015, había muchos comentarios entre familiares, amigos y visitantes y en todo el pueblo. El tacuazín que mataron cerca de la cama del muerto era su nagual. El animal despedazado lo fueron a enterrar en el lugar donde fue el accidente al pie del tronco del árbol.

Pues, yo no muy creía en lo que comentaba la gente acerca del nagual. Pensé que eran mentiras o alguna broma. Pero el domingo, 1 de febrero llegaron conmigo mi hija, Cándida Lesbia, sus hijas, Elena y Oneida, a visitarme. Entonces, yo quería quitarme de la duda, y comenzamos a comentar acerca de lo que pasó con la muerte de Rubén. Ellas me aseguraron todo lo que pasó y lo que vieron esa noche; todo es cierto lo que la gente decía. Ellos me aseguraron que el tacuazín paso sobre sus pies buscando la cama donde estaba el hombre agonizante. Este fue un caso raro o extraño.

—Pedro Cholotío Temó y Juan Francisco

# Tz'utujil Story

## *A Real Deed (Owl Caso)*

BENVENUTO, THE MAN WHO passed himself off [as having] an extraterrestrial power, said that he disappeared in the air and in the clouds and that he transformed into a rainmaker.

This man is a native of San Pedro la Laguna, and is still alive, aged more or less eighty-five years. His real name is Benvenuto Pop. In the years 1950 to 1960, this man deceived many people of San Pedro and San Juan. He said that he had an angelic power, or a heaven-sent [power]. He said that he was able to shake the earth with an angelic power to make rain over the land.

In those times ignorance reigned; many people believed in false things. Benvenuto deceived a lot of people into believing that the man had a supernatural power. At that time Benvenuto was a young man of some twenty-five years. The people of San Pedro and San Juan showed respect and were afraid of him because of all that he said about having an astral force to cause an earthquake or make rain on earth for about eight to ten days as a punishment.

Many people said, "We should not disrespect Don Benvenuto because he has the power of heaven to move the world and a great power of rainmaking." It is true that they respected him a lot. Many men tipped their hat to bid him good morning or good afternoon because nothing less and nothing more, he was the one who made the earth tremble.

This man they knew as "the maker of rain and earthquakes." All the youngsters were obliged to give him reverences, and he placed his hand on the head of the children.

One time, Benvenuto had problems. This was in 1954 when I was thirteen years old. He sold the same land to two buyers. There the problem surfaced;

the buyers presented a complaint against the seller, who then was Benvenuto Pop.

In that time the mayors were the justices of the peace. This man was imprisoned in San Juan. The jail was near the municipality, and the people of the town realized that the man who was the rainmaker was imprisoned. There was commentary that something bad was going to happen.

Benvenuto, they say, motioned to the alguacil to come close to the bars of the jail. "Yes?" said the alguacil, and he drew near the bars. Benvenuto, the prisoner, said, "Tell the mayor that if he does not let me out of jail at night today, the town of San Juan is going to disappear because of a big earthquake, and rain is going to fall with a hurricane." They say the alguacil ran shaking to tell the mayor and the aldermen the worst harm that was going to happen that night if they did not let this man out of jail.

The town was small. The news spread throughout the population that the rainmaker man was in prison. The people of the town gathered, the women crying, to tell the mayor to set free the rainmaker to avoid this evil from coming, or they would blame the mayor for all that was going to happen.

Without much choice, the mayor, regidores, *mayores* [auxiliaries of municipal police in towns with more *indígenas* (Indigenous) people than Ladinos], and alguaciles contributed their money and paid the fine. It was thus when Benvenuto the rainmaker was set free. They took him out of jail about seven at night. They say that he was very grateful for the help of the townspeople, and he told all the people that nothing bad was going to happen; all [would be] peaceful. At this time the mayor was called Marcos.

Some of the people did not believe him [Benvenuto]; they ignored everything this man said. But there were many who believed this man had power.

Thus, Benvenuto came; he enjoyed deceiving the people, especially those of his town. It is said that he gathered the shamans, or *zajorines* (ajcumes), and also he invited their neighbors. He gave them plantains, bananas, mangos, and *patastes* [white cocoa]. He told them that he had brought the fruit from the coast at night after making rain. The shamans and the residents believed that Benvenuto was an envoy from heaven to make rain, and with his great power, he brought the fruit from the coast.

Also, he gave them apples, peaches, pears, and plums, and he said that he carried them from Xelajú [or Xela] of Santa Cruz del Quiché and from Cobán, the cold land. He told them that he was there making rain at night, and he brought the fruit in the mornings for them to eat.

The people stopped believing in the rainmaker when the older guards and alguaciles discovered the fruit that Benvenuto gave the people [was fruit that] some Atitecos carried in canoes over the lake; they came early in the morning to give it to Benvenuto at his house. They say that the Atitecos got confused. They left at midnight from Santiago; at 2:00 a.m. they arrived at the shore of the lake in San Pedro. Then, the patrolmen captured them. They confessed they were fruit-selling merchants and that they always came at 4:00 a.m. to bring their baskets of fruit to Señor Benvenuto. But this time they confused the hour and arrived earlier.

They say that the patrolmen followed the Atitecos to Benvenuto's house. Then they say that this was how it was that the patrolmen proved that that man was a liar—that he brought the fruit from the coast, from Xela del Quiché and from Cobán and [claimed] that he brought them by his astral force in the clouds and in the air. All was a lie of the man!

Now, they do not call him rainmaker. Now they give him the nickname "Benvenuto the owl." They nicknamed him "Benvenuto the owl" because his cheekbones are highlighted. This man lives in the neighboring town with his famous nickname.

Here ends this story.

—Pedro Cholotío Temó

# Cuento tz'utujil

## *Un hecho cierto (caso tecolote)*

BENVENUTO, EL HOMBRE QUE se pasaba con [como tener] un poder extraterrestre, decía que se desparecía en el aire y en las nubes y se convertía como un hacedor de lluvia.

Este hombre es nativo de San Pedro la Laguna la Laguna y todavía vive. Más o menos de 85 años, su verdadero nombre es Benvenuto Pop. En los años 1950 a 1960, este hombre venía engañando a mucha gente de San Pedro y de San Juan. Él decía que tiene un poder de ángel o un enviado del cielo. Decía que él puede hacer temblar la tierra y el poder de ángel para hacer la lluvia sobre la tierra.

En eso tiempo reinaba la ignorancia; mucho de la gente creían en cosas falsas. Benvenuto engaño a mucha gente, creyendo a ese hombre tenía un poder sobrenatural. En este tiempo, Benvenuto era un hombre joven de unos 25 años. La gente de San Pedro y de San Juan le guardaban mucho respeto le tenían miedo por lo que él decía de tener una fuerza astral de hacer un terremoto o hacer llover sobre la tierra por unos 8 o 10 días como un castigo.

Muchos de la gente decían: "No hay que faltarle el respeto a don Benvenuto porque él tiene el poder del cielo de mover el mundo y el gran poder de hacer la lluvia." Es cierto que le guardaban mucho respeto. Muchos de los hombres se quitaban el sombrero para darle los buenos días o las buenas tardes porque nada menos y nada más, era el hombre que hace temblar la tierra.

A este hombre lo conocían como "el hacedor de lluvia y hacedor de temblor." Todos los patojos eran obligados de hacerle reverencia, y él imponía la mano sobre la cabeza de los niños.

Una vez, Benvenuto tuvo problemas. Eso fue en el año 1954 cuando yo tenía 13 años. El vendió a dos compradores el mismo terreno. Allí surgió el problema;

los compradores presentaron la denuncia en contra el vendedor que entonces era Benvenuto Pop.

En ese tiempo los alcaldes eran los jueces de paz. Este hombre quedó preso en San Juan. La cárcel quedaba cerca de la municipalidad, y la gente del pueblo se dio cuenta que el hombre hacedor de lluvia estaba preso. Había comentario que algo mal va a pasar.

Benvenuto, dicen, hizo señas a un alguacil para que se acercara a las rejas, "Sí," dijo al alguacil, y se acercó a las rejas de la cárcel. Buenvenuto, el preso, le dijo, "Dígale el alcade que, si no me saca de la cárcel hoy por la noche, el pueblo de San Juan se va a desaparecer por un gran terremoto, y va a caer lluvia con huracán." Dicen que el alguacil corrió temblando a decirle al alcalde y los regidores el peor mal que va a suceder hoy por la noche si no lo sacan a este hombre de la cárcel.

El pueblo era pequeño. Se regó la noticia en toda la población que el hombre hacedor de lluvia está preso. La gente del pueblo se juntó, las mujeres llorando, para decirle al alcalde que lo dejara en libertad el hacedor de lluvia para evitar que sobre venga ese mal, o lo culpabilizaban al alcalde de todo lo iba a suceder.

Sin tanto remedio, el alcalde, regidores, *mayores* [auxilares de policía municipal en lugares de más María Concepción indígena que ladina], y alguaciles hicieron una contribución con el dinero de ellos pagaron la multa. Es así cuando Benvenuto el hacedor de lluvia quedó en libertad. Lo sacaron de la cárcel más o menos como las 7 de la noche. Dicen que se fue muy agradecido por el apoyo que le dio la gente del pueblo, y le dijo a toda la gente que nada mal va a pasar; todo [sería] tranquilo. En ese tiempo al alcalde se llamaba Marcos.

Una parte de las personas no creían; ignoraba todo lo decía ese hombre. Pero había muchos creían que ese hombre tenía poder.

Así venía Benvenuto; le gustaba engañar a la gente, más a los de su pueblo. Se decía que él juntaba a los chamanes o zajorines (ajcumes), y también, invitaba a sus vecinos. Se los regalaba plátanos, bananos, mangos, *patastes* [cacao blanco]. Les decía las frutas las trajo de la costa por la noche después de hacer lluvia. Los chamanes y los vecinos lo creían que Benvenuto era un enviado del cielo para hacer la lluvia, y con su gran poder traía las frutas de la costa.

También, los regalaba manzanas, duraznos, peras, y ciruelas, y decía que las frutas traían de Xelajú [o Xela] de Santa Cruz del Quiché y de Cobán, la tierra fría. Les decía que allá fue hacer la lluvia por la noche y traer las frutas por las mañanas para que se las comieran.

La gente lo dejaron de creer en el hacedor de lluvia, cuando los guardias, mayores, y alguaciles descubrieron las frutas que Benvenuto regalaba a la gente [era frutas que] unos Atitecos las traían en canoas sobre el lago y venían por las madrugadas a dejárselo a la casa de Benvenuto. Los Atitecos dicen que se confundieron. Salieron a las 12 de la noche de Santiago; a las 2 de la mañana llegaron a la orilla del lago en San Pedro. Luego, los señores de la ronda los capturaron. Confesaron son comerciantes en vender frutas y que siempre venían a las 4 de la mañana a entregar los canastones de frutas al Señor Benvenuto. Pero esta vez, se confundieron por la hora llegaron temprano.

Dicen que los de ronda les siguieron a los Atitecos hasta la casa de Benvenuto. Entonces dicen que así fue los de la ronda comprobaron que ese hombre era mentiroso—que él traía las frutas de la costa, de Xela, de Quiché y de Cobán y que las traía por su fuerza astral en las nubes y en el aire. ¡Toda era una mentira del hombre!

Ahora, ya no le dicen hacedor de lluvia. Ahora le pusieron el apodo "Benvenuto el tecolote." Le pusieron el apodo "Benvenuto el tecolote" porque tienen resaltados los pómulos [de él]. Este hombre vive en el vecino pueblo y con su famoso apodo.

Aquí termina ese cuento.

—Pedro Cholotío Temó

STORY

# The King and His Two Daughters

IN THE WORLD THERE was a king, a bitter and cruel man, who inflicted great punishments on the poor people and enslaved many. Also, he had his two daughters. The king did not want his daughters to marry poor men.

Then the king decreed an order in all the cities and towns that were under his reign, saying, "I have two virgin daughters; I need two young men to be my two sons-in-law who meet the [following] requirements: (1) the same age as my daughters, (2) the same height, (3) the same weight, (4) the same color of eyes (5) the same number of footwear, (6) moles equal to theirs, [and] (7) hairy like them. The two young men who meet these qualifications will be my two sons-in-law. The two will both occupy my throne; they will be the owners of the gold and silver and other riches that I have in my palace," said the king.

Thus it happened; many young men from all parts of the world arrived at the palace of the king. All of them were desirous to be the sons-in-law of the king. Some [were] of the same age but not the same height. Others were the same height but not the same color of eyes. The young ones who had the same color of eyes did not have the same number of shoes. Those with the same number of footwear were not of the same color of eyes. None of the young men weighed the same as the king's daughters, and none of the young men was hairy like the king's daughters. [Therefore,] none of the young men was qualified for the marriage.

The angry king ordered the mayordomo to give twenty-five lashes to each one because none deserved to be the son-in-law of the king. Thus it was; the daughters of the king wanted to get married, but they were unable [to do so] because their father was very angry.

The first daughter of the king left secretly with her husband; [that is to say,] without advising her parents. They left, fleeing from the presence of her father, the king. The woman carried her clothing: *corte* [angle-length skirt], huipil [typical blouse], girdles and combs, and moreover she carried a *tecomate* [gourd jar] of water. Later she told her husband to carry three ears of corn: one of the color white, one of the color yellow, and one of the color black.[10]

"Yes," the husband said, and he took with him the three ears of corn.

When the king and his woman realized that the daughter and her husband had run off, they became furious. They sent all the guards and soldiers to capture and return them to the palace.

The soldiers, guards, and the other people—that is to say, the envoys of the king—now were unable to recognize the daughter of the king because everything had been changed. The three ears of corn had been converted into three beautiful daughters: a white, a brunette, and the third, a black. The daughter of the king and her husband had been gone only three days, and they had three daughters.

The soldiers, guards, and other people returned to tell the king and his wife that indeed they found a couple with three beautiful children, but in appearance it was not their daughter. When the king's wife heard the news, she fainted, saying, "That's my daughter, my son-in-law, and my three granddaughters they should have brought back. Please go back to get them!"

"Yes," said the soldiers, the guards, and the rest of the people, obeying the order.

But the daughter of the king noticed and said to her husband, "My mama ordered more people to come back to get us, but they are not going to be able to do it. I have secretos [magical acts] to defeat them," she said.

Then, she told her husband, "The three girls will be converted again into ears of corn." And thus it was. And she told him to put them on the ground.

The husband did what the woman had told him to do. He put the three ears on the ground. In a little while, a great planted field of milpa [was seen beginning to grain ears of corn. In the middle of the cornfield appeared a *ranchito* [small thatched hut].

Then, the woman said to her husband, "I am converting myself into a virgin and you a sacristan, [and] thus they are not going to be able [to do] anything against us."

The soldiers and the guards arrived and asked the man, "Have you seen around here a couple with three daughters?"

The man answered, "I have not seen anyone. I don't know who you are going around looking for. Here, there is only I, the sacristan, taking care of the virgin who is the protector of the planted cornfield. I don't know anything about what you are walking around looking for."

Without gaining anything, the searchers returned again to the palace to tell the king and his wife that they only found a field planted with corn with a ranchito in the middle with a virgin inside and a sacristan guarding it. The wife of the king exclaimed, "I am dying; I'm dying! What you saw, the milpa that is in ears of corn, those are my three granddaughters! The sacristan guarding, that is my son-in-law, and the virgin in the middle of the rustic farm house, that is my daughter they should have brought back! Return to the place where you saw the milpa! Bring the virgin, sacristan, and three ears of corn so that my daughter, son-in-law, and three granddaughters can come before I die from so much sadness!"

The daughter of the king realized the persecution continued against her because she had the same secretos as her mother. When it dawned, she told her husband to take care of the three ears of corn. The daughter of the king carried a tecomate of water and sprayed it on the ground. This converted it into a small lake. She extended her sash and then a small launch appeared; the two changed their appearance into two old folks fishing in the small lake on a boat.

When the soldiers, guards, and servants arrived at the place, they now did not see the sown milpa; everything had changed. Then, they asked the pair of old folks whether they had seen among the milpa, a virgin and a sacristan inside a ranchito.

The old couple answered, saying, "Señores, you are lost; the place you are looking for is not here. We have been fishing here a long time; we have never seen a planted field of corn. Since we were young, we have been fishermen, and with this work we earn a living." But the truth was that they were not old folks. They only had changed their appearance by way of secretos.

The soldiers, guards, and servants were frightened because indeed they had not found the daughter of the king [and] would be sent to the gallows. They returned again to say that they had not found anyone. The milpa, the virgin, and the sacristan had disappeared.

They only encountered a small lake and a pair of old folks fishing, and they only had three fish. The wife of the king said, "The two old persons fishing are my daughter and my son-in-law; the three fish are my granddaughters. They should have brought them. Without seeing my daughter, I am dying, I am dying."

The wife of the king ordered them to look for them again. "Now, if you find them, take this secreto!" She handed them a handful of hair, her sash, and her comb. "Return to the same place where you had seen the two old persons fishing, extend my faja [sash], put my hair on the ground! And you will see that now you will find them."

"Yes," said the searchers.

They left, but when they arrived, everything had disappeared. Now they did not see the small lake or the pair of old people. All they saw was a plain. Again, the searchers became scared, but then they remembered what the mother of the girl had told them. Then, they dropped on the floor the handful of hair, they stretched out the sash, and they threw [down] the comb. In a blink of the eye, a beautiful garden appeared with lots of flowers where a beautiful woman and a noble hombre with three beautiful daughters were working. At that point, the searchers recognized that it was the daughter, the son-in-law, and the three granddaughters. They were taken to the palace of the king.

When the daughter, the son-in-law, and three grandchildren arrived in the presence of the king and his wife, then he exclaimed, saying, "With my wife and me old, the absence of my daughter left our souls destroyed; my wife and I were not able to eat or sleep for much sadness. Now, my wife and I are happy."

Later, he told his son-in-law, "Oh, dear son-in-law, before, I did not like you; I looked upon you with contempt. But now, you have gained my confidence. Now, you stay on my throne," said the king. He took off his crown, his necklace, and his ring—all gold—and placed them on his son-in-law. Then, he took him to sit on his throne. [And] so it was with his son-in-law. It was not as it was before [when] he despised him for being poor and of small stature. Hence, the former king and his wife threw a great fiesta.

Ultimately, he [the son-in-law] became a great king. The other daughter of the king looked with envy at all the things that were happening to her sister. She did not have a husband, and she left her parents. She began to beg, and that's how she died.

—Pedro Cholotío Temó

CUENTO

# El rey y sus dos hijas

EN EL MUNDO HABÍA un rey, hombre amargo y cruel, quien imponía grandes castigos en la gente pobre y a los esclavizaba mucho. También, tenía sus dos hijas. El rey no quería que sus hijas se casarán con hombres pobres.

Entonces el rey decretó un mandato en toda las ciudades y pueblos que están bajo su reino, diciendo, "Tengo dos hijas vírgenes; necesito dos jóvenes para que sean mis dos yernos que llenan los requisitos: (1) igual edad que mis hijas, (2) igual estatura, (3) pesan igual que mis hijas (4) mismo color los ojos, (5) igual número de calzado, (6) lunares igual que las de ellas, [y] (7) velludos como ellas. Los dos jóvenes que califican las mismas cualidades serán mis dos yernos. Ellos dos ocuparán mi trono; serán ellos los dueños del oro y la plata y demás riquezas que tengo en mi palacio," dijo el rey.

Así pasó; llegaron muchos jóvenes de todas partes del mundo al palacio del rey. Todos ellos estaban deseosos de llegar hacer yernos del rey. Unos [tenían] la misma edad, pero no la misma estatura. Otros eran la misma estatura, pero no el mismo color de ojos. Los jóvenes que tenían el mismo color de los ojos no tenían el mismo número de cazado. Los con el mismo número del calzado no eran del mismo color de ojos. Ninguno de los jóvenes pesó igual que las hijas del rey, y ninguno eran velludas como las hijas del rey. [Por eso,] Ninguno de los jóvenes llegó ser calificado para el casamiento.

El rey enojado mandó al mayordomo a le dieran 25 azotes a cada uno porque ninguno servía para ser yerno del rey. Entonces así fue; las hijas del rey estaban con las ganas de casarse, pero no podían porque su padre el rey era muy enojado.

La primera de las hijas se fue escondidas con su marido; [es decir] sin avisarle a sus padres. Salieron, huyendo de la presencia de su padre, el rey. La mujer se llevó su ropa, corte, huipil [blusa típica], fajas, peines, y además se llevó un tecomate con agua. Luego, le decía a su marido que se llevara con él tres mazorcas, una de color blanca, otra de color amarillo, y una más de color negrita.[10]

"Sí," dijo el marido, y se llevó consigo las tres mazorcas.

Cuando el rey y su mujer se dieron cuenta que se había salida huyendo la hija con su marido, se enojaron demasiado. Mandaron a todos los soldados y guardias para capturarlos que a regresen al palacio.

Los soldados y los guardias y la demás gente, es decir, los enviados del rey, ya no podían reconocer la hija del rey porque todo se había cambiado. Las tres mazorcas se habían convertida en tres hermosas hijas: una blanquita, una morenita, y la tercera una negrita. La hija del rey y su marido solamente tenían tres días haber salido, y contaban con tres hijas.

Los soldados, guardias, y lo demás gente regresaron a decirle el rey y su esposa sí encontraron una pareja con tres hermosas niñas, pero con apariencia no era la hija del rey. Cuando la mujer del rey escuchó estas cosas, se desmayó, diciendo, "Esa es mi hija, mi yerno, y mis tres nietas que deberían haber traído de regreso. ¡Por favor, regresen para ir a traerlos!"

"Sí," dijeron los soldados, guardias y la demás gente, obedeciendo la orden.

Pero la hija del rey se dio cuenta y le dijo a su marido, "Mi mamá mandó más gente regresen para conseguirnos, pero ellas no van a poder hacerlo. Tengo secretos para vencerlos," dijo ella.

Luego, le dice a su marido, "Las tres niñas se conviertan otra vez en tres mazorcas." Y así fue. Y le dijo que colocaron sobre la tierra.

El marido hizo lo que la mujer le había dicho. Colocó las tres mazorcas sobre la tierra. Al ratito, se vio un gran sembrado de milpa (maíz), jiloteando [empezar a granear la mazorca de maíz]. En medio de la milpa apareció un ranchito.

Entonces, la mujer le dijo a su marido, "Yo me convierto en una virgen y tu un sacristán, [y] así no van a poder [hacer nada] en contra nosotros" dijo la hija del rey.

Legaron los soldados y guardias y le preguntaron al hombre, "Ha visto por aquí a una pareja con tres hijas.

El hombre les contestó, "No he visto nada; no sé lo que ustedes andan buscando. Aquí, solamente soy yo, el sacristán, cuidando la virgen que es la protectora del sembrado de milpa (maíz). Yo no sé nada lo que ustedes andan buscando."

Sin lograr nada, los buscadores se regresaron de nuevo al palacio para decirle al rey y su esposa que solamente encontraron un sembrado de milpa en medio había un ranchito con una virgen adentro y un sacristán cuidándolo. La mujer del rey exclamó "¡Me muero, me muero! ¡Lo que ustedes vieron, la milpa que está en elotes, esas son mis tres nietas! ¡El sacristán cuidando, eso es mi yerno, y la virgen en medio del ranchito, esa es mi hija deberían haber traído atrás! ¡Regresan otra vez al lugar donde vieron la milpa! ¡Traigan la virgen, el sacristán, y los tres elotes de maíz para que venga mi hija, mi yerno, y mis tres nietas antes de que me muera de tanta tristeza!"

La hija del rey se dio cuenta la persecución sigue en su contra, es porque tenía los mismos secretos igual que su madre. Cuando amaneció, le dijo a su marido que guardara las tres mazorcas. La hija del rey levaba un tecomate con agua y lo regaba sobre la tierra. Luego se convirtió en una pequeña laguna. Extendió su faja y luego apareció una pequeña lancha; ellos dos cambiaron su apariencia en dos viejitos pescando sobre el pequeño lago en una lancha.

Cuando los soldados, guardias, y criados llegaron en el lugar, ya no se miraba el sembrado de milpa; todo se había cambiado. Luego, preguntaron a la pareja de ancianos si vieron entre la milpa una virgen y un sacristán adentro de un ranchito.

La pareja de viejitos contestó, diciendo, "Señores, ustedes están perdidos; no es aquí el lugar que andan buscando. Nosotros tenemos mucho tiempo de estar pescando; nunca hemos visto sembrado de maíz. Desde joven somos pescadores, y con este trabajo nos ganamos la vida." Pero la verdad era que no eran viejitas. Solamente habían cambiado sus apariencias por medio de secretos.

Los soldados, guardias y criados, asustados porque si no encuentran la hija del rey [y] los mandan a la horca. Se regresaron otra vez a decir que no encontraron nada. La milpa, la virgen, y el sacristán se habían desaparecido.

Solamente encontraron una pequeña laguna y una pareja de ancianos pesando, y solo tenían tres pescados. La mujer del rey dijo, "Los dos ancianos pescando son mi hija y mi yerno; los tres pescados son mis tres nietos. Los hubieran traído. Me muero, me muero sin ver a mi hija," decía la mujer del rey.

La mujer del rey ordenó otra vez los fueran a buscar de nuevamente. "¡Ahora, si [ustedes] las encuentran, toman este secreto!" les entregó un puñado de su cabello, su faja, y su peine!

"¡Regresen al mismo lugar donde vieron a los ancianos, extiendo mi faja, ponga a mi cabello en la tierra! Y verán que ahora si los van encontrar."

"Sí," dijeron los buscadores.

Se fueron, pero cuando llegaron todo se había desaparecido. Ya no se miraba el pequeño lago ni la pareja de ancianos. Solamente se miraba un llano. Otra vez se asustaron los buscadores, pero luego se acordaron lo que les había dicho la madre de la muchacha. Luego, ellos dejaron caer en el suelo el puñado de cabello, tendieron la faja, y botaron [abajo] el peine. En un cerrar y abrir de ojos, pareció un hermoso jardín con una inmensidad de flores donde estaban trabajando una hermosa mujer y un noble hombre con tres hermosas niñas. En ese punto, los buscadores reconocieron que era la hija, el yerno, y las tres nietas. Se los llevaron hacía al palacio del rey.

Cuando la hija, el yerno y las tres nietas llegaron a la presencia del rey y su esposa, entonces el exclamó, diciendo, "Con mi esposa y yo viejos, a la ausencia de mi hija nos dejó destrozada el alma, mi esposa y yo no podíamos comer ni dormir por mucha tristeza. Ahora, nos sentimos felices con mi esposa."

Luego, le dice a su yerno, "Oh, yerno amado, antes no te quería; te miraba con desprecio. Pero ahora me has ganado lo confianza. Ahora te quedas en mi trono," dijo el rey. Se quitó su corona, su collar, y su anillo—todos de oro—y se los colocó a su yerno. Luego, se llevó a sentarlo en su trono. [Y] así fue con el yerno. Ya no era como antes cuando lo despreciaba por ser pobre y de baja estatura." De ahí el ex rey y su esposa a hicieron una gran fiesta.

Por último, [el yerno] llegó a ser un gran rey. La otra hija del rey mirara con envidia todas las cosas que estaba pasando a su hermana. Ella no tuvo marido, y se alejó de sus padres. Se puso a mendigar, y así murió.

—Pedro Cholotío

STORY

# The Woman of the Hunter

THEY SAY THAT IN earlier times, there was a difficulty that happened in life every day. The people of San Juan were extremely poor. In the town, there was no work. It was necessary to go far to look for work on the farms in order to be able to eat.

Then, they say in the town there was a very poor family of a woodcutter who scarcely was able to get the food of the day. The wood he cut in the mountain, he sold in San Pedro and in Santiago, but in order to carry the wood to Santiago, he had to carry [it] by rowing a canoe to cross the lake. His woman sold herbs, and she searched for mushrooms under the trees to earn some *reales* [old Spanish coins]. They say this is how they lived a life of suffering.

Then the man thought and said, "Better that I become a hunter of animals," and thus he did. He prepared traps to catch the animals. He made the traps with cylindrical sticks that he planted in the earth; he put them down in the form of a cage with an entrance that was a little big and where it ended, very small. There was where he put the fruit like bananas, *injertos anonas* [*anona* graft, *sugar* apple graft]. They say that the animal entered to eat the fruit, but from there, he now was unable to leave because the place was very narrow. In other words, it was very reduced; the animals that entered, there they remained; now they could not leave. They were imprisoned in the trap.

When the man arrived, he only killed the animals. Thus, they say, it happened for a long time that man killed many animals such as the raccoon, *pizotes* [coatis], tepezcuinte, rabbits, the [pizote *andasolo* or coati with a white nose (species: *Nasua narica*)] and other animals. Part of the meat was eaten and part was sold in other towns. It was a lot of damage that this man caused on the mountain.

Then, on a Sunday, he told his woman to go with him to the mountain to fetch animal meat.

"Yes," said his woman, and they left.

They were almost there when the man said to his woman, "Stay here. Wait for me."

The man went to where he had put the traps, or the house of the animals. [As the woman waited, there] arrived a dwarf man with a whip hanging from his hand. He asked the woman, "Where is your husband? I want him! I need him right now!"

The woman answered, "My husband has gone a little more ahead to bring a little animal meat to eat; we are poor and do not have the means to buy meat."

The dwarf man answered, "I am the owner [lord] of this mountain. Your husband has done a lot of damage in this place, and so that you will learn, you will now receive twenty-five lashes. And you will remain with me forever in the mountain. Your husband is a murderous man; he has caused a lot of deaths of animals of this place."

The story says the dwarf man gave the woman twenty-five lashes. She was lying on the ground crying; the pain from the lashes was severe.

When the man returned, he found his woman crying. Then, he asked who it was that had hit her. The woman told her husband what she had seen and suffered from the twenty-five lashes. Little by little, the husband consoled his wife, and they headed back. They had walked a little when the woman disappeared [in an act] of magic. They say the husband became insane, only shouting. Running, he returned to the place of the traps, the man crying and looking for his woman on the mountain, but now it was not possible for him to find her. And suddenly, the dwarf man appeared and asked him, "What are you walking around looking for?"

The man replied, "I am looking for my woman; here, she disappeared. A wind took her away, but surely, she must be here on this mountain."

But they say the dwarf man, who is the lord of the mountain and the animals, told the husband of the woman, "Go and walk down. I don't want to see you here. You have done a lot of damage; a lot of animals have perished—you have killed them! Your woman will stay here forever; she will convert into a guardian and caretaker of all the animals on the mountain so that no more thieves will enter this place." That is what the dwarf man, owner and lord of the enchanted mountain, said.

The man arrived at the town to tell the people and relatives all that had happened to them. The next day, the story says that neighbors and relatives went together with the husband to the place of the traps to look for his woman. The husband led the people to the place where his wife was whipped by the dwarf. When they saw there her skirt, blouse, apron, and her comb that she was wearing before she disappeared, they were afraid. And also, they found there her long hairs.

The people began to cry because of all the fright[ful things] that they were seeing. They pondered three versions: the husband killed her; a mountain lion devoured her; or she disappeared in the mountain. The searchers spent the whole day on the mountain looking for that woman; but it was impossible. All the people gathered together to return [to town] because it was late, when suddenly they heard the voice of a woman crying like a lament; all the people went back see if it was she who was crying. But when they arrived where they heard [the voice], there was nothing. It was heard again, but further away. The frightened people did not have the courage to enter deeper into the mountain because it was dark. It was better that they return to the town.

Thus, that is what happened to the woman of the hunter. Now, it is believed that she is the guardian crying on the mountain. The place where this happened is called Xe Patzia'k in Tz'utujil; that is to say, in Spanish, the place where the clothing of the woman was found. In order to arrive at this place, it takes an hour and a half, and truly, one hears the sad voice of a woman crying.

—Pedro Cholotío Temó

CUENTO

# La mujer del cazador

DICEN QUE, EN LOS tiempos de antes, era una pena [que] pasar la vida cada día. La gente de San Juan era extremadamente pobres. En el pueblo, no había trabajo. Hay que ir lejos a buscar trabajo en las fincas para poder comer.

Entonces, dicen que en el pueblo había una familia de un leñador muy pobre a puras penas conseguían la comida del día. La leña que cortaba en la montaña, lo vendía en San Pedro y en Santiago, pero para llevar la leña a Santiago, tenía que llevarla en canoa para atravesar el lago remando. Su mujer vendía hiervas y buscaba hongos debajo de los árboles para ganarse unos reales. Dicen que así pasaban la vida, vida de sufrimiento.

Entonces el hombre pensó y dijo, "Mejor me convierto en un cazador de animales," y así lo hizo. Preparó trampas para atrapar a los animales. Las trampas los hacía con palos rollizos que los sembraba en la tierra; lo dejaba en forma de una jaula con una entrada que era un poco grande y donde termina era muy angosta. Allí era donde él ponía las frutas como bananos, injertos anonas. Dicen que el animal entraba para comerse las frutas, pero de ahí ya no podía salir porque el lugar era muy estrecho. En otras palabras, era muy reducido; los animales que entraban, allí se quedaban; ya no podían salir. Allí, se quedaban presas en la trampa.

Cuando el hombre llegaba, solo a matar a los animales. Así, dicen que pasó por mucho tiempo; ese hombre mató a muchos animales, como el mapache, pizotes [coatis], tepezcuinte, conejos, el andasolo [pizote o coatí de nariz blanca, (especie: *Nasua narica*)] y otros animales. Parte de la carne se lo comía y parte lo vendían en otros pueblos. Era mucho el daño que ocasionó ese hombre en la montaña.

Entonces, en un día domingo le dijo a su mujer para que se fuera con él a la montaña para ir a traer carne de animal."

"Sí," dijo la mujer, y se fueron.

Un poco faltaba para llegar cuando el hombre le dijo a su mujer, "Quédate aquí. Me vas esperar."

El hombre se fue donde tenía puesto las trampas, o la casa de los animales. Allí, donde la mujer se había quedado, llegó con ella un hombre enano con chicote colgado de la mano. Le preguntaba a la mujer, "¿Dónde está tu marido? ¡Yo lo quiero él! ¡Lo necesito ahorita mismo!"

La mujer, le contestó, "Mi marido se ha ido un poco más adelante a traer un poco de carne de animal para comer; somos pobre y no tenemos como para comprar carne."

El hombre enano le vuelva a decir a la mujer, "Yo soy el dueño de esta montaña. Tu marido ha hecho mucho daño en este lugar, y para que aprendas, ahora te toca 25 azotes. Y te quedas conmigo para siempre en la montaña. Tu marido es un hombre asesino; ha causado muchas muertes a los animales de este lugar."

El cuento dice que el hombre enano le pegó los veinticinco chicotazos a la mujer. Ella quedó tirada en el suelo (tierra) llorando; era mucho el dolor de los azotes.

Cuando regresó el hombre, encontró a su muer llorando. Luego, él peguntó que es lo que le ha pegado. La mujer le contó al marido todo lo que había visto y sufrido los veinticinco chicotazos. Poco a poco, la mujer fue consolado por su marido, y se vinieron de regreso. Habían caminando poco cuando la mujer se desapareció como un arte de magia. Dicen que el marido se puso loco, gritando solo. Corriendo se regresó hasta el lugar de las trampas, el hombre llorando [y] buscando a su mujer en la montaña, pero ya no fue posible encontrarla. Y de repente, se le apareció el hombre enano, y le preguntó "¿Que es lo que anda buscando?"

E hombre le contesta, "Estoy buscando a mi mujer; aquí, se desapareció un viento se la llevó, pero sin duda aquí ha de estar en esta montaña."

Pero dicen que el hombre enano, [quien] es el señor dueño de la montaña y de los animales, le dijo al marido de la mujer, "Anda y baja de regreso. No te quiero ver aquí; haz hecho mucho daño. ¡Muchos de los animales se han perdido—los has matado! Tu mujer se quedará aquí para siempre; ella se convertirá en guardiana y cuidadora de todos los animales en la montaña para que no entren más ladrones en este lugar." Eso es lo que dijo el hombre enano, dueño y señor de la montaña encantada.

El hombre llegó al pueblo a decirle a la gente vecina y familiares todo lo que había sucedido con ellos. Al otro día, dice que los vecinos y familiares se fueron juntos con el marido hasta al lugar de las trampas para buscar a su mujer.

El marido llevó la gente hasta al lugar donde su mujer fue azotada por el enano. Lo que les causó temor era cuando vieron allí su corte, su güipil, el delantal y su peine que tenía puesto antes de desaparecer. Y allí también se encontraban sus largos cabellos.

La gente comenzó a llorar de tanto miedo de todo lo que estaban viendo. Se pusieron a pensar tres versiones: su marido la mató; fue devorado por un león; o se desapareció en la montaña. Los buscadores, todo el día pasaron en la montaña buscando a esa mujer; pero no fue posible. Se juntaron toda la gente para regresar [al pueblo] porque ya era tarde cuando de repente oyeron la voz de una mujer llorando como un lamento; toda la gente se regresó para ver si era ella la que estaba llorando. Pero cuando llegaron donde oyeron [la voz], no hay nada. Se dejo oír otra vez, pero más lejos. La gente asustada no se animó entrar más al fondo de la montaña porque estaba oscuro. [Era] mejor se regresaron al pueblo.

Así, eso fue que pasó con la mujer del cazador. Ahora, se cree que ella es la guardiana llorando en la montaña. El lugar donde sucedió se llama Xe Patzia'k en tz'utujil; es decir, en español, el lugar donde se encontró la ropa de la mujer. Para llegar a este lugar, se hace una hora y media y, de verdad, se oye la voz triste de una mujer llorando.

—Pedro Cholotío Temó

# Tz'utujil Story

## *The Woman Who Buried the Devil*

IT IS SAID THAT in a town lived a woman who did not have a husband; her parents told her that it would be better for her to have a husband because her father and mother now were very old and then the daughter would remain in solitude. For that reason, they told her it would be better for her to have a house-mate.

Finally, the woman was convinced to marry a man, and she told her parents that yes, she would be able to marry a man, but only one who had money.

Her mother told her, "Daughter, how are you going to know which of the men has a lot of money?"

She answered her mother, "Mama, in order to know which one of the men has money, he must have gold teeth."

The mother answered, "Daughter, but in our town, there are no men who have gold teeth."

The woman told her mother, "Mama, my husband is going to have money and gold teeth." That is what she said, that she would have to marry a man with gold teeth.

The woman met a man with gold teeth; his mouth gleamed because his teeth were pure gold. But it is said that it was the devil who converted into a man in order to deceive the woman. When the woman saw a man with teeth of gold, she fell in love with him, but it was not really a man—it was the devil. The woman was very content because she found the man of her wish; she wanted very much to have a husband with gold teeth.

So it was that the woman married the man with gold teeth; she had the best fiesta when it was her wedding reception. But the old folks, that is to say, her parents, became very sad. They sensed something bad was going to happen to their daughter, thinking that their son-in-law was not a good man, that their daughter's marriage was not good.

They were right, because this woman married the devil. The first night when they were going to bed, the woman took off her skirt and blouse, preparing to lie down with her husband. Also, the man took off his clothing and began to take apart his body. By pieces, he took off his head and put it on the pillow; his legs and all his body converted into wood. Now he was not a man.

The woman began to shout to call her parents and neighbors to come to see what was happening with their son-in-law, who converted into wood. That is when they [realized] that the man who turned into wood was the devil. The parents and neighbors burned the wood, but they say that when the wood was burning, in the flames was heard a laugh. There, they verified that it was the devil who was laughing in the flames of the fire.

The next day, the husband appeared again with gold teeth, but the woman was very afraid of him. But as he was the devil, he convinced her again, and he told her, "I am the husband of gold teeth as you wanted him. Well, I am your husband, and you are my woman. You have to learn to coexist with me. I convert into many qualities—into persons, into animals, and I change into serpents when I wish. I have a lot of power. When I want, I am here; and when I want, I am far away. Do not be afraid; I have money to give you. And you also are going to convert into a woman with gold teeth." That is to say, the woman was going to transform into a female devil.

But the woman, thinking about what she was going to do to free herself of the devil, asked her husband, "When you convert into an animal, can you speak?"

The man said, "Yes, I can talk; I can scream; I can do whatever I want in this world." So he answered his wife. The woman was sorry to have married a man with gold teeth and that now she could not liberate herself from the evil because her husband was not a man. The woman had a lot of fear since the first night when they went to bed and the man transformed into wood and they burned it and he laughed in the flames because for him the fire was nothing. For the woman, it was a big problem when she felt the man and he was already asleep with her, and after a while, he disappeared and became many things.

The story says that again a great snake was with her on the bed—it was her husband, the devil. The woman screamed for help, and the serpent laughed at her, and in a little while, disappeared. Now, the woman could neither eat nor sleep, only thinking in her disgrace to see when he was going to die to be free of the evil.

She, pondering and pondering, finally went to a thinker, or wise man, to consult about what she ought to do to free herself from the man with gold teeth.

**The *Secreto* that the Wise Man Gave Her**

"Prepare a big clay jar and place near the bed a black cloth and a *pita* [cord] of maguey! When your husband converts into a serpent, tell him to get into the clay pot! And when the snake is inside the pot, you cover it up with the cloth, tie it up with the maguey rope, and turn it upside down! During the night, bury it in the middle of the cemetery! And you'll see that you're going to be free of this demon." So said the wise man.

The woman did everything the wise man told her. Then the man with gold teeth arrived again with his woman. The woman asked him to turn himself into a snake.

"Yes," said the man. He became a big snake, and his woman asked him to get inside the clay jar.

"Yes," said the serpent. He got inside the jar with the black cloth, and she tied it up with maguey rope and turned it upside down while she waited for midnight to bury it in the cemetery.

Inside the jar the serpent man whistled, asking the woman to take him out of the jar. She heard in the jar a man crying, and he said if she would not take him out of the jar, it would be the end of her life. At midnight, the woman carried the jar upside down and dug a hole in the center of the cemetery and there left buried the man with gold teeth who was the devil.

The grandmothers and grandfathers said do not covet things, because all the bad desires have a bad ending. After being buried in the cemetery, that man with gold teeth did not return. [Not] until then did the woman free herself from evil.

—Juan Upán Ovalle and Pedro Cholotío Temó

I, Pedro, gave the name of this story although indeed the old folks called this story "The Man with Gold Teeth."[11]

# Cuento tz'utujil

## *La mujer que enterró el diablo*

SE DICE QUE EN un pueblo vivió una mujer que no tenía marido; sus padres le decían que sería mejor para ella tener su marido porque su papa y su mama ya eran muy viejos y entonces la hija quedaría en la soledad. Por eso razón, le decían sería mejor para ella tener a su compañero de hogar.

A fin, la mujer se convenció de casarse con un hombre, y les dijo a sus padres que sí, ella podría casarse con un hombre, pero solo con uno que tenía dinero.

Su mamá le dijo, "¿Hija, como lo vas hacer para saber quien de los hombres tiene mucho dinero?"

Ella le contestó a su mamá, "Mamá, para saber cuál de los hombres tiene dinero, debe tener dientes de oro."

La mama le contestó, "Hija, pero en nuestro pueblo, no hay hombres que tienen dientes de oro."

La mujer le dijo a su mama, "Mamá, mi marido va a tener dinero y dientes de oro." Eso es lo que decía que tendría que casar con un hombre de dientes de oro.

La mujer conoció a un hombre con dientes de oro; su boca brillaba porque tenía la dentadura de puro oro. Pero se dice que era el diablo que se convirtió en un hombre para engañar a la mujer. Cuando la mujer vio al hombre de dientes de oro, se enamoró de él, pero no era hombre de verdad—era el diablo. La mujer se puso muy contenta porque ya encontró el hombre de su deseo; ella deseaba mucho tener un marido de dientes de oro.

Así fue que la mujer se casó con el hombre de dientes de oro; tuvo la mejor fiesta cuando fue la recepción de su boda. Pero los viejitos, es decir, los padres de la muchacha, se pusieron muy triste. Presentían algo mal iba a pasar a su hija, pensando que su yerno no era un buen hombre, que el casamiento de su hija no era bueno.

Todo fue cierto lo que presentían los viejitos porque esa mujer se casó con el diablo. La primera noche cuando se iban a dormir, la mujer se quitó su corte y su huipil, preparándose para acostarse con su marido. También, el hombre se quitó su ropa y comienza a desarmar su cuerpo. Por piezas, se quito la cabeza la puso sobre la almohada; sus piernas y todo su cuerpo se convirtió en madera. Ya no era hombre.

La mujer comenzó a gritar a llamar a sus padres y vecinos para que venir a ver lo que está pasando con yerno que se convirtió en madera. Allí es cuando pensaron que el hombre se volvió madera es el diablo. Los padres y vecinos quemaron la madera, pero dicen que cuando la madera estaba quemando, en las llamas se oía una risa. Allí comprobaron que era el diablo el que estaba riendo en las llamas del fuego.

Al día siguiente, apareció otra vez el marido de dientes de oro, pero la mujer le tenía mucho miedo. Pero como era el diablo, la convenció de nuevamente, y le dijo, "Yo soy el marido de dientes de oro como lo querías. Pues yo soy tu marido, y eres mi mujer. Tienes que aprender a convivir conmigo. Yo me convierto en muchas cualidades—en personas, en animales, y me convierto en serpiente cuando quiero. Tengo mucho poder. Cuando quiero, estoy aquí; y cuando quiero, estoy más allá lejos. No tengas miedo; yo tengo dinero para darte. Y tú también te vas a convertir en una mujer de dientes de oro." Es decir, la mujer se iba a transformer en una diabla.

Pero la mujer, pensando en lo que iba a hacer para librarse del diablo, le preguntó a su marido, "¿Cuándo te conviertes en animal, puedes hablar?"

El hombre dice, "Sí, yo puedo hablar; puedo gritar, y puedo hacer lo que quiero en este mundo." Así que contestó a su mujer. La mujer era arrepentida de haber casado con un hombre de dientes de oro y ya no podía librarse del mal porque su marido no era hombre. Mucho miedo tuvo la mujer desde la primera noche cuando se iban a dormir y el hombre se convirtió en madera y lo quemaron y se reía en las llamas del fuego para él no era nada el fuego. Para la mujer, fue un gran problema cuando sentía el hombre y ya se encontraba dormido con ella, y al rato. se desaparecía y convertía en muchas cosas.

El cuento dice que la otra vez gran serpiente estaba con ella en la cama—era el marido, el diablo. La mujer gritaba para ayuda, y la serpiente se reía de ella, y al ratito se desapareció. Ahora, la mujer ya no podía comer ni dormir, solo pensando en su desgracia a ver cuando se va a morir para librarse del mal. La mujer, pensando y pensando, al fin se fue con un hombre pensador, o sabio, para consultar que debería de hacer para librarse del hombre de dientes de oro.

## El *secreto* que le dio el sabio

"¡Prepara una tinaja grande de barro y ponte cerca de la cama una tela negra y una *pita* [cuerda] de maguey! ¡Cuando tu marido se convierte en serpiente, dile que se meta adentro de la tinaja de barro! ¡Y cuando la culebra está adentro de la tinaja, tú la tapa con la tela, la amarra con pita de maguey, y la pon de boca abajo! ¡Por la noche, la entierra en el centro del cementerio! Y verás que te vas a librar de este demonio." Así le dijo el sabio.

La mujer preparó todo lo que el sabio le había dicho. Entonces el hombre de dientes de oro llegó otra vez con su mujer. La mujer le pidió que se convirtiera en serpiente.

"Sí," dijo el hombre. Se volvió una gran culebra, y su mujer le pidió se metiera adentro de la tinaja de barro.

"Sí," dijo la serpiente. Se metió en la tinaja con la tela negra, y la mujer amarró con la pita de maguey y lo puso boca abajo mientras esperaba la media noche para ir a enterrarlo en el cementerio.

Adentro de la tinaja el hombre serpiente daba silbidos, pidiendo a la mujer que lo sacara de la tinaja. Se oía que en la tinaja lloraba un hombre, y decía si no lo sacaba de la tinaja, sería el fin de su vida. A la media noche, la mujer se llevó la tinaja boca abajo y abrió un hoyo en el centro del cementerio y allí lo dejó enterrado el hombre de dientes de oro que era el diablo.

Las abuelas y abuelos decían no hay que codiciar cosas porque todos los deseos malos tienen mal fin. Después de enterrado en el cementerio, ya no volvió ese hombre de dientes de oro. [No] hasta allí la mujer se libró del mal.

—Juan Upán Ovalle y Pedro Cholotío Temó
Yo, Pedro, puse el nombre de este cuento, aunque sí, los viejitos contaban este cuento "El hombre de dientes de oro."[11]

*CASO*

# Holy Friday, an Elder with a Cane Blinds a Hunter

DON JUAN GONZÁLES CHOROR of eighty-six years of age [had] parents [who] were natives of San Juan la Laguna. He says that he grew up and worked more on the coast when he was young. His parents, Basilio Gonzáles and Ignacia Choror, worked a long time for the fincas [farms] of Chicacao. Leaving the farms, they arrived in Panyebar, aldea of San Juan la Laguna.

Don Juan says that in the year 1950 he was alguacil of the aldea, *ad honorem* [honorary, unpaid]. From the aldea he came and took turns for eight days in the town, and eight days he worked for himself, going to work at the farms in order to earn a little more money. He said that he worked mainly on the fincas of Chicacao and Santo Tomás la Unión.

He says that twenty-five years ago a strange thing happened on a finca of Santo Tomás la Unión. He says that living on a finca is not the same as living in a town. Living in a town, one enjoys going to church or [walking] in the procession on Semana Santa [Holy Week]. But those who live on the fincas are not able to go. The only diversion is to go to the banks of the rivers or to go to the mountain to hunt animals with dogs, with slings, or with shotguns, [and] sell the meat or eat it.

Then on a Good Friday, a man who always liked the hunt went to the mountain with his sling and his three dogs to look for animals. Well, he says that his father told him not to go, for it being the most sacred day, something bad could happen to him. But the muchacho said that nothing bad was going to happen, and he went to the mountain on that day, Holy Friday.

When that man was already on the mountain with his three hunting dogs to kill some deer or whatever other animals he found, suddenly a hillside of the mountain opened, and from there came out many animals—mountain lions, jaguars, deer, *tepescuintles* [brown rodents the size of a rabbit with black stripes on their backs], armadillos, pizotes, rabbits, wild pigs, and many more of that mountain came out running in groups, and they disappeared in the air. So it went for half an hour. The dogs now were not able to walk. All of them were trembling, they wanted to get between the legs of their owner. And neither could the muchacho walk; his body remained paralyzed, seeing and experiencing these strange things.

And suddenly, he says that from the same place where the animals left, or better said, after the animals had left, an old man with a cane in his hand came out and spoke to the hunter, saying, "Muchacho, what did you come to look for on this mountain? You could not take a day to rest in your house[?] Don't you know that today is the most sacred day—big and small, rich and poor are remembering the death of the son of God, and you killing my animals. From now on, you will be blind together with your three dogs."

Thus, it happened—the hunter man and his dogs remained blind. Now they were not able to leave from where they were; they were unable to walk. There on the mountain, they remained on the day, Friday, and during the night. Saturday, at sunrise, the family, seeing that the man did not arrive home, asked for help from his kin and neighbors. They went to the mountain to look for him. They found him seated on the ground together with his three dogs, but now he was unable to look at them, but he spoke to them. They carried him on their backs to his house. There, he began to tell them all that happened—a man came out of the mountain who left them blind.

Thus, it happened that the hunter and his three dogs remained blind, but they did not live anymore. The man died, and also his three dogs died.

This *caso* happened with the friends of Juan Gonzáles on one of the fincas of Santo Tomás la Unión.

—don Juan Gonzáles Choror

CASO

# Viernes Santo, un viejo con un bastón ciega cazador

DON JUAN GONZÁLES CHOROR de 86 años de edad [tenía] padres [que] eran oriundos of San Juan la Laguna. Él dice que creció y trabajó más en la costa cuando eran joven. Sus padres, Basilio Gonzáles y Ignacia Choror, trabajaron mucho tiempo por las fincas de Chicacao. Saliendo de las fincas, llegaron a Panyebar, aldea de San Juan la Laguna.

Don Juan dice que en el año 1950 fue alguacil de la municipalidad, *ad honorem* [honorario, no remunerado]. De la aldea venía y hacía turno por ocho días en el pueblo y ocho días trabajaba para él mismo, ir a trabajar a las fincas para poder ganar unos centavos más. Él dijo que trabajó más en las fincas de Chicacao y Santo Tomás la Unión.

Él dice que hace veinticinco años pasado sucedió una cosa extraña en una finca de Santo Tomás la Unión. Él dice vivir en una finca no es igual vivir en un pueblo. Vivir en un pueblo uno se divierta va a la iglesia o [andando] en la procesión en la Semana Santa. Pero los que viven en las fincas no pueden salir. La única diversión es ir a la orilla de los ríos [o] ir a la montaña a cazar animales con perros, con hondas o con escopetas, [y] vende la carne o se la comen.

Entonces en un viernes Santo, un hombre que siempre le gustan la cacería se fue a la montaña con su honda y sus tres perros para buscar animales. Pues, dice que su papa le dijo no saliera por ser el día más sagrado; le puede pasar alguna cosa mal. Pero el muchacho dijo que nada mal va a pasar, y se fue a la montaña en ese día Viernes Santo.

Cuando ese hombre se encontraba ya en la montaña con sus tres perros cazadores para matar algún venado o cualquier otro animal él encontró, de repente una ladera de la montaña abrió, y de allí, salían muchos animales—leones, tigre, venados, tepescuintles [roedores marrones del tamaño de un conejo con rayas negras en el lomo], armadillos, pizotes, conejos, coche monte, y muchos más de ese cerro salían por grupos corriendo, y se desaparecían en el aire. Así pasó como por media hora. Los perros ya no podían caminar. Todos temblando, se querían meterse entre las piernas de su dueño. Y el muchacho tampoco podía caminar; su cuerpo quedó paralizado, viendo y viviendo estas cosas extrañas.

Y de repente, dice que del mismo lugar de donde salían los animales, o vale más decir, después de haber salido los animales, salió un hombre viejo con un bastón en la mano le habló al cazador, diciendo "¿Muchacho, que vienes a buscar aquí en esta montaña? No has podido guardar un día para descansar en tu casa. No sabes que hoy es el día más sagrado—grandes y chiquitos, ricos y pobres están recordando la muerte de hijo de Dios, y tu matando a mis animales. Desde ahorra, tu quedarás ciego junto con tus tres perros."

Así se hizo—el hombre cazador y los perros se quedaron ciegos. Ya no pudieron salir de donde estaban; no podían caminar. Allá en la montaña, se quedaron en el día viernes, y durante la noche. Amanecer sábado, la familia, viendo que el hombre no llegaba a su casa, pidieron ayuda a los familiares y vecinos. Se fueron a la montaña para buscarlo. Lo encontraron sentado en el suelo junto con sus tres perros, pero ya no podían mirarlos, pero les hablaba. Los trajeron cargados hasta su casa. Allí era donde comenzó a contarles todo lo que pasó—un hombre viejo salió de la montaña que los dejó ciego.

Así, pasó con el cazador y sus tres perros que quedaron ciegos, pero no vivieron más. El hombre se murió, y también se murieron los perros.

Este caso pasó con los amigos de Juan Gonzáles en una de las fincas de Santo Tomás la Unión.

—don Juan Gonzáles Choror

# The Tale of Señor Sebastián Ujpán

WE HAVE KNOWN SEÑOR Sebastián Ujpán of San Pablo la Laguna for many years. A son of his comes to dance in the group of the Mexicans [Dance of the Mexicans].

In January of this year, 2017, Señor Sebastián Ujpán came to me to invite us to go to lunch at his house on the twenty-fifth of January, the same day of the apostle San Pablo. Señor Sebastián Ujpán was chatting about two hours with me. The señor is seventy-three years old.

He told me of the suffering of residents of the neighboring town of San Pablo la Laguna in the years of 1981 to 1982, when it was the time of the military commissioner, Pascual Petzey, nicknamed *amees* [ame's]; that is to say, cat burglar.[12] Don Sebastian says he and his sons were frowned upon [maltreated] by the military commissioner. Two of them were sent to the military detachment in Santiago Atitlán, accused as guerrillas merely for not giving money to the military commissioner. He himself came to the house of the people to frighten them by telling them that their names were already are on a blacklist and to be prepared because in the night they would be kidnapped and disappeared once and for all.

Don Sebastián says, "The persons persecuted cried night and day; they sold their lands, treasures, pigs, and *chompipes* [turkeys]. The money was delivered to the then–military commissioner, Pascual Petzey." He said that that money was delivered to high military chiefs of the detachment in Santiago Atitlán so that their names would be taken off the blacklist and they would be free of persecution. It was all a lie, the money he asked from the people was for him.

Another clever trick of the military commissioner [was that] he had a list of the people who lived a little better. He [Santiago] says that he told them every fifteen days, they had to give two or three turkeys for the lunch of the high [senior] bosses of the army; he threatened the persons if they refused to comply with this demand.

But he [Sebastián] says that not all of the people had turkeys. They had to go to Nahualá or to Totonicapán to buy the turkeys to give to the *amees*. Don Sebastián says that this man said he carried up to ten turkeys in big baskets for the food of the colonels, but it all was a lie. He says that he took them to sell in the hotels in Panajachel and in the capital—it was a business of the man. Sure, he said that he had a lot of contact with jefes of the military detachment. They [the bosses] said that they [the people] had to obey the orders of the commissioners. Many people were denounced as guerrillas, and they punished them for fifteen to twenty days.

Don Sebastián says that in that time, 1981 to 1982, there was a fear of sleeping in one's own house because Pascual threatened the people to take money from them. He says that he had contact with the mayor, Bartolo Petzey; they put many people in jail. It makes him sad to remember, said Sebastián.

One of the victims was Señor Pedro Xajil. At that time, he was a member of Catholic Action and [an] honorable and hard-working man who enjoyed the respect of many people. The military commissioner threatened to get money from him.

Pedro Xajil did not give the money they asked for because it was an extortion, or because he did not have it. One night, he was taken from his house by the commissioners to torture him. They carried him off to put him on an anthill during the night. He says they left him tied with rope to an avocado tree. There was no one who could help him until it dawned. Then, he was helped by the first persons who went down to irrigate their cultivations on the shore of the lake. He [Sebastián] says that Señor Pedro Xajil was alive, but all his body was swollen and bruised from the stings of thousands of ants. He was not able to speak because his tongue had swollen. Indeed, he was able to see because he closed his eyes when the ants bit him. It was an unbearable punishment. They said they carried him on their backs to his house. It took many days to recover his health; it was deplorable what the *Pableños* [people of San Pablo] saw.

Don Sebastián says that some of the people who supported the commissioners but that some residents got together, that is to say, the ones more affected, to give the jefe of the commissioners a beating. Three men and three women of the tallest and stoutest monitored the place where Pascual passed when he went to inspect his coffee trees near where a small river passes. On a morning when Pascual was passing by, the three men and the three women came out from the woods and they all grabbed him; the men grabbed his hands and feet while each one of the women urinated on his face and in his mouth and made him swallow the urine of the women. That was the punishment that they gave him, and he [Sebastián] says they told him, "If you molest us anymore, we are going to burn you!"

How did Pascual Petzey end up? He [Sebastián] says that he was very astute. After losing his fame as jefe of the military commissioners, he became a *curandero* [curer]. He said that he was able to cure the most difficult illnesses, that he knew many medicinal plants.

Don Sebastián says that Pascual Petzey lost the confidence of the people of the town. No one believed what he said about being a healer. He went to the towns to deceive the people. [Sebastián] says that in San José Poaquil, Chimaltenango, he was able to deceive the people. He began to cure a woman who suffered from sickness. To cure her, he asked for Q3,000. The family of the sick person only had Q2,000. They owed Q1,000. But Don Sebastián says that the sick woman died. Pascual had not realized that the sick woman had already died. He arrived again at San José to collect the Q1,000. Well, the family did not tell Pascual that the sick woman under his treatment already died. They received him with much respect as a curandero. They prepared a lunch for him. He ate lunch well, and they gave a Q1,000 adjustment for the value of his work without his knowing that they had put poison in the food. He was able to walk, and he came to die on the Inter-American Highway. He [Sebastián] says that inside the pocket of his trousers, he had Q1,000. His family went to bring his body [home] without [any investigation]. Don Sebastián says the notice went out how the ex-military commissioner died. Don Sebastián finished saying, "The people of the town were very happy when this man died."

I asked Don Sebastián if he would allow me to write this story as a tale. He said, "Yes, you can write it," and for that reason, I wrote this story.

—Sebastián Ujpán

# El cuento del señor Sebastián Ujpán

NOS CONOCEMOS SEBASTIÁN UJPÁN de San Pedro la Laguna por muchos años. Un hijo de él viene a bailar en el grupo de los mexicanos [Baile de los Mexicanos].

En enero de este año 2017, El Señor Sebastián vino conmigo para invitarnos para que fuéramos almorzar en su casa el 25 de enero, el mero día del apostal San Pablo. El Señor Sebastián estuvo platicando como dos horas conmigo. El señor es de 73 años.

Me cuenta de los sufrimientos de los vecinos del vecino pueblo of San Pablo la Laguna en los años 1981 to 1982, cuando era la época de comisionado militar Pascual Petzey, apodado *amees* [ame's]; es decir, gato ladron.[12] Don Sebastián dice que él y sus hijos fueron mal visto [maltratado] por el comisionado militar. Dos de ellos fueron enviados al destacamento militar en Santiago Atitlán, acusados como guerrilleros solo por no darle dinero al comisionado. El mismo llegaba a la casa de la gente para atemorizarles con decirles que sus nombres ya están en la lista negra que se preparen porque por la noche serán secuestrados y se desaparecerán de una vez.

Don Sebastián dice, "las personas perseguidas lloraban de noche y de día; vendían sus terrenos, terneros, cerdos, y *chompipes* (pavos). El dinero se lo entregaban al entonces comisionado militar, Pascual Petzay. Él decía que ese dinero se lo entregaba a altos jefes militares en el destacamento en Santiago Atitlán para que sus nombres sean quitados de la lista negra y quedaban en libertad de la persecución. Todo era mentiras; el dinero que pedía a la gente era para él.

Otra astucia del comisionado militara [era que] él tenía una lista de las personas que viven un poco bien. Él [Santiago] dice que les decía que cada 15 días, tenían que dar dos o tres chompipes para el almuerzo de los altos [mayor] jefes del ejército; amenazaba a las personas si se negaba cumplir lo que él ordenaba.

Pero dice [Sebastián] que no toda la gente tenía chompipes. Tenían que ir a Nahualá o Totonicapán para comprar los pavos para darselo al amees. Don Sebastián dice que ese hombre decía que él lleva hasta diez chompipes en canastos grandes para la comida de los coroneles, pero todo era mentira. Dice que lleva a vender en los hoteles en Panajachel y en la capital [Guatemala City]—era un negocio del hombre. De verdad, dice que tenía mucho contacto con los jefes del destacamento militar. Decían [los jefes] que tenían [la gente] que obedecer las ordenes del comisionado. Mucha gente fue denunciada como guerrilleros, y les daban castigo por 15 a 20 días.

Don Sebastián dice que, en ese tiempo, 1981 a 1982, había miedo de dormir en su propia casa porque Pascual amenazaba a la gente para sacarles dinero. Dice que tenía contacto con el alcalde, Bartolo Petzey; metían a mucha gente en la cárcel. Le da tristeza recordar decía don Sebastián.

Una de las victimas fue el Señor Pedro Xajil. En ese tiempo, era miembro de la Acción Católica y [un] hombre honrado y muy trabajador que gozaba el respeto de mucha gente. Él comisionado militar amenazó para sacarle dinero.

Pedro Xajil no dio el dinero que le pedían porque era una extorsión, o porque no lo tenía. Una noche fue sacado de su casa por los comisionados para torturarlo. Se lo llevaran a ponerlo en un hormiguero durante la noche. Dice que lo dejaron amarrado con lazo a un árbol de aguacate. No había nadie que pudiera ayudarlo hasta que amaneció. Entonces, fue ayudado por las primeras personas que bajaron a regar sus cultivos a la orilla del lago. Dice [Sebastián] que el Señor Pedro Xajil estaba vivo; pero todo su cuerpo esta hinchado y amoratado por el piquete de millares de hormigos. No podía hablar porque su lengua la tenía hinchada. Sí, podía ver porque dice que cerro sus ojos cuando le picaba las hormigas. Era un castigo insoportable. Decían que cargado se lo llevaron a su casa. Tardo muchos días en recuperar su salud; fue deplorable lo que vieron los Pableños.

Don Sebastián dice que había uno parte de la gente que apoyaban a los comisionados pero que se juntaran unos vecinos; es decir, los más afectados, para darle una golpiza al jefe. Tres hombres y tres mujeres de las más altas y gordas, controlaron el lugar donde siempre pasa Pascual cuando de iba a ver sus cafetos cerca donde pasa un pequeño rio. En una mañana cuando iba pasando Pascual, del monte salieron los tres hombres y las tres mujeres entre todos lo agarraron; los hombres le agarraron las manos y los pies mientras las mujeres cada una se orinaban en la cara y en la boca [y] le obligaron que tragara el orín de las mujeres. Esto era el castigo que le dieron, y [Sebastián] dice que le dijeron: ¡Si molesta más, lo iban a quemar!"

¿Como terminó Pascual Petzey? [Sebastián] dice que era muy astuto. Después de perder la fama de ser jefe de los comisionados militares, se pasó a curandero. Él decía que puede curar enfermedades más difíciles, que conocía muchas plantas medicinales.

Don Sebastián dice que Pascual Petzy ha perdido la confianza con la gente del pueblo. Nadie le crecía lo que él decía de ser curandero. Se fue a los pueblos a engañar a la gente. [Sebastián] dice que en San José Poaquil, Chimaltenango, pudo engañar a la gente. Él comenzó a curar a una mujer que padecía de enfermedad. Para curarla, el pidió Q3,000. La familia de la mujer enferma solamente tenía Q2,000. Le quedaron debiendo Q1,000. Pero don Sebastián dice que la mujer enferma se murió. Pascual no se había dado cuenta que la mujer enferma ya se había muerta. Él llegó otra vez a San José para cobrar Q1,000. Pues, la familia no le dijeron Pascual que la señora que estaba bajo su tratamiento ya murió. Lo recibieron con mucho respeto como un curandero. Le preparan un almuerzo. Almorzó bien, y le dieron Q1,000 ajuste del valor de su trabajo sin saber si adentro de la comida le echaron veneno. Pudo caminar, y se vino a morir en la carretera interamericana. Dice [Sebastián] que adentro de la bolsa de pantalón, tenía Q1,000. La familia lo fueron a traer su cadáver sin hacer averiguaciones. Don Sebastián dice salió la noticia como fue la muerte del comisionado ex-militar. Don Sebastián termina diciendo, "La Gente del pueblo se alegran mucho cuando murió ese hombre."

Yo le dije don Sebastián si él permite que yo escribiera este cuento como una leyenda. Él me dijo "Sí puedes escribirlo," y por eso escribí este cuento.

—Sebastián Ujpán

# The Wise and Powerful

THEY SAY THAT IN the world a man who was wise walked around, thinking of leaving the world flat. That man did not eat or drink; where he passed, the earth remained flat.

But, the story says that there was another man wiser than the one who came from the other side of the sea. He asked the first, "What are you doing?"

He answered, "I am flattening the [ground] because there are many hills, ravines, and so that all will be level, I am working."

The other wise man tells him, "Hombre, you are thinking badly; don't do that. If all the world were flat, the people would die because of big floods. The hills, ravines, and the volcanoes help us so that the rivers run toward the ocean. Stop doing it." In a little while the man who was leveling the world converted into a big rock.

The wiser man took to the road, walking through the world. The story says that he reached a farmer who was sowing corn. The wise and powerful man asked, "What are you planting?"

The farmer answered, "Señor, I am a poor farmer; here, I am planting maize; I am hoping for a blessing from heaven so that my sowing will give me a good harvest."

The wise and powerful man replied, "Bring a little seed; I'm going to plant some plots." Thus, he did; he planted a plot of maize in each corner of the land. Then, he told the muchacho, "Come, we are going to rest a little under this tree."

Thus, they rested a while. Having rested a while, they saw the crop of milpa that covered the ground, *jiloteando* [coming into ear]. It was a wonder what they were seeing. The farmer joyfully shouted, "You are a god of the world! Let me go with you; I want to follow you!"

But the wise and powerful [man] told him, "You can't go with me. I don't have a house to sleep in or money to buy sustenance. Moreover, there is no one to harvest your crops; thus, you cannot go with me."

The wise and powerful one continued on his road through the world until reaching another man who was kneading flour to make bread. They say that at this time the bread did not come out like the bread of today. The wise and powerful man said to the one who was kneading, "Son, what are you doing? If you want, I can help you a little."

"Very well, Señor, thank you if you want to help me; here is the dough. You can make some bread," said the baker.

The wise man began to shape the bread, and he put it in the oven. A little later, the best bread came out. Loaves have never come out like the loaves that the wise man took out.

The baker said, "Señor, if you would like, stay here with me making bread. I know that you have the power to make many things."

The wise one told him, "I can't remain here with you. It is that I must go around the world to help those who receive me in their homes."

The baker replied, "I will go with you; I know you are very powerful."

He answered him, "You cannot; it is that I have to walk a lot. I showed you how to make the best bread; may your work be blessed and fruitful." Yet for that reason, the bakers have a job that is very blessed in the world.

The wise one continued walking through the world until arriving at the house of a man who was fabricating caites, and he said, "My son, what are you doing?

The sandal maker said, "Señor, here I am making caites to sell," and he grabbed a pair of sandals he gave to the wise man. He told him, "Here is a pair of sandals for you to put on."

The señor said, "Thanks, Son, you covered my feet," and he put on the sandals. Because the wise one walked barefoot, he replied, "Your work is blessed and multiplied." For that reason, they say that the work of sandal makers and cobblers is a good work in the whole world. The wise one went walking more until he met with another man who was disposing [cutting down] trees; more clearly, he was clearing a piece of land to plant. The wise man asked him, "Son, what are you doing?"

The muchacho very angry and with bad humor answered him, "What do you care what I'm doing? It is my [concern]; there is no need to ask if I am going to plant bramble, rocks, or brush—you have nothing to do with me."

The wise man told the muchacho, "Son, if this is what you want to cultivate, that is what the earth will produce for you." The story says that the wise man [walked away]. The ground where the man was working was covered with big rocks, bramble, lots of brush, serpents, and coyotes.

The story says that the muchacho could barely break away from where he was working. Very angrily he said, "I am going to look for that man and kill him."

He gathered the people of his town and he went to show them how the land where he was working was. The townspeople got upset; they went looking for the wise man to kill him. But he realized they were chasing him and soon they would catch him.

The wise one told a woman who was herding sheep, "Please I want to hide among your sheep because some enemies are looking for me to kill me."

The woman said, "Señor, you can hide among the sheep without problems."

The wise and powerful man got between the sheep and became a big sheep much bigger than all the [other] sheep. The enemies arrived and asked the lady, "This way, we saw a man. Where did he hide? We are looking for him to kill him; he caused a lot of damage to a piece of land."

The woman answered, "Señores, I have not seen the man that you are looking for, only my sheep. You can look there [to see] if he is among the sheep."

The angry enemies did not find anyone and continued on their way. The lamb converted again into a person and said to the woman, "Many thanks for helping me, and in exchange, what do you ask from me?"

"A blessing for my animals and pasture for them," said the woman.

"Very well," said the powerful and wise man.

He embraced one of the lambs and kissed it and kissed the ground and said, "These sheep shall multiply; this place shall be green forever." In a little while, hundreds of sheep could be seen, and the place became greener.

The woman shouted with joy so that people came to see everything that had happened to her.[13]

—Pedro Cholotío Temó

# El sabio y poderoso

DICEN QUE EN EL mundo andaba un hombre que era sabio, pensando de dejar plano el mundo. Ese hombre no comía ni bebía; donde el pasaba quedaba plano la tierra.

Pero el cuento dice que había otro hombre más sabio que el que venia del otro lado del mar. Le pregunto al primero ¿"Qué es lo que está haciendo?"

Él le contestó "Estoy aplanando [la tierra] porque hay muchos cerros, barrancos, y para que todo quede plano, estoy trabajando."

El otro sabio le dice, "Hombre estás pensando mal; no hagas eso. Si todo el mundo fuera plano, la gente del mundo se moriría por las grandes inundaciones. Los cerros, los barrancos y los volcanes nos ayudan para que los ríos corran hasta al mar. Dejé de hacerlo." Al ratito el hombre que estaba aplanando el mundo se convirtió en una gran roca.

El hombre más sabio agarró su camino, andando por el mundo. El cuento dice que llegó con un campesino que estaba sembrando maíz. El hombre sabio y poderoso le preguntó, "¿Hijo que estás sembrando?"

El campesino le contestó, "Señor, soy un pobre campesino; aquí, estoy sembrando maíz; espero una bendición del cielo para que mi siembra me dé una buena cosecha."

El hombre sabio y poderoso el volvió a decir, "Traiga un poco de semilla; voy a sembrar unas matas." Así, lo hizo; el sembró una mata de maíz en cada esquina del terreno. Luego, le dijo al muchacho, "Venga, vamos a descansar un poco debajo de este árbol."

Así, se descansaron al rato, de haber descansado, vieron el sembradío de milpa que cubría el *terreno jiloteando* [saliendo de la mazorca]. Era una maravilla lo que estaba viendo. ¡El campesino de alegría gritó "¡Tú eres un dios del mundo! ¡Déjame ir contigo; quiero seguirte!"

Pero el hombre sabio y poderoso le dijo, "No puedes ir conmigo. Yo no tengo casa donde dormir ni dinero para comprar el sustento. Además, no hay quien recoge tu cosecha; así, que no puedes ir conmigo."

El sabio y poderoso siguió su camino por el mundo hasta llegar con otro hombre que estaba amasando harina para hacer el pan. Dicen que en ese tiempo los panes no salían como los panes de ahora. El hombre sabio y poderoso le dijo al que estaba amasando, "¿Hijo, que es lo que estás haciendas? Si quieres, te ayudo un poco."

"Muy bien, Señor, gracias si quieres ayudarme, aquí está la maza. Puedes hacer cuantos panes," dijo el panadero.

El sabio comenzó a figurar los panes, y los metió en el horno. Al ratito, salieron los mejores panes. Nunca habían salido panes, así como los panes que sacó el hombre sabio.

El panadero le dijo, "Señor se quieres, quedarte conmigo hacienda pan. Sé que tienes poder de hacer muchas cosas."

El sabio le dijo, "No puedo quedarme contigo. Es que tengo que andar por el mundo a ayudar a los que me reciben en sus casas."

El panadero le volvió a decir, "Señor, me iré contigo; que eres muy poderoso."

Él le contesta, "No se puede; es que tengo que andar mucho. Ya te enseñé hacer los mejores panes; bendecida y fructífero tu trabajo." Más por eso razón, los panaderos tienen un trabajo de mucha bendición en mundo.

El hombre sabio siguió andando por el mundo hasta llegar a la casa de un hombre que estaba fabricando caites y le dice "¿Hijo mío, que es lo que estás haciendas?"

El caitero le contesto, "Señor, aquí estoy fabricando caites para vender, y agarró un par de caites se lo regalo al hombre sabio. Le dijo, "Señor, aquí, este par de caites para que se los ponga."

El señor le dijo, "Gracias, Hijo, me cubriste los pies," y se lo puso los caites. Porque el hombre sabio andaba descalzo, el vuelvió a decir, "Tu trabajo es bendito y multiplicado." Por eso, dicen que el trabajo de los caiteros y zapateros es un buen trabajo en todo el mundo.

El hombre sabio a fue caminado más hasta encontrase con otro hombre que estaba botando (talando) árboles; más claro, se encuentra limpiando un terreno para sembrar. El hombre sabio le preguntó, "¿Hijo, que es lo que estás haciendo?"

El muchacho muy airado y con mal humor le contestó, "¿Que te importa lo que estoy haciendo? Es mío [preocupación]; no hay porque preguntar si voy a sembrar zarza, rocas, o maleza—nada tienes que ver conmigo."

El hombre sabio le dijo al muchacho, "Hijo, si eso es lo que quieres cultivar, eso es lo que te producirá la tierra." El cuento dice que el hombre sabio se fue caminando. La tierra donde estaba trabajando el hombre se cubrió de grandes rocas, zarza, mucha maleza, serpientes, y coyotes.

El cuento dice que el muchacho a puras penas pudo desprenderse de donde estaba trabajando. Muy enojado dijo, "Voy a buscar a eso hombre y lo voy a matar[lo]."

Juntó la gente de su pueblo y les fue a enseñar como quedó el terreno donde estaba trabajando. La gente del pueblo se molestó, salieron a buscar al hombre sabio para matarlo. Pero se dio cuenta que a él lo anduvieron persiguiendo poco falta para que lo agarrarían.

El sabio le dice a una señora que estaba pastoreando abejas, "Por favor, quiero esconderme entre tus ovejas, porque unos enemigos me andan buscando para matarme."

La señora le dijo, "Señor usted puede esconderse entre las ovejas sin problemas."

El hombre sabio y poderoso se metió entre las ovejas y se convirtió un gran borrego más grande que todas las [otras] ovejas. Llegaron los enemigos y le preguntaron a la señora, "Por aquí, vimos a un hombre. ¿Dónde se metió? Nosotros lo andamos buscando para matarlo; ha causado mucho daño en un terreno.

La señora les dijo, "Señores, yo no lo he visto a ese hombre que ustedes lo andan buscando, solamente mis ovejas. Pueden buscar allí [para ver] si está entre las ovejas.

Los enemigos enejados no encontraron nada [y] siguieron su camino. El borrego se convirtió otra vez en persona y le dice a la mujer, "Muchas gracias por ayudarme, y a cambio, ¿que me pides dijo el sabio a la señora?"

"Una bendición para mis animalitos y pasto para ellos" dijo la señora.

"Muy bien," dijo el hombre poderoso y sabio.

Abrazó uno de los corderos lo besó y besó la tierra y dijo, "Multiplicado sean estas ovejas y que verdea este lugar para siempre." Al ratito, se miraban cientos de ovejas, y el lugar se puso más verde.

La señora de alegría grito para que la gente llegó a ver todo lo que ha pasado con ella.[13]

—Pedro Cholotío Temó

# The Characotales, a Real Story

SEÑOR PEDRO SICAJAU TOPÓZ was born in the canton, Los Churuneles 2, Sololá.[14] He is pure Kaqchikel Maya who understands some words in Castilian [Spanish] but not others. This señor comes to see me whenever he can when he comes to work [in San Juan] forty days before returning to his village.

On a break, we began to chat on the patio of my house, and he told me this real tale. He says that there in his cantón, Los Churuneles 2, lived a woman that was a characotel [a person who can turn into a nagual or animal form of a person or spirit and act as a spy or do evil; similar to a witch] who transformed into a cat. How weird that she became an animal, but during the day!

Well, the neighbors always saw a cat leave that house, go into the woods, and disappear. It went far away to other hamlets.

Well, the people of other villages had their doubts that the animal was on the prowl in the patio of their house. What they did not know was whether it was a characotel because they always said that there were persons who transformed into animals, but during the nights. Pedro says that this woman changed into an animal during the day and got inside the houses to see and hear what it was that the owners were doing and saying. The cat woman took notice where they left clothing and where they kept the things to eat. That was the work that the cat woman did.

That woman was the jefa [boss] in charge of a group of women characoteles. The people who lived near the house of that woman always saw that, upon nightfall, in that house four cats came out; the neighbors were bothered, and they asked what was happening there. Because when they came out, there were four cats, and when they returned, there were four women—when they left, they were cats, and when they returned, now, they were women, with suitcases in their hands [in which] they carried huipiles, cortes, shirts, *típicos* [traditional trousers]. That was what they robbed in the nights.

The following day, the other women left, minus the owner, with their suitcases in their hands. The neighbors arrived to ask her, "Who are these women who remained with you during the nights?"

She said that they were her kin who live in other villages and they came just to visit her and stayed there. But the neighbors realized that they were characoteles. The suitcases that they carried had all that had been stolen at night.

Many people complained in the nearby villages and hamlets [about] the loss of their dress clothing. Some had some quetzales of money that they lost inside their house. The people put out an alert to catch the thieves, but there were no thieves. Only four cats came. At dawn, there was the alarm that in other homesites they had been robbed of many things.

When the people went to the capital city [Sololá] of the Department of Sololá, they recognized their typical blouses, skirts, shirts, and trousers for sale in a shop. The people told the owner of the shop that all the clothing that was in the shop had been stolen from their homes.

The gentleman answered them, "I don't know if it's yours; three women who are *paisanas* [countrywomen] from Sololá come to sell it to me."

The people were left with the suspicion that from inside that house a cat left at ten past nine in the morning and returned in the afternoon and that the cat was the owner of the house. And they doubted that it was during the day that the cat woman discovered where people left their things so that she and her three companions could go and rob them at night.

There in the canton, Los Churuneles 2, Pedro Sicayau says that a señora sold a piece of land for Q25,000. The woman did not know what to do with the money; she was afraid to take it to the bank. If she kept the money inside her house, thieves could rob her. Finally, she buried the money in the ground below an avocado tree that was near her house, unaware that the cat woman knew what she was doing.

The following day, the señora carried a clump of güisquil to plant in the place where she had buried the money. She did it so as not to forget the place. But when the woman arrived, they had already taken out the money. Only the pieces of rags and nylon remained, which was an alarm in the family. Who, but who, had stolen the money? Finally, they [remembered] that the previous day there was a cat above the *temascal* [sweat house] seeing everything the woman did to bury the money. Then he [Pedro Sicajua] says that the family asserted that that cat was a characotel and thief.

During the night, the family and neighbors gathered and went to the hamlet where this cat woman lived, because there had been news among the people that she was a characotel, robbing the houses and the homesites. Pedro says when they arrived, they opened the door and entered to look for the money, but now they only found Q6,000, whereupon they thought that the four cat women had divided it among themselves. Pedro says that they did not find the cat woman in her house. She went doing her work, nor did she realize that the people went to recover part of the money.

Pedro Sicajau says that those four women who converted into cats did a lot of evil. The people of the canton, Los Churuneles 2, got together and planned to kill those four cats that had stolen so much in the canton and in the hamlets. Pedro says that the plan was thus: The harmed persons asked for help from a group of persons who had arms in their homes; those men who were among the guerrillas. Well, on one night, they killed the four cats that were the women characoteles.

When it dawned the following day, the cat woman appeared dead in her house with her tongue and eyes out. Now, she no longer looked like a cat; now, she was in her form of [a] woman. The people of this canton did not make a fuss. They went to bury her in the cemetery. Without doubt, the other three went to die in their houses because since this time, there have been no robberies.

—Pedro Sicajau Topóz, who says that he also experienced this case.

# Los characotales, una historia real

EL SEÑOR PEDRO SICAJAU Topóz nacido en el cantón, Los Churuneles 2, Sololá.[14] Él kaqchikel maya puro que entiende algunas palabras en castellano [español] pero no otras. Este señor viene a verme siempre que puede cuando viene a trabajar [en San Juan] durante 30 días antes de regresar a su pueblo.

En un descanso, empezamos a platicar en el patio de mi casa, y me cuenta este caso real. Él dice, que allá en el cantón, Los Churuneles 2, vivía una mujer que era characotel que convertía en gata. ¡Cómo raro que ella se convertía en animal, pero de día!

Pues, los vecinos siempre miraban que de esa casa siempre salía un gato que se metía a dentro del monte y se desaparecía. Se iba lejos en otros caseríos.

Pues, la gente de otros pueblos tenía sus dudas de que en el patio de su casa el animal gateara. Lo que no sabían si era [una] characotel porque siempre se dice que hay personas que se convierten en animales, pero por las noches. Pedro dice que esa mujer en el día es cuando se cambia en ser animal y se metía en los sitios y en las casas para ver y oir que es lo que hacer y lo que dicen los dueños de la casa. La mujer gata se fija donde dejan la ropa y donde guardan las cosas de comer. Eso era el trabajo que hacia la mujer gata.

Esa mujer era la jefa o encargada de un grupo de mujeres characoteles. La gente que vivían cerca de la casa de esa mujer siempre miraba que, al entrar la noche, en esa casa salían cuatro gatas; los vecinos se molestaban y se preguntaban qué es lo que está pasando allí. Porque cuando salían, eran cuatro gatas, y cuando regresaban eran cuatro mujeres—cuando salían eran gatas y cuando regresaban ya eran mujeres, con maletas en las manos traían güipiles, cortes, camisas y pantalones típicos. Eso es lo que robaban por las noches.

Al día siguiente, salieron de esa casa las otras mujeres, menos la dueña, con las maletas en la mano. Los vecinos llegaban a preguntarle "¿Quiénes son estas mujeres que se quedaban con usted durante las noches?"

Ella decía que eran sus familiares que vivan en otras aldeas llegan solo para visitarle allí se quedaban. Pero los vecinos se dieron cuenta que eran characoteles. Las maletas que llevaban tenían toda que la roban por las noches.

Mucha gente se quejaba en las aldeas y caseríos cercanos [acerca de] la perdida de sus ropas de vestir. Algunos tenían unos sus quetzales de dinero y se perdía adentro de la casa. La gente se puso en alerta para agarrar a los ladrones, pero no hay ladrones. Solamente pasaban cuatro gatos. Al amanecer, [había] la alarma en otros sitios que se habían robado muchas cosas.

Cuando la gente fue en la cabecera [Sololá] de[l] departamento] de Sololá, reconocieron sus güipiles, cortes, camisas y pantalones típicos que estaba de venta en una tienda. La gente le dijo al dueño de la tienda que toda ropa que está en la tienda les ha sido robado de sus viviendas.

El señor les contestó, "Yo no sé si es de ustedes; tres mujeres que son paisanas de Sololá vienen a vendérmelo."

La gente se quedó con la duda de que desde dentro de esa casa salió una gata a las nueve y diez de la mañana y entraba por la tarde y que la mujer gata era la dueña de la casa. Y dudaban que fuera durante el día que la mujer gata descubriera dónde dejaba la gente sus cosas para que ella y sus tres acompañantes pudieran ir a robarles por la noche.

Allá en el cantón, Los Churuneles 2, Pedro Sicajau dice que una señora vendió un terreno por Q25,000. La mujer no sabía qué hacer con el dinero; tenía miedo de llevarlo al banco. Si guardaba el dinero dentro de su casa, los ladrones podrían asaltarla. Al fin, la señora enterraba el dinero en la tierra debajo de un aguacatal que está cerca de su casa, sin darse cuenta que la mujer gata sabía lo que estaba haciendo.

Al día siguiente, la señora se llevo una mata de güisquil para sembrar en el lugar donde había enterrado el dinero. Lo hizo para no olvidar el lugar. Pero cuando la señora llegó, ya lo habían sacado el dinero. Solo quedaba los pedazos de trapos y naylón, que fue una alarma en la familia. ¿Quién, pero quién ha robado el dinero? Al fin, pensaron que el día anterior sobre el temascal estaba echada una gata viendo todo lo que la señora hizo para enterrar el dinero. Entonces [Pedro Sicajau] dice que la familia aseguró que esa gata era characotel y ladrona.

Por la noche, los familiares y vecinos se juntaron y se fueron hasta al caserío donde vivía es a mujer, porque había noticias entre la gente que ella es characotel, robando en las casas y en los sitios. Pedro dice cuando llegaron, abrieron la puerta entraron a buscar el dinero, pero ya solo encontraron Q6,000 y donde se pensaron que lo habían repartido entre las cuatro mujeres characoteles. Pedro dice que la mujer gata no se encontraba en su casa. Anda hacienda su trabajo, ni se dio cuenta de la gente que fueron a recuperar parte del dinero.

Pedro Sicajau dice que era mucho el mal que esas cuatro mujeres que se convertían en gatas hacían. La gente del cantón, Los Churuneles 2, se juntaron e hicieron en plan para matar a esas cuatro gatas que tanto robo cometido en el cantón y en los caseríos. Pedro, dice que el plan fue así: las personas perjudicadas pidieron favor a un grupo de personas que tenían armas en sus casas, esos hombres que estuvieron en la guerrilla. Pues, en una noche mataron las cuatro gatas que eran mujeres characoteles.

Cuando amaneció el día siguiente, la mujer gata apareció muerta en su casa con la lengua y los ojos hacían afuera. Ya, no se miraba como gata; ya era su forma de [una] mujer. La gente de ese cantón no hizo bulla. La fueron a enterrar en el cementerio. Sin duda, las otras tres se fueron a morir a sus casas, porque desde ese tiempo, no ha habido robos.

—Pedro Sicajau Topóz quien dice que también él lo vivió este caso.

# True Visions and Beliefs

[THIS IS] A REAL story, or tale [*caso*] of a Tz'utujil Maya of San Pedro la Laguna about the belief in the dueños [owners, lords, gods] of the hills and volcanoes. Señor Juan Televario Puac seventy-five years of age [is] a friend and companion from [my earlier] work on the cotton farms.

Mister Juan tells [about] three certain facts that have happened to the people of San Pedro. Don Juan believes what the grandmothers and grandfathers said that indeed the lords, owners, of the hills and volcanoes exist. When the grandmothers and grandfathers told this story, it was sacred to them. In other words, they, the grandparents, left us good things; they told us stories about the enchanted hill and others. Little by little, they [the stories] are disappearing; now, they are no longer.

In these times, the people no longer respect Mother Earth—dueña of the natives. Don Juan says that when he was young, his grandparents had a lot of respect for Santo Mundo [Sacred World, Earth]. Before the sowing of corn and beans, they went to the slope of the volcano, and in the places where they sowed their cultivations, they presented an offering of candles, myrrh incense, and aguardiente to ask for forgiveness. This they offered to the owner and lord and administrator. The offering was to ask permission so that nothing bad would happen to the workers, to avoid the bad [evil] hour.

Don Juan says [reiterated to emphasize], "This kind of costumbre has been lost. The people don't respect [them]; now they don't value the costumbres and values of our grandmothers and grandfathers. More for that reason, many strange things are happening to our people," says don Juan.

Don Juan Televario relates that in San Pedro la Laguna, there are three enchanted places where many strange things have happened to the people of the town. Many have died a sudden death. There are three locations: (1) Xe' kaq powoon, (2) Pa chojoob', and (3) Chiriij kaq jaay that are enchanted places that are believed to be dangerous.[15] The men arrive good and healthy to work in those places. Suddenly, they fall ill and cannot walk. There, they lie on the ground; the family comes to get them; the following day, they die.

Don Juan says in this year, 2017, there have been three cases: (1) Mr. Anibal Gonzáles and his sons went to fetch firewood at one of these places. He fell and was not able to get up. His sons brought him [home] in a pickup; the following day, he died. (2) What happened to Señor Buena Ventura Toy [was that] he went to clean milpa in Chiriij kaq jaay. At work he fell sick. They went to get him; in three days, he died. (3) Señor Domingo Tepas Yojcóm went to pick coffee, and he was not able to return. They went to get him. He lasted a month, but he could not speak. Thirty days he remained in a coma, and he passed away.

There is a belief of the native Tz'utujiles; that is to say, the grandparents said, and those who are still alive say that in the volcanoes and in the hills, there are administrators, [like] mayordomos, and *caporales* [leaders], who are guarding, watching like an invisible *ronda* [patrol].[16] [That is to say,] they are the ones who watch over and take care of Mother Earth.

The [ronda] that leaves the volcano passes to the hills, and the ronda that leaves the hills passes to the volcano. It penetrates the hearts and brains of people; they are struck down and they fall wounded. That's why they no longer get up and [why they] die from vomiting a lot of blood. But they say that is what happens when a man comes to sleep with a strange woman, and also when a man is disgusted with his work, or when he remains just fighting in his house. That is when the round of the world falls upon him. It is very dangerous; no medicine or doctor can help him.

Well, they say that the rondas of the volcanoes are not the same, depending on the places. There are very strong rondas and others less strong. The strong rondas do not have cures. The weaker rondas have cures. For infidelity, they [the adulterers] are hit by the ronda. If the infidelity is in the mountains or among the cafetales [coffee plants], there is where the bad hour [time] comes. The unfaithful woman must go to identify the place where she sinned with the man. [For the] cure or secreto, in the place where the woman was lying, they [the woman and the man] dig a hole about twelve to fifteen inches and scoop out handfuls of dirt. They put the dirt in a jug and add water to it. The man and woman begin to drink earth tea, [and] with that they free themselves from death.

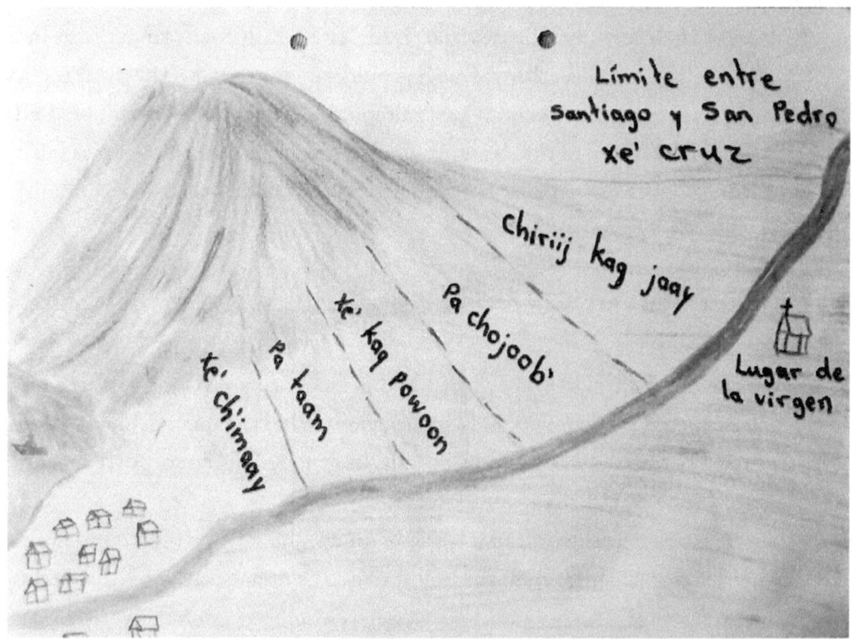


*Map* 3. Map of the places at foot of San Pedro volcano made with the help of a teacher who understands and writes Tz'utujil / Los lugares al pie del volcán San Pedro hechos con la ayuda de un profesor que entiende y escribe tz'utujil

## The Fate of Jerónimo Quiacain

I, Pedro, am going to comment a little about this story. Eight years ago, a son-in-law of Gerado Cotúc, called Jerónimo Quiacain, husband of Josefa, was my neighbor. His real name was Jerónimo, but he was better known as Fidel. He was a retired teacher and councilor of the municipality. There were rumors that he had many lovers—he liked women. Jerónimo was a native of San Pedro, but he came to marry in San Juan. He had land in Chiriij kaq jaay, which is on the slope of San Pedro Volcano.

One day in the month of November, he got up very early. Josefa served her husband bread and coffee at six in the morning. He grabbed his bicycle and went to inspect his milpa. On the side of the asphalt road, he put down his bicycle and entered the milpa to see how the harvest was doing.

There he was struck down by the ronda of the volcano. He managed to get back to where he had left the bicycle, [but] he could not walk anymore.

At 8:00 in the morning, the news arrived. The family went to get him in a pickup, and he still was breathing. But he could no longer talk. They wanted to take him to a specialist in Xelajú (Quetzaltenango), [but] on the road, he died. The news arrived in town of the death of Fidel at 10:00 a.m., when the news [also] spread throughout the town that he was shot by the ronda because of infidelity. He shed a lot of blood when he died.

## Don Juan Televario Puac Tells Another True Case

One time the boy Santiago was ordered by his father to go to look for firewood in the place called Xe' kaq powoon. [The story] says that the muchacho really did not want to go because it was Sunday. Finally, he grabbed his lasso, porter's strap, and machete, took to the road, and left.

When he arrived at the hill, in a blink of an eye, he saw a child about twelve years of age leaving the hill. Then the boy spoke to Santiago, saying, "Muchacho, where are you going?"

Don Juan says that Santiago, trembling with fear, answered, "I have to look for firewood in this place."

The child replied, "Come, follow me! We have to see what my father says because he is the dueño of this place. Now, let's go!"

Santiago had to obey; he went walking, following the child of enchantment. [The story] says the child [was] dancing and laughing, going around Santiago many times. At that moment, Santiago lost consciousness. When he recovered his memory, he found himself in a strange place at Xe' cruz [the boundary between Santiago and Pedro]. He could not see the sun; indeed, it was clear, but he could not see the hills or the volcano. It was an immense place. The child took Santiago to where a very old man was seated on a *descansador* [a chair, or luxury armchair, such as those used by senior officials.]

Then [the story] says that the boy said to the señor who was seated, "Here, I bring you this man who has done so much damage, cutting many trees and killing many animals."

"Fine," said the señor who was sitting in the big armchair. He got up from his chair, took Santiago, [and] opened a door. There, showing Santiago, the dueño of the hill said, "Here [are] these men and women; these are my workers. They plant corn and beans; they cut a lot of trees in this place."

Santiago saw many men and women with their heads tied with typical cloths, and women with heads covered with aprons. A big, round, rock served them as a table. Over the rock they burned incense, myrrh, and candles, and knelt, offering as a sacrifice the things that were on the rock.

The señor, dueño of the hill, said to Santiago, "What you are seeing are my servants. In life, they sowed corn and beans; they cut down many trees, but they always asked for permission, as you are seeing. I gave them good harvests—an abundance of corn and beans. Now, they are fine here," said the señor. "Let's go!" he said.

Santiago followed him. He [the señor] opened another door of the dueño of the hill; there were the lions, tigers, coyotes, and wolves—[a] horrible place. The animals ate human flesh; with their fangs they broke the bones of the dead. The señor told Santiago "What you are seeing, these things are certain; they are not dreams. The people who die in this place come to serve as food for the animals."

The lord of the hill told Santiago, "Let's go," and he opened another door where there was a chair of gold, and the lord sat down on the chair. The room of the señor of the gold chair was like an office.

The lord seated in the gold chair said to Santiago, "You have to return, walking, and tell your parents all that you have seen in this place. Within four days, you will be here and you will be the server and office boy of this place."

Again, Santiago, brought back by the same child, says that he looked at the place, and it was not the same spot where he had been intercepted [captured] at Xe' kaq powoon, which is about eight kilometers from Xe' cruz. When the family of Santiago realized he had not arrived and it was already late, they went to look for him, but it was impossible.

The following day, they advised the town and the church; many people left to form a rescue party, thinking that he had fallen into some ravine or had been devoured by some wild animal. They looked for him for four days. They found him in a rock portal, [that is,] rock above and rock below. He could not go up or down, and the strangest thing, says don Juan, that his body was encased in a vine. Santiago's screams and pleas for help was what alerted those who were walking by looking for him. Well, Santiago says that he felt as if had been two or three hours that he had been lost, but it really had been four days.[17]

After having rescued him, they carried him to his house. Don Juan says that there Santiago related everything that happened to him and what he had seen inside the hill. [Don Juan] says that Santiago could neither eat nor drink. Now, he was not able to sleep. In three days, he died. Many people believe that his spirit remains in the hill, Xe' kaq powoon.

## The Case of the Hill, Pa chojoob'

Don Juan Televaro Puac told another case of the hill, Pa chojoob', that is in the western part between Santiago Atitlán and San Pedro. Walking on foot, it takes three hours [to get there]. The mountains of Pa chojoob' are on the slope of the volcano. The Pedranos call it "Chua Nimajuyú."

This tale concerns the dueños, administrators, mayordomos, and alguaciles of the world. Don Juan says one time a man who is called Francisco always left from his house at four in the morning to arrive early at his work on the hill, Pa chojoob'. Francisco was a farmer [who] lived by the harvests that Mother Earth gave him, such as corn, beans, and other cultivations. He says that he walked on foot six hours daily.

One time, leaving the road, he ascended the paths to Pa chojoob'. He says he had a half hour to go [when] on the path, he encountered a young person about fifteen years old carrying in his hands a gold chain, with his face, feet, and hands all red. He was wearing a velvet suit and a cap, all colored red and with fringes of gold. Then, he says he [the young person] began to dance around him. Francisco was very scared; now, he was unable to walk. His entire body was *aguado* [lax, weak, without movement], and he fell to the ground.

He says that the enchanted young person told him, "Don't be afraid; get up; follow me! I will take you to my lord, the owner of this place."

He says that Francisco, between fear and horror, said, "What is it that I am seeing? Could it be that I am alive, or am I now dead?"

He says that he had to follow the enchanted young person, dancing with his gold chain in front, and Francisco was walking behind. In a few minutes, Francisco lost consciousness without knowing what way he was going. When he regained consciousness, he now found himself in a strange place, seeing a man like a king seated on a gold chair. Then, the red-colored, enchanted person says to the señor seated in a chair of gold. "Here, I bring this man who has done much damage in this sacred place."

"Very well," said the lord who was in a gold chair, and he spoke to Francisco in an echoing voice, "Boy, you have done much damage in this place. Come!" he told him. He opened a door of a corral encompassing deer, lions, pizotes, raccoons, and snakes of different sizes. Among the animals, there were some injured.

The señor of the gold chair says to Francisco, "I am the owner and lord of this place; you have done much damage in this place. You have killed a lot of my animals. Also, you have cut down many trees without asking for permission."

Francisco was not able to reply; he felt a great, horrifying coldness in his whole body. The lord opened the door of a store that looked like a warehouse, where there was a lot of piles of gold. [There were also] many suits of the Dance of the Conquest, Dance of the Deer, and Dance of the Monkey. Also, he showed him other kinds of suits of rainmakers, all velvet in different colors with gold fringes.

The lord told him again, "You will have to come [back] to this place to take care of it. You will be the alguacil and messenger. Here, come to rest the señores, the rain makers, those who work in the clouds, those who work in the air, [and] those who watch and care for the hills and the volcano. They are the naguales [spirits] of the volcano and of the enchanted hills."

Then he told Francisco, "You have to go back and to tell the other people all you have seen in this place. You have one year to live, and soon you will be here as a tithe and first fruits [offering to Mother Earth] of everyone who causes harm to this sacred place."

Then, he [don Juan] says that the young person with red skin appeared again. "Follow me!" he told Francisco. Always with his gold chain in his hand [and] dancing, he took Francisco back. But Francisco lost consciousness again. When he recovered his memory, he was in a ravine at the foot of the volcano at Xe' cruz.

The family asked for help from many people. Also, the *bomberos* [firefighters] worked, but not until three days were they able to rescue him. He says that he does not remember how long he was inside the enchanted hill called Pa chojoob'.

Francisco told many people everything that had happened to him, mainly to those who had cultivations in Pa chojoob', that it would be better if they presented a Mayan ceremony so that they not suffer the same as happened to him. He [don Juan] says that Francisco was sick for a year. His family fought a lot and did many Mayan ceremonies, but they were unsuccessful. And he died. It is believed his spirit is in the hill Pa chojoob'[18].

—Juan Televario Puac

# Visiones y creencias ciertas

[ESTA ES] UN RELATO, o cuento real [caso], de un maya tz'utujil de San Pedro la Laguna, la creencia acerca de los dueños de los cerros y volcanes. El señor Juan Televario Puac de 75 años de edad [es] un amigo y compañero de [mi] trabajo [anterior] en las fincas algodoneras.

El señor Juan relata [acerca de] tres hechos ciertos lo que ha[n] sucedido con la gente de San Pedro. Don Juan crece lo que decían las abuelas y abuelos que sí existen los señores, dueños, de los cerros y volcanes. Cuando los abuelos y las abuelas contaron esta historia, fue sagrada para ellos. En otras palabras, ellos, los abuelos, nos dejaron cosas buenas; nos contaron historias sobre el cerro encantado y otros. Poco a poco van despareciendo [las historias]; ahora, ya no son.

En estos tiempos, la gente ya no respeta la madre tierra—dueña de las naturales. Don Juan dice: cuando era joven sus abuelos tenían mucho respeto al Santo mundo. Antes de la siembra del maíz y el frijol, se iban a la falda del volcán, y en los lugares donde sembraron sus cultivos presentaban ofrendas, candelas, incienso mirra, y aguardiente para pedir perdón. Esto lo ofrecían al dueño y señor y administrador. La ofrenda era para pedir permiso para que nadie mal sucede con los trabajadores, para evitar la mala hora.

Don Juan dice [reitera para enfatizar]: "Esta clase de costumbre se ha perdido. La gente no [los] respeta; ya no valoran las costumbres y valores de nuestras abuelas y abuelos. Más por eso, muchas cosas extrañas están sucediendo con nuestra gente," dice don Juan.

Don Juan Televario relata que en Sean Pedro la Laguna, hay tres lugares encantados donde han sucedidos muchas cosas extrañas con la gente del pueblo. Muchos han muerto de muerto repentina. Hay tres lugares: (1) Xe'kaq powoon, (2) Pa chojoob', (3) Chiriij kaq jaay que son lugares encantados que se cree son peligrosos.[15] Los hombres llegan buenos y sanos a trabajar en esos lugares.

Repentinamente, caen enfermos ya no pueden caminar. Allí, se quedan tirado en el suelo; la familia les llega a traer; al día siguiente, se murieron.

Don Juan dice en ese año 2017 ha sucedido tres casos. (1) El señor Aníbal Gonzáles junto con sus hijos se fue a carrear leña en uno de esos tres lugares. Se cayó y no pudo levantar. Los hijos se lo trajeron en un picop [camión de reparto]; al día siguiente, murió. (2) Lo que pasó con el señor Buena Ventura Toy, salió a limpiar milpa en Chiriij kaq jaay. En el trabajo cayó enfermo. Lo fueron a traerlo; a los tres días, falleció. (3) El señor Domingo Tepas Yojcóm se fue a cortar café, ya no pudo regresar. Se lo fueron a traerlo. Dilató un mes, pero ya no pudo hablar. Los treinta días se quedó en coma, y se murió.

Hay una creencia de los nativos tz'utujiles; es decir, los abuelos decían, y dicen, los que todavía están con vida, que en los volcanes y en los cerros hay administradores, [como] mayordomos [enlaces entre el juez y los mayordomos secundarios que son miembros de base de una cofradía] y caporales (líders), que andan cuidando, vigilando como una ronda [patrulla] invisible.[16] [Es decir,] ellos son los que vigilan y cuidan a la Madre Tierra.

La [ronda] que sale del volcán pasa a los cerros, y la ronda que sale de los cerros pasa al volcán. Penetra los corazones y cerebros de las personas; los fulminan y caen heridos. Por eso, ya no se levantan y se mueren por vomitar mucha sangre. Pero dicen que eso pasa cuando un hombre llega a dormir con una mujer extraña, y también cuando el hombre va disgustado con su trabajo, o solo peleando se mantiene en su casa. Eso es cuando la ronda del mundo le toca. Es muy peligroso; ni medicina o médico puede ayudarle.

Pues, dicen que las rondas no son iguales, depende de los lugares. Hay rondas muy fuertes y otros poco fuertes. Las rondas fuertes no tienen curación. Las rondas poco fuertes tienen curación. Por infidelidad, eran [los adúlteros] alcanzado por ronda. Si la infidelidad fue entre el monte o entre los cafetales, allí es donde les toca la mala hora. La mujer infiel tiene que ir a enseñar el lugar donde [ella] pecó con el hombre. [Para la] curación o secreto, en el lugar donde estuvo acostado, ellos [el hombre y la mujer], escarban un hoyo como de 12 a 15 pulgadas y sacar puñadas de tierra. La tierra la ponen en un jarro, le agregan agua. El hombre y la mujer se ponen a tomar té de tierra, [y] con eso se liberan de la muerte.

## El destino de Jerónimo Quiacan

Yo, Pedro, voy a comentar un poco acerca de este relato. Ocho años pasado, un yerno de Gerardo Cotúc, se llamaba Jerónimo Quiacain, esposo de Josefa, era mi vecino. Su mero nombre era Jerónimo, pero él era más conocido como Fidel. Era un maestro jubilado y estaba de concejal de la municipalidad. Había rumores que tenía muchas amantes—le gustaba las mujeres. Jerónimo era nativo de San Pedro, pero se vino a casar en San Juan. Tenía terreno en Chiriij kaq jaay, que está en la falda del Volcán de San Pedro.

Un día mes de noviembre, se levantó. Josefa le sirvió café y pan a su esposo a las seis de la mañana. Agarró su bicicleta [y] se fue a ver la milpa. En la orilla del camino asfaltado, él dejó la bicicleta y entró adentro la milpa para ver comó estaba la cosecha.

Allí fue donde fue fulminado por la ronda del volcán. Logró salir donde había dejado la bicicleta, [pero] ya no logró caminar.

A las ocho de la mañana llegó la noticia. La familia lo fue a traer en un picop, [y] todavía tenía aliento, pero no pudo hablar. Lo quisieron llevar con un especialista en Xelajú (Quetzaltenango) [pero] en el camino murió. La noticia llegó en la población de la muerte de Fidel a las diez de la mañana, donde [también] corrió por todo el pueblo la noticia que fue tiroteado por la ronda por infidelidad. Arrojó mucha sangre al morir.

## Don Juan Televario Cuenta otro caso real

Una vez el muchacho, Santiago, fue ordenado por su padre para ir a buscar leña en el lugar, Xe' kag powoon. [El cuento] dice que el muchacho no muy quería [ir] por ser día Domingo. Al fin agarró su lazo, mecapal, y su machete, agarró camino, y se fue.

Cuando llegó en el cerro, en un abrir y cerrar de ojos, vio salir del cerro a un niño como de unos doce años. Luego, [el niño] le habló a Santiago, diciendo: "¿Muchacho, a dónde vas?"

Don Juan dice que Santiago, temblado de miedo, le contestó, "Tengo que buscar leña en este lugar."

El niño le vuelve a decir, "Ven y sígueme; [tenemos] que [ver lo que] dice mi padre porque él es el dueño de este lugar. Ahora vamos," dijo.

Santiago tuvo que obedecer; se fue caminando, siguiendo al niño del encanto. [El cuento] dice que el niño [era] bailando y riendo dando muchas vueltas alrededor de Santiago. A ese momento, Santiago perdió el conocimiento. Cuando Santiago recuperó su memoria, ya se encuentra en un lugar extraño at Xe' cruz [límite entre Santiago y San Pedro]. No podía ver el sol; sí, había claridad, pero no podía ver los cerros ni el volcán. Era un lugar inmenso. El niño lo llevó a Santiago hasta donde estaba sentado un señor muy viejo en un descansador [una butaca de lujo, como las que usan los altos funcionarios].

Luego [el cuento] dice que el niño le dijo al señor que estaba sentando, "Aquí, traigo este hombre que tanto daño ha hecho, cortando muchos árboles y matando muchos animales. "Bien," dijo el señor que sentada en la gran butaca. Se levantó de su silla, se llevó a Santiago, [y] abrió una puerta. Allí, mostrando Santiago, el dueño del cerro diciendo, "Aquí, [están] estos hombres y mujeres; estos son mis trabajadores. Ellos sembraron maíz y frijol; cortaron muchos árboles en este lugar."

Santiago vio a muchos hombres y mujeres con la cabeza amarrada con telas típicas, y las mujeres cubrían la cabeza con sus delantales. Una gran piedra redonda les servía como una mesa. Sobre la piedra quemaban el incienso, mirra y candelas, se ponían de rodilla, ofreciendo como sacrificio las cosas que estaban sobre la gran piedra.

El señor, dueño del cerro le dijo a Santiago, "Lo que está viendo son mis sirvientes. En vida, sembraron maíz y frijoles; talaron muchos árboles, pero siempre pidieron permiso, como ves. Les di buenas cosechas—abundancia de maíz y frijoles. Ahora están bien aquí," dijo el señor. "¡Vamos!" dijo. Santiago lo siguió. Abrió [el señor] otra puerta [d]el dueño del cerro; había los leones, tigres, coyotes, y lobos—[un] lugar horrible. Los animales comían carne humana; con sus colmillos quebraban los huesos de los muertos. El señor le dijo a Santiago, "Lo que estás viendo, estas cosas son ciertos; no son sueños. Las personas que mueren en este lugar vienen hacer comida por los animales.

El dueño del cerro le dijo a Santiago, "¡Vamos!" y abrió otra puerta donde se encuentra una silla de oro, y el señor se sentó en la silla. La habitación del señor de la silla de oro era como un despacho.

El señor sentado en la silla de oro le dijo a Santiago, "Tiene que regresar, andando, y dígales a tus padres todo lo que has visto en este lugar. Dentro de cuatro días, estará aquí y será el servidor y mandadero de este lugar."

Otra vez, Santiago traído de regreso por el mismo niño, dice que él miró el lugar, y no era el mismo lugar donde se había interceptado (capturado) en Xe' kaq powoon, que está a unos ocho kilómetros de Xe' cruz. Cuando la familia de Santiago se dio cuenta de que no había llegado y ya era tarde, fueron a buscarlo, pero fue imposible.

Al día siguiente, dieron aviso en el pueblo y en las Iglesias; salieron mucha gente para su rescate, penando que se había caído en algún barranco, o había sido devorado por algún animal salvaje. Buscaron por él para cuatro días. Lo encontraron en un portal roca, [es decir,] roca arriba y roca abajo. No podía subir ni bajar, y los más extraño, dice don Juan, que su cuerpo estaba enrayado en un bejuco. Los gritos de Santiago y pidiendo ayuda fue lo que alertó a los que pasaban buscándolo. Bueno, Santiago dice que sintió como si hubieran pasado dos o tres horas que se había perdido, pero en realidad habían sido cuatro días.[17]

Después de haberlo rescatado, se lo trajeron para su casa. Don Juan dice que allí Santiago contó todo lo que ha pasado y lo que ha visto adentro del cerro. [Don Juan] dice que ya no comió ni bebió. Ya, no pudo dormir. A los tres días se murió. Mucha de la gente cree que su espíritu se había quedado en el cerro Xe', kag' powoon.

## El caso del cerro, Pa chojoob'

Don Juan Televario Puac contó otro caso del cerro, Pa chojoob' que está en la parte poniente entre Santiago Atitlán y San Pedro. Caminando a pie, se hace tres horas [para llegarlo]. Las montañas de Pachojoob' están en la cuesta del volcán. Los Pedranos le llaman *Chua* nimajuyú.

Este cuento se relaciona con los dueños, administradores, mayordomos, y alguaciles del mundo. Don Juan dice una vez un hombre que se llama Francisco siempre salía de su casa a las cuatro de la mañana para llegar temprano a su trabajo en el cerro Pa chojoob'. Francisco era campesino [quien] vivía de las cosechas que le daba la madre tierra como el maíz, frijol, y otros cultivos. Dice que caminaba a pie seis horas diarias.

Una vez dejando la carretera, subía por las veredas hasta Pa chojoob'. Dice que le fallaba media hora para llegar [cuando] en la vereda, se encontró con un joven como de quince años, llevando en sus manos una cadena de oro, con el rostro, los pies y las manos todo rojo. Tenía puesto un traje de terciopelo y una gorra todo de color rojo y flecos de oro. Luego, dice que se puso a bailar a su alrededor. Francisco se asustó; ya no podía caminar. Se quedó aguado todo su cuerpo, y se cayó en la tierra.

Dice que el joven encantado le dijo, "No te asustes; levanta; sigueme. Te llevaré con mi señor, el dueño de este lugar."

Dice que Francisco dentro del temor y el miedo decía "¿Qué es lo que estoy viendo? ¿Sería que estoy vivo, o estoy ya muerto?" decía.

Dice que fue obligado de seguirle al joven encantado, bailando con su cadena de oro adelante, y Francisco iba atrás. En unos minutos, Francisco perdió conocimiento sin saber en que camino pasó. Cuando recuperó conocimiento, ya se encontraba en un lugar extraño, viendo a un hombre como un rey sentado en una silla de oro. Luego, el joven encantado de color rojo le dice al señor que está sentado en la silla de oro: "Aquí, traigo este hombre que ha hecho mucho daño en este lugar sagrado."

"Muy bien," dijo el señor que estaba en la silla de oro, y le habló a Francisco con una voz con eco, diciendo, "Muchacho, tú has hecho mucho daño en este lugar. ¡Ven! le dijo. Abrió la puerta de un corral donde están encerrados los venados, leones, pizotes, mapaches, culebras de diferentes tamaños. Entre los animales, había algunos heridos.

El señor de la silla de oro le dice a Francisco, "Yo soy el dueño y señor de este lugar; tú has hecho mucho daño en este lugar. Tú has matado a mucho de mis animales. También, has cortado muchos árboles sin pedir permiso."

Francisco no podía contestar; sentía un gran frio espeluznante en todo su cuerpo. El señor abrió la puerta de un local que se parece una bodega donde había mucho oro por montones. [Había] mucho traje del Baile de la conquista, Baile del venado, y Baile del mico. También, le enseño otra clase de trajes de los hacedores de lluvia, todo de terciopelo de diferentes colores con fleques de oro.

El señor le volvió a decir, "Tú tienes que venir a este lugar a cuidarlo. Serás el alguacil y mandadero. Aquí, vienen a descansar los señores, los hacedores de lluvia, los que trabajan en las nubes, los que trabajan en el aire, [y] los que vigilan y cuidan en los cerros y en el volcán. Son ellos los naguales del volcán y de los cerros encantados."

Luego le dijo a Francisco "Tienes que regresar y decirle a la demás gente todo que has visto en este lugar. Tienes un año de vida, y pronto estarás aquí como un diezmo y primicia [ofrenda a la Madre tierra] de todos los que causen daño este lugar santo."

Luego, él [don Juan] dice que apareció otra vez el joven de piel rojo. "¡Sígame!" le dijo a Francisco. Siempre con su cadena de oro en la mano [y] bailando, lo trajo a Francisco de regreso. Pero Francisco perdió otra vez su conocimiento. Cuando él recobró su memoria, estaba en un barranco al pie del volcán en Xe Cruz.

La familia pidió ayuda a mucha gente. También, trabajaron los bomberos, pero hasta los tres días pudieron rescatar. Dice que no recuerda cuanto tiempo estuvo adentro del cerro encantado llamado Pa chojoob'.

Francisco le contó a mucha gente todo lo que le había pasado, más a los que tienen cultivo en Pa chojoob', que sería mejor si presentan una ceremonia maya para no sufrir como lo que le pasó a él. Él [don Juan] dice que Francisco durante un año estuvo enfermo. La familia luchó mucho [y] hizo muchas ceremonias mayas, pero no se lograron. Y se murió. Se cree que su espíritu está en el cerro Pa chojoob'.[18]

—Juan Televario Puac

# The End of the Dance of the Deer

THE DANCE OF THE Deer is 100 percent Mayan and folkloric.[19] It is a pity that all this is lost; it only remains in the stories of us who are sixty years of age or more. I say that it is a folkloric dance [that is] 100 percent Mayan. I am going to relate a little of the structure of the small marimba that was used in this kind of dance; it is a material [that is] 100 percent vegetarian. The resonance box they formed with gourds of different sizes for a different sound from peak to the bass. To make the skeleton, or frame, a dry and strong vine was used about two inches thick. They formed it when they had just cut it to facilitate [bending it] because if the vine is already dry, it cannot be bent.

Below the vine, the gourds are placed, and above the same vine the planking is placed. With that, it takes the form of a small marimba. The player carries his own instrument. With a typical sash tied on the same gourd, they put the sash on the arms of the player. In the same processions, the same man carries the marimba and at the same time plays the old sounds that no longer exist. This kind of music is performed by two men, he of the marimba and he of the flute.

The flute is made of reed, about eighteen inches long and two inches thick with six holes for the air to pass through. The cane is covered with bees wax so that air will not leak. In the year of 1951, when I was ten years old, they presented the Dance of the Deer for the last time with this kind of folkloric music. The players were natives of San Pedro la Laguna [named] Don Juan Chavajay and Don Mariano Puac. The one who taught us the dance was Don Felix Gonzáles Pop. The three already died. Don Nicolás Cholotío Pérez, brother of my Uncle Pedro Cholotío Pérez, was then the tutor of the dance.

This kind of dance is made up like this: the two little old ones. The little old man [who] is married in the dance is called Ta-ta Culax, in Spanish one says Ta-ta, or Papá Nicolás. The little old woman is the wife of Ta-ta Culax [who] in the dance is named Nan-Katal, or Mamá Catarina in Spanish. These two are the ones who lead the dance; they form it in two lines. From there come the two who come out like little dogs, one on each side. The first is called Q'eju'm, in Spanish "Darkness." The second is named Amós; that is to say, "beautiful." From there come the two shepherd boys; that is to say, the two young herdsmen. It is better to say [that these] two orphans were not the sons of the old folks. The little dogs were two boys between ten and twelve years [of age]. Then that time in the year 1951, I was one of the little dogs. The other was my friend, Domingo Mendoza. We are both still alive.

Then the mountain lions, jaguars, and monkeys formed a row, the four deer in the middle of the row. The old ones with canes dance and dance. The old Ta-ta Culax relates his life, that they had no children because his woman is sterile. For that reason, the orphans live with them whom they love very much, just like their two puppies. He says that they are very poor and don't have money or land. They just live hunting animals like the monkeys, lions, and deer. He speaks in the Tz'utujil language.

Then he begins to dance with his woman. Across from them go the two dogs, dancing as if they were guarding them so that the jaguars and mountain lions do not harm them. But in their [the dogs'] distraction, they [the tigers and lions] carry Catarina on their backs to hide her. The animals make faces as if they want to eat her. Then Ta-ta Culax leaves with his two dogs to rescue his woman. Also, they [the jaguars and mountain lions] carry him on their backs. The jaguars and mountain lions act as if they want to eat him. The old man shouts and asks for help, calling for his woman and his two dogs. Then, they go out to save his life, and they return dancing.

I am writing this story of the Dance of the Deer that already disappeared in this region of Guatemala. This change took place last year, when December 21, 2012, was celebrated. The association of those who call themselves spiritual guides, or Mayan priests, wanted to present the Dance of the Deer. They called me to a meeting to ask me to collaborate with them. I told them with much pleasure I am able to teach them and organize the dance, but it was not possible for them to obtain the players of the marimba or the flute. They say that in Cobán and in Ixcán there is a group of players, [but] the distance is too far. For that reason, they were unable to present this kind of dance.

The focus of the dance is the running or hunting of the deer. The old man tells his woman to give tortillas to the dogs, because they have to leave with him to

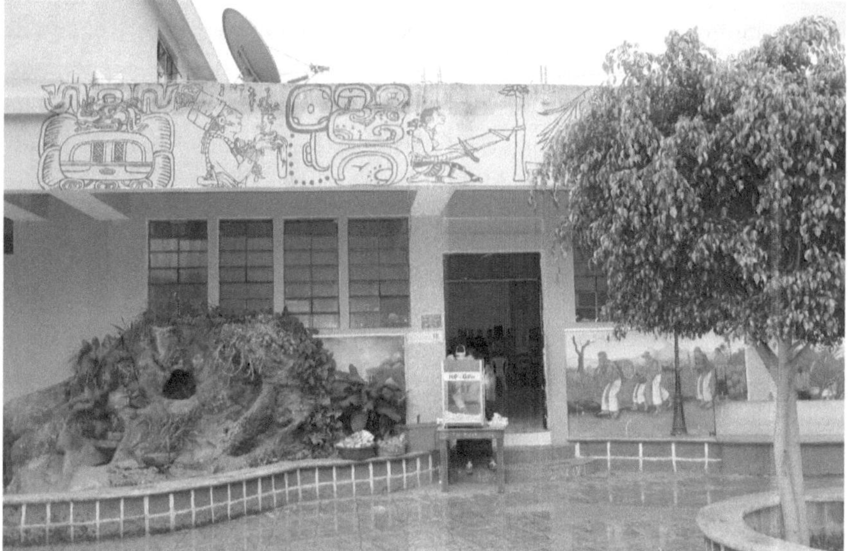

*Figure* 10. Recreational center in the town center of San Juan showing a mural of men playing the flute and drum at lower right of the photo / Centro recreativo en el Centro del pueblo de San Juan mostrando un mural de hombres tocando la chirimía [la flauta] y tambor en parte inferior derecho a de la foto

hunt animals in the mountain. The old woman acts as if she is giving food to the dogs; she dances with them, telling them to take care of their owner (the old one), telling them not to leave him alone because the animals can kill him in the mountain. They begin to dance, the two old ones; then, the old man says goodbye to his wife, saying, "I am going to the mountain to hunt the deer. You stay here in the rustic house with the two children, and I will take the two dogs."

Then the old man begins to mention the names of all the hills and mountains, asking those in charge and caretakers of the Santo Mundo to open the doors and windows and for the shepherds to let out the deer where they are kept. At the same time, he asks permission of the lord of Santo Mundo so that the mountain lions and jaguars do not hurt him; he acts as if he were doing a costumbre [ritual]. But the true costumbre, he had done three times previously.

The old man leaves, shouting, whistling, and mentioning the name of all the hills and mountains in search of the animals. The deer and monkeys are now hiding. The little dogs get to looking for the animals, and the old man acts as if he were killing them. The deer fall, and they act as if they were dead. The grandparents said that it is necessary to make and present [a] costumbre for the Santo Mundo because the old man mentions the names of all the places and that one cannot mock or play with the names of the hills and mountains. They (the grandparents) said many went crazy on the main day of the fiesta.

## Here in the Year 1951

The old ones in the Dance of the Deer, Ta-ta Culax, Andrés Cholotío Vázquez; Mamá Catarina, Diego Cholotío Hernández, already died. The little dogs, Pedro Cholotío Temó and Domingo Mendoza Bizarro, we are living. The shepherd boys were Diego Pérez Morales, still living, [and] Raymundo Ramos, already died. The four who came out like deer were then Antonio Nanichoc Coché, alredy died; Francisco Pérez Ujpán, already died; Pedro Quem, already died; and Luciano Cholotío Sumosa, he lives. Jaguars: Clemente Temó, Francisco Toc; monkeys: Delfino Navichoc, Andrés Mendoza García, they live. There are more that I can't remember. I forgot some because the time already has passed, more than sixty years. This is a real story.

—Pedro Cholotío Temó

# El final del baile del venado

EL BAILE DEL VENADO es 100 porciento maya y folclórico.[19] Es una lástima que todo está perdido; solo queda en la historias de nosotros los de está edad de 60 años para arriba. Yo digo que es un baile o danza folclórico 100 porciento maya. Voy a relatar un poco de la estructura de la pequeña marimbita que se usaba en esta clase de baile; es un material [que es] 100 porciento vegetal. La caja de resonancia lo formaban con tecomates de diferentes tamaños para un sonido diferente desde el pico hasta el bajo. Para hacer el esqueleto, o armazón, se usaba un bejuco seco y fuerte más o menos dos pulgadas de grueso. Lo formaban cuando lo acaban de cortar para facilitar [la flexión] porque si el bejuco ya seco no se puede doblar.

Debajo del bejuco, están colocados los tecomates, y sobre el mismo bejuco está puesto la tablazón. Con eso, se da la forma de una pequeña marimba. El tocador lleva su propio instrumento. Con una faja típica amarrada en el mismo bejuco, se ponen la faja en los hombros del tocador. En las mismas procesiones, el mismo hombre lleva la marimbita y al mismo tiempo toca los sones viejitos que ahora ya no hay. Esta clase de música es ejecutada por dos hombres, él de la marimbita y él de la flauta.

La flauta está hecha de cañaveral más o menos 18 pulgadas de largo y de grueso más o menos dos pulgadas con seis agujeros para que repercuta el aire. La caña está tapada con cera de abeja para que no se fugue el aire.

En el año de 1951 cuando yo tenía 10 años, lo presentaron por última vez el baile del venado y con esa clase de música folclórica. Los tocadores eran oriundos de San Pedro la laguna [nombrado] don Juan Chavajay y don Mariano Puac. El que nos enseñó el baile o la danza fue don Félix Gonzáles Pop. Los tres ya murieron. Don Nicolás Cholotío Pérez, hermano de mi abuelo Pedro Cholotío Pérez, fue entonces el tutor del baile del venado.

Esta clase de baile se forma así: los dos viejitos. El viejito que es el marido en el baile se le llama Ta-ta Culax, en español se dice Ta-ta, o Papá Nicolás. La viejita es la esposa de Ta-ta Culax [que] en el baile se le llama Nan-Katal, o mamá Catarina en español. Los dos son los que encabezan el baile; lo forman de dos filas. De allí, vienen los dos que salen como perritos, uno en cada lado. El primero se llama Q'eju'm, en español, Oscuridad. El segundo se le llama Amós; quiere decir, hermoso. De allí vienen los dos zagales; es decir, los dos jovencitos pastores. Vale más decir [que estos] dos huérfanos no eran hijos de los viejitos. Los perritos eran dos niños entre 10 y 12 años. Entonces esa vez en año 1951, yo fui uno de los perritos. El otro fue mi amigo, Domingo Mendoza. Los dos todavía estamos vivos.

Luego los leones, tigres, y micos se ponen en fila, los cuatro venados en el centro de las dos filas. Los viejitos con bastón bailan y bailan. El viejito Ta-ta Culax cuenta su vida, que ellos no tuvieron hijos es porque su mujer es estéril. Más por eso, con ellos vivan los dos huérfanos que los quiere mucho, igual que sus dos perritos. Cuenta que son muy pobres y no tienen dinero ni terreno. Únicamente vive cazando animales como los micos, leones, y venados. Lo relata en dialecto tz'utujil.

Luego comienza a bailar con su mujer. Atrás de ellos, van los dos perritos bailando como que si los estuvieran cuidando para que los tigres y leones no les hicieran daño. Pero en sus descuidos, se la llevan [tigres y leones] cargada a la mamá Catarina para esconderla. Los animales hacen muecas como que se la quieren comerla. Luego, sale Ta-ta Culax con sus dos perritos a rescatar a su mujer. También, se lo llevan [los tigres y leones] cargado al viejito. Tigres y leones hacían como que se lo querían comer, el viejito, gritaba pidiendo auxilio, llamando a su mujer y a sus dos perritos. Luego, salen a salvarle la vida y regresan bailando.

Escribo esta historia del baile del venado, ya se desapareció en esta región de Guatemala. Este cambio paso del año pasado cuando se celebró el 21 de diciembre 2012. La asociación de los que se dicen guías espirituales, o sacerdotes mayas, quisieron presentar el baile de venado. Me llamaron en una reunión para pedirme que colaborara con ellos. Yo les dije con mucho gusto puedo enseñarles y organizar el baile, pero no fue posible para ellos conseguir a los tocadores de la marimbita ni él de la flauta. Dicen que en Cobán y en Ixcán hay un grupo de tocadores, [pero] la distancia es demasiado lejos. Más por eso no pudieron presentar esta clase de baile.

El centro del baile, es el correr o cazar del venado. El viejito le dice a su mujer que les dé tortilla a los perritos, porque con el tienen que salir a cazar animales en la montaña. La viejita hace como que estuviera dando de comer a los perritos; baila con ellos, diciendo que cuiden a su dueño (el viejito), que no lo dejen solo porque los animales lo pueden matar en la montaña. Comienzan a bailar, los dos viejitos; luego, el viejito se despide de su mujer diciéndola, "Me voy a la montaña a cazar el venado. Tú te quedas aquí en el ranchito con los dos patojos, y yo me llevo a los dos perritos.

Luego el viejito comienza a mencionar el nombre de todos los cerros y montañas, pidiendo a los encargados y cuidadores del Santo Mundo a que abren los puertas y ventanas y a que los pastores dejan salir a los venados de donde los tienen guardados. Al mismo tiempo, pide permiso al dueño del Santo Mundo para que los leones y tigres no le hagan daño, hace como que estuviera hacienda costumbre. Pero la verdadera costumbre ya lo había hecho tres veces con anterioridad.

El viejito sale gritando, silbando, y mencionando el nombre de todos los cerros y montañas en busca de los animales. Los venados y micos ya estaban escondidos. Los perritos se meten a buscar a los animales, y el viejo hace como que los estuviera matando. Los venados caen, y hacen como que estuvieran muertos. Los abuelos decían que es necesario hacer y presentar [una] costumbre para el Santo Mundo porque el viejito menciona los nombres de todos los lugares y que uno no puede burlarse ni jugar con los nombres de los cerros y montañas. Ellos (los abuelos) decían muchos se quedado locos en el mero día de la fiesta.

## Aquí en el año 1951

Los viejitos en el baile del venado, Ta-ta Culax, Andrés Cholotío Vásquez; Mamá Catarina, Diego Cholotío Hernández, ya murieron. Los dos perritos, Pedro Cholotío Temó y Domingo Mendoza Bizarro, estamos vivos. Los zagales eran Diego Pérez Morales, está vivo, [y] Raymundo Ramos, ya murió. Los cuatro que salieron como venados eran entonces Antonio Navichoc Coché, ya murió; Francisco Pérez Ujpán, ya murió; Pedro Quem, ya murió; y Luciano Cholotío Sumosa, él, vive. Tigres: Celemente Temó, Francisco Toc; micos: Delfino Navichoc, Andrés Mendoza García, viven. Hay más quien no recuerdo. Se me olvidaron algunos porque el tiempo ya han pasado, más de 60 años. Este es una historia real.

—Pedro Cholotío Temó

# The Witch C'oxol

*An Ancient Legend*

THIS TALE CAME TO be as a real story, told by the great-grandparents of my wife who were named Juana Bizarro and Diego Pérez Ramos. They were grandparents of the father of my wife, Diego Pérez Có. He told us what our great-grandparents spoke of, things as they were before. He says that inside the hill, K'istalin, there was a lot of wealth; there was gold and silver. Well, the ancient Tz'utujiles, when they worked in Xe K'istalin and in Chua Suj, under the rocks, they found pieces of gold and silver. They kept it in their chests like a treasure of the enchanted hill. It was like this when corn, beans, yuca, sweet potatoes, and everything that was planted abounded. There was no shortage of rain; there was abundant harvest.

With the arrival of the Spaniards, all was lost—they told the native people they came from God; they know Heaven; and they know Hell. Also, they said that there is a place called purgatory where the spirits of the dead are suffering, burning day and night. There is no one to help them. The Spaniards told the native people that they could save the spirits of the dead from Hell or from purgatory in exchange for money. That is to say, the Indigenous people had to pay the Spanish priests money to rescue the spirits of the deceased from the eternal fire of all their grandmothers and grandfathers, their fathers, [and] kin so that they do not suffer more in Hell.

But the Indigenous people lacked money. Then, the Spaniards told the Indigenous people that they would accept the gold and silver in order to rescue the spirits of the deceased from the fire of Hell. It was thus when the natives handed over all the gold and silver that they had laid aside to the Spanish priests. It was like a means of deceit or lie what they said to liberate the spirits of the dead. [But] the natives became very sad and crying when they knew that their parents, kin, and grandparents were burning. More for that reason, they delivered all [the gold and silver] they had.

This deception remained like a plague, and it still exists. [For example,] the second of November [All Soul's Day] of each year, the people of my town pay the catechists some money. [This is] for the prayer of a responsory [or response], sung or prayed, they say to help the blessed souls achieving their rescue from Hell or purgatory. Those who do this know that it is a lie—[that it is] to obtain money.

Speaking of Cerro k'istalin, the great-grandparents said that the K'istalin Hill is an enchanted hill of much power that gave a lot of wealth to the people of earlier times. They say that inside the enchanted hill there were a lot of costumes of the Dance of the Bull, Dance of the Deer, [and] Dance of the Monkeys. Well, they say that earlier there was a dance called "Lebal." That dance was forgotten. It had disappeared when those who practiced the Lebal dance died.

This is always related to the enchanted hill K'istalin. The great-grandparents said when King Tecún Umán was in the world; that is, when he was alive, with him was a shaman (*aj-iitz*) [also spelled *aj'iitz*], or brujo [witch], who was called C'oxol, [who was] a strong and enchanted man.[20] They say that he had a lot of communication with the lords of the enchanted hills and that he was of the color red; that is, his body was completely red. He was in charge of making the costumbres, ceremonies, hexes, or witchcraft so that nothing bad would happen to the king, Tecún Umán.

But he [Diego Pérez Có] says that everything was the opposite. The great king, Tecún Umán, died. He lost the war [with the Spaniards]. He says that the enchanter, aj-iitz, who also was called C'oxol, cursed all the costumbres and witchcraft he had done for the king—not one was worth anything.

After everything, it is said that the witch with the name C'oxol came to dwell in the hill, K'istalin, place of enchantment. The locals saw him dancing in the place called Chua Cruz, more or less half up the hill, K'istalin, with a small dummy and a gold chain in one hand and small hatchet in the other and with a silver incensory, dancing over an enormous stone in the place, Chua Cruz.

It is said that in that time the town did not have a name as it does now. It was known as Chua Sanik Juyú, in Spanish, Land of the Ants. In the afternoons, he [Diego Pérez Có] says the aj-iitz C'oxol was seen dancing. When the people would want to see him up close, then he went inside the enchanted hill. He did not want to be seen up close. The aj-iitz C'oxol was very upset.

At night he would stand on the huge stone in Chua Cruz, shouting insults at the people of the town, saying things like, "Women and men of this arrogant place, eaters of rotten fish and crabs, you have your *dormilones la[s] cabeza[s]* [sleepyheads] up your ass! You are pigs who do not bathe!" It was an insult and outrage what he said to the residents. He [Diego Pérez Có] says that townspeople were tired of the insults and outrages. All the people of the place gathered. Among them were evil people with naguales [animal forms] who converted into eagle hawks, buzzards, and owls. Others changed into wolves, coyotes, monkeys, wild cats, and in kinkajous. Together they made the decision to attack the enchanted witch C'oxol.

One night again, the enchanted sorcerer began to insult, or mistreat, the locals. They angrily converted into their respective naguales. Those who had wings flew. Also, those who could not fly [came along]. Together, they went to capture the witch C'oxol. They strapped him and whipped him with lemon branches with thorns until they drew blood. There, they left him lying on the great stone in Chua Cruz. They thought that they had killed him, but because he was a charmed sorcerer, they were unable to kill him. Soon after, he returned to insult and scandalize. He did not allow the people of the town to sleep.

The people of the town felt molested because of the insults and scandals that did not leave them alone. Angry one night, they met [and] then converted into their naguales and went to capture C'oxol, the magical witch. He [Diego Pérez Có] says they carried him into the air and circled many times above the town. At a very high altitude, after spinning him many times in the air, they finally dropped him on an enormous stone in a place called Patinoy Atz'am. That is where the enchanted sorcerer fell. The naguales thought he had died, but he did not die. He only fractured many parts of his body. He [Diego Pérez Có] says [it was only then that] he [C'oxol] stopped insulting because of the blows and wounds he had suffered on the big flattened stone. It is now seen in the place Patinoy atz'am.

Well, it is said that brujo C'oxol, enchanted man, abandoned the hill, K'istalin, and left closed the doors and windows to all the riches of the magical K'istalin hill. The grandmothers and grandfathers have said that after the witch C'oxol, the enchanted man of great power, abandoned the K'istalin hill, one night he was

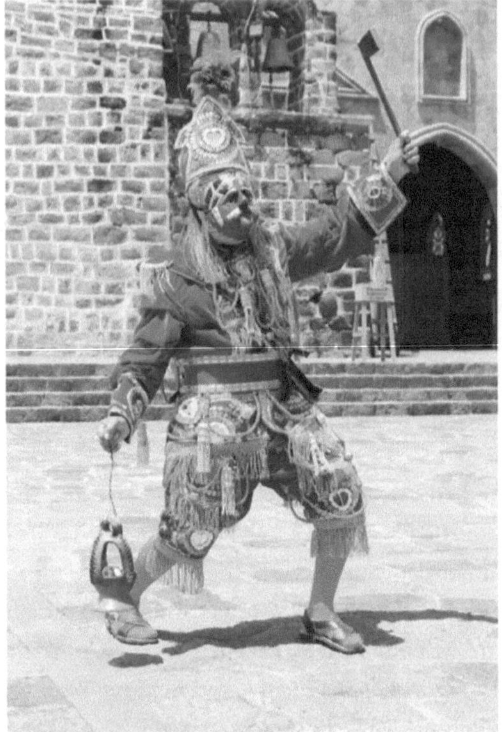

*Figure* 11. Pedro's son, Clemente, dances in front of the Catholic church in San Juan dressed as Witch C'oxol. A woman who is a shaman lent Pedro the costume. / El hijo de Pedro, Clemente, baila frente a la iglesia Católica en San Juan vestido como aj-iitz C'oxol. Una mujer que es chamán le prestó el traje a Pedro.

heard crying bitterly and sadly, and from there, nothing else was heard of him.

It is believed, and so say our grandparents, that the inhabitants of this place are suffering poverty because of all the evil the ancient Tz'utujiles caused the witch C'oxol. It is said that the witch C'oxol carried all those riches of K'istalin Hill to Bocoó Hill and to Ruchi chi [juyú] Hill. These are found in Chichicastenango and Santa Cruz del Quiché. More for that reason, it is said that the people of Chichcastenango and of Santa Cruz del Quiché have many riches that they have obtained from the two enchanted hills, and in those towns, there are many witches that are dedicated to making witchcraft.[21]

—Juana Bizarro y Diego Pérez Ramos

# El *aj-iitz* C'oxol

*Una leyenda antigua*

ESTE RELATO VINO SER como un cuento real relatado por los tatarabuelos de mi esposa que se llamaban Juana Bizarro y Diego Pérez Ramos. Eran abuelos del padre de mi esposa, Diego Pérez Có. Él nos relataba lo que contaban nuestros tatarabuelos cosas como eran antes. Él dice que adentro del cerro, K'istalin, había mucha riqueza; había oro y plata. Pues, los antiguos tz'utujiles, cuando trabajaran en Xe K'istalin y en Chua Suj, debajo de las piedras (rocas), encontraban pedazos de oro y plata. Lo guardaban en sus cofres como un tesoro del cerro encantado. Era así cuando abundaba el maíz el frijol, la yuca, el camote, y todo lo que se sembraba. No había escases de lluvia; había abundante cosecha.

Con la llegada de los españoles, todo se perdió—le decían a la gente natural ellos venían de parte de dios; conocen el cielo, y conocen el infierno. También, decían que hay un lugar que se llama purgatorio donde lo espíritus de los muertos están sufriendo, quemándose de día y de noche. No hay quien los ayude. Los españoles decían a la gente natural que ellos pueden rescatar los espíritus de los muertos del infierno o de purgatorio a cambio de un dinero. Es decir, los naturales tenían que pegarles a los sacerdotes españoles dinero a como un medio para rescatar los espíritus de los difuntos del fuego eterno de todo sus abuelas y abuelos, sus padres, [y] parientes para que no sufran más en el infierno.

Pero los naturales carecían de dinero. Entonces, los españoles decían a la gente indígena, ellos reciben el oro y la plata para rescatar los espíritus de los difuntos del fuego del infierno. Es así cuando los naturales entregaron a los sacerdotes españoles todo el oro y la plata que tenían guardado. [Fue] como un medio de engaño o mentira lo que decían de liberar los espíritus de los muertos del infierno. [Pero] los naturales se pusieron muy tristes y llorando cuando supieron que sus padres, parientes y abuelos, se están quemando. Más por eso, entregaron todo [el oro y la plata] lo que tenían.

Este engaño quedó como una plaga, [y] existe ahora. [Por ejemplo,] el segundo de noviembre de cada año, la gente de mi pueblo paga a los catequistas un dinero para el rezo de un responsorio, cantada o rezado, dicen que para ayudar a las benditas ánimas logrando su rescate de infierno o purgatorio. Lo[s] que hacen esto saben que es una mentira—[que es] como un medio de obtener dinero.

Hablando de cerro K'istalin, los tatarabuelos decían que el cerro K'istalin es un cerro encantando y de mucho poder que le daba mucha riqueza a la gente de antes. Dicen que dentro del cerro encantado había mucho traje del baile del torito, baile del venado, [y] baile de los micos. Pues, dicen que antes había un baile se llámala "Lebal." Ese baile se quedó en olvido. Despareció cuando murieron los que practicaban el baile Lebal.

Este siempre se relaciona con el cerro encantado K'istalin. Los tatarabuelos decían cuando el rey Tecún Umán estuvo en el mundo; es decir, cuando esta con vida, con él estuvo un chamán (*aj-iitz*) [also spelled *aj'iitz*], o brujo encantado que se llamaba C'oxol, [que era] un hombre fuerte y encantado.[20] Dicen que tiene mucha comunicación con los dueños de los cerros encantados y que él era del color rojo; es decir, su cuerpo era todo rojo. Él era encargado de hacer las costumbres, ceremonias; maleficios o brujerías para que nada mal pasará al rey Tecún Umán.

Pero dice [Diego Pérez Có] que todo fue al contrario. Se murió el gran rey, Tecún Umán. Perdió la guerra [con los españoles]. Dice que el brujo (*aj-iitz*), que también se llama C'oxol, maldijo todas las costumbres y bujerías que había hecho en favor del rey—ninguna valió nada.

Después de todo, se dice que el brujo con el nombre C'oxol se vino a morar (vivir) en el cerro K'istalin, lugar encanto. Los lugareños lo miraban bailando en el lugar llamado Chua Cruz, más o menos a media cuesta del cerro, K'istalin, con un pequeño muñeco y una cadena de oro en una mano y en la otra con una pequeña hacha y con un incensario de plata, bailando sobre una enorme piedra en el lugar Chua Cruz.

Se dice que en ese tiempo el pueblo no tenía el nombre como ahora. Se conocía como Sanik Juyú, en español, Tierra de las hormigas. Por las tardes, dice [Diego Pérez Có] que se miraba el *aj-iitz* C'oxol, bailando. Cuando la gente lo querían ver de cerca, luego se internaba adentro del cerro encantado. No quería que lo vieran de cerca. El *aj-iitz* C'oxol, se molestaba mucho.

Por las noches se ponía sobre la enorme piedra en Chua Cruz, gritando insultos a la gente del pueblo diciendo [cosas] así: "Hombres y mujeres, haraganes de este lugar, comedores de pescado y cangrejos podridos, tienen los dormilones la[s] cabeza[s] [cabezas soñolientas] en el culo. Son cerdos que no se bañan." Era un insulto y escándalo lo que decía a los pobladores. Dice [Diego Pérez Có] que los del pueblo [eran] cansados de los insultos y escándalos. Se reunieron toda la gente del lugar. Entre ellos había gente mala con naguales que convertían en águilas gavilanes, zopilote, y búhos. Otros que se convertían en lobos, coyotes, micos, gatos de monte, y en micoleones. Entre todos dice que tomaron una decisión de atacar al brujo C'oxol encantado.

Una noche otra vez, el brujo encantado comenzó a insultar o maltratar a los lugareños. Ellos muy enojados se convirtieron a según sus naguales [formas espirituales o formas animales]. Los que tenían alas volaron. Se fueron también los que no podía volar. Entre todos, fueron a capturar al brujo C'oxol. Los atraparon y azotaron con ramas de limón con espinas hasta que sacaron sangre. Allí, lo dejaron tendido sobre la gran piedra en Chua Cruz. Ellos creyeron que lo habían matado, pero como era brujo encantado, no lo pudieron matar. Al poco tiempo, volvió a insultar y escandalizar. No los dejaba dormir a las personas del pueblo.

La gente del pueblo se sentía molestos por los insultos y escándalos que no los dejaba tranquilos. Enojados una noche, ellos reunieron [y] luego se convirtieron en sus naguales y se fueron a capturar al brujo C'oxol encantado. Él [Diego Pérez Có] dice que se lo trajeron en el aire y dieron muchas vueltas en el aire sobre el pueblo. A una altura bien alto, después de darle muchas vueltas en el aire, al fin se lo dejaron caer sobre una enorme piedra en un lugar llamado Patinoy Atz'am. Allí es donde se vino a caer el brujo encantado. Los naguales pensaron que se había muerto, pero no se murió. Solamente se fracturó muchas partes de su cuerpo. Él [Diego Pérez Có] dice que no hasta allí dejó de insultar por los golpes y heridas que había sufrid en la gran piedra aplanada. Ahora se ve ahora en el lugar, Patinoy atz'am.

Pues, se dice que el brujo C'oxol, hombre encantado, abandonó el cerro K'istalin y dejó cerrada las puertas y ventanas de todas las riquezas del cerro encantado "K'istalin." Las abuelas y abuelos han dicho que cuando el brujo C'oxol, hombre encantado de mucho poder, abandonó el cerro K'istalin, una noche se le oyó llorando amargamente y muy tristemente, y [después] de ahí, ya no se oyó de él.

Se cree, y así lo decían nuestros abuelos, los pobladores de este lugar estamos sufriendo la pobreza por causa de todo mal que los antiguos tz'utujiles le causaron al brujo (*aj-iitz*) C'oxol. Se dice que todas esas riquezas del cerro K'istalin, el brujo C'oxol se llevó al cerro Bocoó y al cerro Ruchi chi juyú. Estos se encuentran en Chichicastenango y Santa Cruz del Quiché. Más por eso, se dice que la gente de Chichicastenango y de Santa Cruz del Quiché tienen muchas riquezas que han obtenido de los dos cerros encantados, y en esos pueblos, hay muchos brujos que se dedican a hacer brujería.[21]

—Juana Bizarro y Diego Pérez Ramos

# Mayan Folktale

*Origin of the Marimba*

A TZ'UTUJIL TALE SAYS that earlier, neither the marimba nor the *tun* [traditional drum] nor the chirimía [traditional flute] existed. Then, it says a king was the one who ruled in the highlands. That is to say, he had the power over the K'iche's, Kaqchikeles, and Tz'utujiles.

It says that the king had his two daughters, one of them called Xuul and the other named Sanik.[22] The two were beautiful and joyous who sang and danced in the house of their father. It says that the king lived in mansions that did not have padlocks. Only he knew how to [magically] open and close his house.

The daughters were already grown, but their father, the king, did not want his daughters to have husbands. He only wanted them to be the joy of the house. The two princesses remained locked inside the house. Their father did not want them to marry because all the men of the towns were poor, and it would be a loss of prestige. More for that [reason], he had locked them up.

Outside, you could hear the songs and dances the sisters did inside their house. It was very pleasant, [and it] also warmed the hearts of those who listened.

The story says that the sisters had a great desire to escape, but they were not able to do so. In an oversight of the king, the two sisters left from where they were locked up, and they said goodbye to their mother. She told them, "Be careful because your father, upon realizing it, will order many people to capture you, but do not worry. Take this secreto [magical act or object]," giving them a handful of her tangled hair, "and when the captors are near, throw the secreto back at them;" that is, the handful of hair. Thus, they [the girls] did it when they saw that a lot of people were chasing them to capture them. They left the secreto behind. After a while, when they looked back again, they saw that behind them [were] ravines, rocks, and brambles. Up to there, the people remained and they were not able to pass. They returned to tell the king that his two daughters disappeared and that they [the people] could barely return.

The king told them to go again tomorrow. "Bring me my two daughters if you do not want to be burned to death." The people became sad.

The woman of the king became sad because her two daughters left home, but the story says that she had her nagual and certain secretos. When he [the king] was sleeping in his place [close to] where his woman was sleeping, she left the arm of her grinding stone beside the king. In case the king felt it, or better said, if he awoke, the stone appeared as if it were his wife. The story says that she did so to leave to see her daughters. When she arrived in the place, Xuul and Sanik were in a cave, singing and dancing. Then they embraced their mother, [saying,] "You are our mother; we don't want to return home. Here, we are well, seeing the stars and contemplating the sky with our song and dance."

Their mother tells them, "Tomorrow, the king is going to order many people to capture you, but do not worry. Here is the secreto. I leave you my sash and my leather caites. When you see many people coming, spread out my sash and place my guaraches [sandals] on a rock. You will see that these people cannot capture you."

"Fine, mama," said the two sisters.

The following day, the king ordered all the people of the town to look for and bring them [back]. When the captors were nearing the cave, the two daughters of the king did what their mother had told them to do. They placed the guaraches on the rock and spread out the sash. These turned into [mountain] lions, tigers, serpents, [and] huge rocks so that no one was able to enter that cave. The people were frightened and, because of the great fear, had to return to tell the king all that they had suffered—they were almost going to be food for the animals.

In the night, the story says that the mother went again to the cave to see her two daughters. When she got near, the muchachas were singing and dancing inside the cave. They embraced and she told them, "I am going to wear my sash and guarachas."

They said, "Mamá, how will we defend ourselves? Without doubt, they will come again tomorrow to get us."

Their mother told them, "Do not worry; I will be with you. My two daughters, I will stay here forever, and they will not move you nor take you back to the house."

Later, the story says that the two princesses converted into trees of different sizes, and in their foliage, you could hear the joy of the marimba, the drum, and the chirimía [traditional flute].

Then their mother told them, "Here you will stay forever, and you will be the joy of our people." More for that reason, they say that they extract the marimba, drum, and chirimía from the trees.

*Sanik*, in Spanish, means *hormiga* [ant]. Hormigo is a tree not very big; [it is] like a bush. It is only found on the coast, and with its wood they make the marimba. But our grandparents said that in this kind of tree, there are many hormigueras [ants' nests]; from the ant came this name that now they call *palo del hormigo* [reddish, durable wood of the hormigo tree ] as a relic of the nation as part of the Guatemala cultural heritage.[23]

—Pedro Cholotío Temó

# Cuento maya

## *Origen de la marimba*

UN CUENTO TZ'UTUJIL DICE que antes no existía la marimba [tambor tradicional] ni el tun ni la chirimía [flauta tradicional]. Entonces, dice que un rey era él que gobernaba en el altiplano. Es decir, él tenía el poder sobre los k'iche's, kaqchikeles, y tz'utujiles.

Dice que el rey tenía sus dos hijas, una de ellas se llamaba Xuul, y la otra se llamaba Sanik].[22] Las dos eran hermanas hermosas y alegres que cantaban y danzaban en la casa de su padre el rey. Dice que el rey vivía en casonas que no tenía candados. Solo él sabía cómo abrir y cerrar [mágicamente] su casa.

Las hijas ya eran grandes, pero su padre (el rey) no quería que sus hijas tuvieran marido. Únicamente él las quería ser la alegría de la casa. Las dos princesas permanecían encerradas adentro de la casa. Su padre no quería que se casaran porque todos los hombres de los pueblos eran pobres, y sería un desprestigio. Más por eso [razón], las tenía encerradas.

Afuera, se escuchaba los cantos y las danzas que hacían adentro de la casa. Era bien alegre [y] también alegraba los corazones de los que oían.

El cuento dice que las hermanas tenían tanto deseo de escapar, pero no podían. En un descuido del rey, las dos hermanas salieron de donde estaban encerrados, y se despidieron de su madre. Ella les dijo, "Cuídense porque su padre al darse cuenta mandará mucha gente para capturarlas, pero no tengan pena. Lleven este secreto," dándolas un puñado de su pelo enredado, "y cuando los captores están cerca, tiren atrás el secreto;" es decir, el puñado de pelo. Así lo hicieron [las chicas] cuando vieron que mucha gente que andaba las perseguía para capturarlas. Ellas dejaron tirado atrás el secreto. Al rato, cuando volvieron a ver atrás, vieron que detrás de ellos había barrancos, rocas, y zarzas. Hasta allí, quedaron la gente y ya no pudieron pasar. Se regresaron a decirle al rey que sus dos hijas se desaparecieron [y] que apenas pudieron ellos [la gente] regresar.

El rey dijo mañana se van otra vez. "Me traigan a mis dos hijas si no quieren morir quemados." La gente se puso tristes.

La mujer del rey se puso triste porque sus dos hijas se fueron de la casa, pero el cuento dice que ella tenía su nagual y ciertos secretos. Cuando el [el rey] estaba durmiendo en su lugar [cerca de] donde dormía la mujer, dejó el brazo de su piedra de moler a la par del rey. Por si el rey lo sintiera, o bien dicho, si se despertara, la piedra apareció como que si fuera su esposa. El cuento dice que así lo hizo ella se fue a ver a sus hijas. Cuando llegó en el lugar, Xuul y Sanik estaban debajo de una cueva, cantando y danzando. Luego abrazaron a su madre, "Tu eres muestra madre; no queremos regresar a la casa. Aquí, estamos bien, viendo las estrellas y contemplando el cielo con nuestro canto y danza.

Su mamá les dice, "Mañana, el rey va a mandar mucha gente para captúralas, pero no tengan pena. Aquí está el secreto. Les dejo mi faja y mis caites de cuero. ¡Cuando ven venir mucha gente, tended mi faja y cuelgad mis guarachas en la roca! Veréis que esta gente no las puede capturar."

"Bien, mamá," dijeron las dos hermanas."

Al día siguiente, el rey mandó a toda la gente del pueblo que las buscara y las trajera [de regreso]. Cuando los captores se estaban acercando a la cueva, las dos hijas del rey hicieron tal como su mamá les había dicho. Colgaron las guarachas en la roca y tendieron la faja. Estos se volvieron leones, tigres, serpientes, [y] grandísimas rocas para que nadie podía entrar en esa cueva. La gente se asustó, y por el gran miedo, tuvieron que regresar a decirle al rey, todo lo que sufrieron—por poco iban ser comida por los animales.

Por la noche, el cuento dice que la madre se fue otra vez a la cueva a ver a sus dos hijas. Cuando se acercaba, las muchachas estaban cantando y danzando a dentro de la cueva. Se abrazaron y les dijo, "Voy a llevar mi faja y mis guarachas."

Ellas dijeron, "Mamá como nos defendemos sin duda que mañana nos vienen a traernos."

Su mamá las dijo, "No tengan pena; yo estaré con ustedes. Mis dos hijas aquí te quedaras para siempre, y no os moverán ni os regresarán a la casa."

Al rato, el cuento dice que las dos princesas se convirtieron en árboles de diferentes tamaños, y en sus follajes, se oía lo alegre de la marimba, el tun y la chirimía [flauta tradicional].

Entonces su madre las dijo, "Aquí os quedaréis para siempre, y os seréis la alegría de nuestros pueblos." Más por eso, dicen que la marimba, el tun y la chirimía lo sacan de los árboles.

Sanik, en español, quiere decir hormiga. Hormigo es un árbol no muy grande; [es] como un arbusto. Solo se encuentra en la costa, y con su madera hacen la marimba. Pero nuestros abuelos decían que en esta clase de árboles, hay muchas hormigueras; de la hormiga salió este nombre que ahora le llaman *palo de hormigo* [madera rojiza y duradera del árbol hormigo] como una reliquia de la nación como parte del patrimonio cultural de Guatemala.[23]

—Pedro Cholotío Temó

# A Mysterious Tale of the Matapalo Tree

THERE ARE MANY MYSTERIOUS things. We people know that there are strange things, but we don't know the origin [of] the occult things within Mother Earth.

In other regions of Guatemala, the matapalo tree they call "amate." In Tz'utujil [and] in Kaqchikel, we call it "po'j." This kind of tree doesn't require much humidity; its roots stick on the stones [rocks]. [Because] its wood is very weak, it doesn't serve for construction. It only serves for firewood. What is not known [is] how it is connected with nature—in other words, Mother Earth.

It is the titular fiesta of San Lucas Tolimán. In San Lucas lives my sister Petrona Vásquez Cholotío of seventy-three years [of age]. She invited us to spend the fiesta with her. My wife and I accepted the invitation.

With her, we remembered the death of don Ángel Hernández Ujpán, who died the tenth of October, eight days ago, commenting on what the people said, that the death of Señor Ángel Hernández was for cutting down a matapalo tree in an enchanted place.

Petrona assures me that indeed there is a matapalo tree, or "po'j" in Tz'utujil, in enchanted places, and she began to tell, or relate a story.

She says that in San Lucas Tolimán, there is an enchanted place about two kilometers from the town. In that place there was a big matapalo tree, or po'j tree, [also] in Kaqchikel. It was an enormous tree that was positioned over a big rock. She says below the rock, the place looked very beautiful. Many people arrived in this place to rest, to study. There were people who carried their candles or *veladores* [short, thick candles] and left them lit as a present to the Holy Mother Earth. She says that the people of other towns regarded it as a sacred place.

Petrona told me that it is said that the owner of the sacred place was very poor. He did not care [about it] and had abandoned it. She says that the land was sold to a rich man of the same town. The new owner of the land, as he was very rich, did not want the people come to rest. The new owner of the land, as he was rich, did not allow anyone to enter. As he was the richest, he paid *mozos* [workers] to clean the land, and ultimately wasted the big matapalo tree. The po'j served as firewood. It provided a large amount of firewood, and later, it was a big problem.

Petrona told me that in a few days, the rich man became insane in the same place that he squandered the po'j tree. Sometimes, or at times, he runs away, and at times, he starts laughing. The mozos ask what is happening to him. They say that the señor said that when he runs out is when he sees many men and women calling him to run with them. But, she says, the mozos do not see anyone. She says they ask him why he begins to laugh. He says many men and women begin to laugh with him. But the strangest thing [is] the mozos do not see anyone.

At night when he slept, suddenly he got up and went out running. He said that the men and women obligated him to leave running. But she says that the family saw nobody and was very preoccupied for all that was happening to the señor.

As he had a lot of money, they took him to the doctors in Mazatenango and in Antigua, Guatemala. But he was not cured. Finally, they took him to a sorcerer in Samayac, the land of the sorcerers. Well, the witch of Samayac told the family [that] the sick one now did not have his spirit, only his body. His spirit now was with the blessed animals, and he was going to be mad for the rest of his life.

At the request of the family, the sorcerer from Samayac came to San Lucas to cure the sick person. Well, the witch worked with black magic when he arrived at the enchanted place where the man had destroyed the matapalo. The witch told the family to look for a good, fat pig and three roosters, and told them to dig a grave in the ground of the same enchanted place.

The family prepared all that the sorcerer asked for. All [was] ready. The hour of twelve at night arrived, and the sorcerer told the sick man to push the pig and three roosters into the ditch [grave], and the workers buried the animals with dirt. So alive they buried them. Patrona says that was healing of the rich man. She told me that this man was cured of the insanity. Now, he lives well, but he spent a lot of money.[24]

—Patrona Vásquez Cholotío

# Un cuento misterioso del árbol matapalo

HAY MUCHAS COSAS MISTERIOSAS. Nosotros las personas sabemos que hay cosas extrañas, pero no sabemos el origen [de] las cosas ocultas dentro de la madre tierra.

En otras regiones de Guatemala, el árbol matapalo lo llaman "amate." En tz'utujil [y] en kaqchikel, lo llamamos "po'j." Esta clase de árbol no requiere tanta humedad; sus raíces se pegan sobre las piedras (rocas). [Porque] su madera es muy débil, no sirve para construcción. Únicamente sirve para leña. Lo que no se sabe [es] como está conectado con la naturaleza—en otras palabras, la madre tierra.

Es la fiesta titular de San Lucas Tolimán. En San Lucas vive me hermana Petrona Vásquez Cholotío de 73 años [de edad]. Ella nos invitó para que fuéramos a pasar la fiesta con ella. Mi esposa y yo aceptamos la invitación.

Con ella recordamos la muerte de don Ángel Hernández Ujpán; él se murió el 10 de octubre, ocho días pasado, comentando lo que la gente decía que la muerte del Señor Ángel Hernández es por talar un árbol de matapalo en lugar encantado.

Petrona me asegura que, si hay árbol de matapalo, o "po'j" en tz'utujil, en lugares encantados, y me comienza a contar o relatar un cuento.

Dice que, en San Lucas Tolimán, hay un lugar encantado casi dos kilómetros del pueblo. En ese lugar había un gran árbol de matapalo, o "po'j" [también] en kaqchikel. Era un árbol enorme que estaba puesta sobre una gran roca. Dice que debajo de la roca se miraba el lugar bien hermoso. Llegaba mucha gente en este lugar para descansar, para estudiar. Había gentes que llevaban sus candelas o veladoras y lo dejaban encendidas como un presente a la Santa madre tierra. Dice que la gente de otros pueblos lo tenían como un lugar sagrado.

Petrona me dijo se dice que el dueño del lugar sagrado era muy pobre. No le daba importancia [sobre eso], y él lo tenía abandonado. Dice que el terreno le fue vendido a un hombre rico del mismo pueblo. El nuevo dueño del terreno, como es muy rico, no quería que la gente llegara a descansar. El nuevo dueño del terreno, como el era rico, no dejaba entrar a nadie. Como era el más rico, pagó mozos a limpiar el terreno, y por último botó el gran árbol matapalo. El po'j le sirvió para leña. Dio una gran cantidad para leña, y más tarde, era un gran problema.

Petrona me dijo que, a los pocos días, el hombre rico se puso loco en el mismo lugar donde botó el árbol po'j. Por ratos, o por momentos, se va corriendo, y por momentos, se pone a reír. Los mozos le preguntaban qué es lo está pasando con él. Dicen que el señor decía que cunado sale corriendo es cuando el miraba a muchos hombres y mujeres lo estaban llamando para correr con ellos. Pero, dice que los mozos no miraban nadie. Ella dice que le preguntaban porque se ponía a reír. Él dice que muchos hombres y mujeres se ponen a reír con él. Pero lo más extraño [es] los mozos no veían nada.

Por las noches cuando dormía, de repente se levanta y salía corriendo. Él decía que los hombres y mujeres le obligan para que saliera corriendo. Pero ella dice que la familia nada miraba y estaba muy preocupada por todo lo que estaba pasando con el señor.

Como tiene mucho dinero, se lo llevaron con los médicos en Mazatenango y en Antigua Guatemala. Pero no se curó. Al fin, se lo llevaron con un brujo en Samayac, la tierra de los brujos. Pues, el brujo de Samayac le dijo a la familia [que] el enfermo ya no tiene su espíritu; solamente el cuerpo. Su espíritu ya está con los animales benditas, y se queda loco por el resto de su vida.

Al ruego de la familia, el brujo de Samayac vino a San Lucas para curar al enfermo. Pues, el brujo trabaja con la magia negra cuando llegó en el lugar encantado donde el hombre había botado el matapalo. Él brujo dijo a la familia que buscaron una cerdo bien gordo y tres gallos, y les dijo que abrieron una tumba en la tierra en el mismo lugar encantado.

La familia preparó todo lo que el brujo pidió. Todo [estaba] listo. Llegó la hora 12 de la noche, y el brujo dijo al hombre enfermo que empujaron el cerdo y los tres gallos adentro de la zanja (tumba), y los mozos enterraron con tierra a los animales. Así vivos los enterraron. Patrona dice que fue así la curación del hombre rico. Me dijo que ese hombre se curó de la locura. Ahora, vive bien, pero gastó mucho dinero.[24]

—Patrona Vásquez Cholotío

# Glossary / Glosario

**ad honorem:** Honorary, unpaid. Honorario, no remunerado
**aguado:** Lax, weak, without movement
**aguardiente:** Firewater, cane liquor, sugarcane rum
**ajau, ahau, ajawor, or aajaaw:** Owner; lord, god, lord of heaven, or sky, and lord of the world, or earth.
**aj-iitz or aj'iitz:** Witch. Brujo, chamán
**ajkuum:** Shaman. Chamán
**alcalde:** Head. Jefe
**aldea:** Village
**alguacil:** Bailiff, runner, attendant
**amate:** Ficus jimenezii: tree of the most massive of the Guatemalan flower (Armas 1991:10). Ficus jimenezii: árbol de los más corpulentos de la flor
**amees** [ame's]: Cat burglar
**andasolo:** *Pizote or coati of a white nose (species: Nasua narica)*
***anonas:*** Aromatic, beefy fruit of the anono (sugar apple) tree, which is very tempting
***Atiteco, Atiteca:*** Male, female inhabitant of Santiago, Atitlán; female inhabitant of Santiago, Atitlán
**atol:** Ritual corn drink. Bebida ritual de maíz
**bomberos:** Firefighters
**brujo, bruja:** Witch, sorcerer
**búho:** Owl. Tecolote
**cafetales:** Coffee groves
**caites:** Typical leather sandals. Sandalias típicas de cuero
**Camino a la Felicida:** Road to Happiness
**campesino:** Countryman; peasant; farmer
**cantón:** Small village, aldea, administrative unit
**caporales:** Leaders
**cargado:** Carried on one's back

**caso:** Genre of a folktale based on true events. Género de un cuento basado en hechos reales

**caso:** Case, instance, occurrence, affair; subject

**chamán:** Shaman. Ajkuum

**characotales:** Persons who can transform into her or his nagual and do evil things

**chirimía:** Traditional flute in Tz'utujil and in Spanish flute. Flauta tradcional en Tz'utujil y en español flauta

**chompipes:** Turkeys. Pavos

**cofrades:** Brothers within a religious fraternity. Hermanos dentro de una fraternidad religosa

**cofradías:** Religious brotherhoods. Hermandades religiosas

**corte:** Traditional wrap-around skirt

**costumbres:** Customs; rituals. Ceremonias; ritos

**cuerdas:** .178 acre each

**cusha:** Abbreviation for cushusha, clandestine aguardiente. Abreviatura de cushusha, aguardiente clandestino

**cuta:** Short snake. La culebra corta

**descansador:** A chair, or luxury armchair, such as those used by senior officials. Una butaca de lujo, como las que usan los altos funcionarios

**diezmo:** Tithe

**dormilones las cabezas:** Sleepyheads

**dueña:** Owner; lady, goddess

**dueño:** Owner; lord, god

**finca:** Farm

**fiscal:** Person in charge of the local Catholic church where there is no resident priest; an official

**flor de muerto:** Wild plant whose yellow flowers the people use to adorn the tombs on the Day of the Saints (Armas 1991:98); marigold

**guaro:** Home brewed *aguardiente; plain distilled liquor*

**guatemalteca:** Guatemalan

**güisquil:** *A climbing plant whose fruit is the size of an orange.* Chayote: Choyota edulis. Chayote, una planta trepadora cuyo fruto es del tamaño de un naranja

**hormiga:** Ant

**hormigo:** Tree Platymiscuim spp.: macacauba, Maacawood, orange agate

**incensario de baño:** Bath [purification or cleansing] censer

**ik:** Day, sun wind. Día, sol, viento

**injertos anonas:** Annona graft (sugar apple graft)

**jiloteando:** Beginning to grain ears of corn. Empezando a granar la mazorca de maíz

**Juaneros:** People of San Juan

**juez:** Vice-head; judge

**malignos:** Devils

**mayordomo:** Rank-and-file member of a cofradía

**mayores:** Auxiliaries of municipal police in towns with more indígenas [indigenes, natives] people than Ladinas or Ladinos. Auxilares de policía municipal en lugares de más población indígena que ladinas o ladinos

**matapalo** tree: "Amate" in other regions of Guatemala; in Tz'utujil [and] in Kaqchikel, "po'j"

**micoleón:** Kinkajou (mammal related to the racoon that is arboreal and nocturnal with big eyes and a long, prehensile tail and yellowish brown fur). Mamífero emparentado con el mapache que es arbóreo y nocturno con ojos grandes y una cola larga, prensil y pelaje pardo amarillento

**micoleones:** Kinkajous (plural of micoleón). Plural de micoleón

**milpa:** Cornfield

**morería:** Workshop in which costumes and implements are made and rented for the Moorish and conquest dances

**mozos:** Servants

**muchacha:** Young woman

**muchacho:** Young man

**naguales:** The animals or spirits into which people can convert; owners. Los animales o espíritus en los que las personas pueden convertirse; dueños

**nagualismo:** La gente tiene un nagual que es un espíritu o un animal

**nixtamal:** Corn cooked in lime or ash water

**octavo:** Eighth of a liter

**oxlajuj;** Oxlajuuj: Thirteen

**palo:** Tree standing or felled. Árbol en pie o derribado

**palo del hormigo**: Reddish, durable wood of the hormigo tree. Madera rojiza y duradera del árbol hormigo

**Pedranos:** People of San Pedro

**perraje:** Blanket of cotton or wool

**pita:** Cord. Cuerda

**pizotes:** Carnivorous mammals with a long snout and tail that nimbly climb the trees, similar to coatis. Mamíferos carnívoros con un hocico y una cola largos que trepan ágilmente a los árboles, similares a los coatis

**potreros:** Wide open spaces between the houses where children play and where the people keep chickens and large animals. Amplios espacios abiertos entre las casas donde juegan los niños y donde la gente tienen gallinas y animales grandes

**principales:** Elders; dignitaries

**quetzal:** Guatemalan currency; beautiful bird with iridescent, green tail

**regidores:** Councilmen

**retoños:** Offspring (descendencias, descendants); children, kids

**rojiza:** Reddish

**ronda:** Patrol; round of the world, or earth; patrol of the volcano. Patrulla

**sanik:** In Spanish, means hormiga (ant). Sanik, en español, quiere decir hormiga

**Santo Mundo:** Sacred World, Earth

**secreto:** Magical objects or acts. Objetos o actos mágicos

**síndico:** Syndic, legal representative, trustee

**sitio:** Homeplace

**suj** tree: Suuj, sare, conacaste tree

**tacuazín:** Opossum. Zarigüeya

**taltuza:** Rat-like rodents that bore long tunnels in the ground; gophers. Roedores similares a las ratas que perforan largos túneles en la tierra; ardillas terrestres

**teclados:** Keyboards

**tecomates:** Gourds. Guardias

**tepezcuinte or tepezcuintle:** Brown rodent the size of a rabbit with black stripes on its back

**traje:** Suit, costume, outfit, dress

**tun:** Traditional drum

**veladores:** Short, thick candles

**xuul:** Chirimia

**xuul q'ojoom:** Chirimía drum, or drum of the chirimía. Tambor de chirimía, o tambor de la chirimía

**zacate:** Grass, herb, generic name for several species of grass that serve as pasture and forage and curing the sick. Hierba, yerbas

# Notes

1. As I have said, the blending of native religion and the early Catholicism introduced by the Spanish friars is most obvious in the cofradías, religious brotherhoods that have as a major obligation the sponsoring of saints and burying the dead (Sexton 1992b:xix–xx).

Each cofradía has an alcalde (head), and the more active cofradías have a juez (vice-head) and a first mayordomo (a liaison between the juez and secondary mayordomos who are the rank-and-file members). Men climb the ranks by periodically bearing a cargo, or office, for a year. Holding an office requires them to redistribute their wealth because they are expected to spend their money on food and drink for fiestas that honor the saints. Thus, a member's financial responsibilities may make him poor in wealth but rich in social status. So it is a wealth-leveling mechanism. But because richer families get their sons through the ranks faster than poor families, it may be a stratifying mechanism, especially in land-wealthy communities.

Men who successfully fulfill both high religious and political offices may become known as principales, or town elders, who are consulted on civil and religious matters. Although the principal's whole family shares the prestige of his high status, wives and children enjoy this status only vicariously.

2. This is what anthropologists have identified as the civil-religious hierarchy in which there is mandatory unpaid service in both religious and civil offices. By the time men climb the highest ranks, they may be financially poor because of all of the expenses holding these offices but rich in social status in their communities.

Pedro said that his most difficult obligation for this office of alguacil was to drop off and bring correspondence to the departmental government, the Court of First Instance or income administration. Going and returning on foot from San Juan to Sololá took ten hours round trip. Also, he said he had to go to make the firewood for the family of the municipal secretary who was a Ladino. On June 6, 1976, Pedro also began to serve as *síndico* (syndic, legal representative; trustee), the second-highest elected office after mayor in San Juan la Laguna (Sexton 1984:40). He did not mention this office in his current summary "My Life in the Community."

3. Pedro's following account on November 21, 2022, of the Virgin Mary, or Virgin of the Conception, healing his knee helps to explain his devotion to this saint:

"Also, my wife and I are very devoted of visiting the mother of Lord Jesus, Holy Mary. I had been suffering from a knee. I went to the doctors; they sent me to the national hospital of Sololá.

"The result of the exam told me that the cartilage of my knee is very worn. That is why when I walk the bones collide. They gave me a medicine for six months, and finally they told me what I had left was a knee operation and they would have to put a prosthesis on me. But the cost of operation and material is Q18,000, and I would have to go a hospital in Antigua, Guatemala. But Q18,000 is very expensive. I am not able with that quantity of money; I don't have the money. I was only able to buy the medicine to take for nine months. I suffered a lot; I walked a block, [and] then I tired. For a while, I abandoned my works in the field. My knee hurt a lot; I was not able to walk well.

"Always with my prayers [I was] asking Jesús Sacramento and Virgin María for relief from my illness. In the prayers, my wife, Nicolasa, accompanied me.

"One night I dreamed while I was sleeping—a señora appeared to me in the dream and told me: 'Pedro, I see you very preoccupied and sad about the pain in your knee. If you want, I am going to heal you. With me are medicine and rods [narrow rods, needles, and syringes].'

"In the dream, I told her: 'Madam, how do you know that I have a knee injury?'

"She tells me in the dream: 'I saw you in the hospital when the doctor told you the operation costs Q18,000—I am going to cure you, [and] it doesn't cost you five centavos to look at your knee.'

"I showed her my knee was very swollen and it hurt a lot. The lady from her shawl took out a syringe with a needle from the needles they used earlier, but it had no liquid or medication, only the needle with the syringe entered into my knee.

"In the dream, I shouted [and] the lady told me 'Calm down; you're cured.' She touched her hands on my knee.

"In my dream, I wanted to kiss her hand. She told me, 'Don't touch me.'

"When I woke up, my heart was pounding a lot. I felt that my knee weighed a lot, and [I felt] a sharp pain.

"In my dream I said, 'What happened? Who is the woman who spoke to me in the dream? She is not Ladina.' A different woman was wearing a corte as the women in the region wear. She was wearing a white blouse with long hair, not braided; she spoke to me in Tz'utujil.

"When my dream ended, I sat on the edge of my bed to pray, now not sleeping at all. When it dawned, I told my family what I dreamed and what happened to me.

"A few days later, I started to walk. I abandoned the cane. Now I can walk; I can work in the field. For me, this was a miracle of Virgin Mary and Jesus Sacramentado."

4. For this tale, see "Francisco Sojuel and General Jorge Ubico: A Tz'utujil Tale" in *The Dog Who Spoke and More Mayan Folktales* (Sexton et al. 2010:56–59). For another tale about the miracles of Sojuel and Ubico, see "The Legend of Francisco Sojuel: A Tzutuhil Story," in *Heart of Heaven, Heart of Earth* (Sexton and Bizarro 1999:82–87).

Neither Diego Mendosa nor Pedro gave "*Caso*: Francisco Sojuel Warns of Hurricane Stan" a title. I did it based on the content of the story.

5. There are twenty days in a month of the Mayan calendar, which range from zero to nineteen or one to twenty, depending on the source. In the latter, the names of the numbers

are from one to thirteen and then repeat themselves, in consecutive order seven more times, adding up to twenty. Each day also has its own individual names with possible individual meanings. See Marco and Marcus (De Paz 1991:34) in *Calendario Maya: El camino infinito del tiempo*, and Monro S. Edmonson (1988:236) in *Book of the Year: Middle American Calendrical Systems.*

In response to my query, Pedro writes "the ancient shamans used [spelled] 'Ajpub.' Nowadays, they use [spell] 'Ajpú.'" For both spellings, also see Juan Felipe Dayley et al. (1996: 11) in *Diccionario Tz'utujli.*

For another tale that deals with the significance of Paru-chi Abaj, see "The Story of the Enchanted Place, Paru-chi Abaj," in *Heart of Heaven, Heart of Earth and Other Mayan Folktales*, Sexton and Bizarro Ujpán (1999:67–70).

6. For another interesting story about a deer who got away from a hunter, see "Otomi Parables, Folktales, and Jokes" (Russell Bernard and Jesús Salinas Pedraza 1976) in *International Journal of American Linguistics*, Native American Texts Series, 1, no. 2.

7. The piece is jade with gold. It is a fortune that the goddess of the hill gave the woman. It is said that she was not able to sell or give it to another person. It is like a talisman that can be kept inside the house. With this fortune, the woman was cured of her illness; everything changed for her family. Her husband began to plant corn and beans and went out to harvest [crops] in abundance. And the señora began to raise chickens and sheep and sold them to the people. With those jobs, they obtained good earnings. In other words, one can say the jade with gold was like a magnet to bring people to a business. Also, one can say it was a secreto.

8. Cuah Suj appears to be a K'iche' name even though it is just outside of downtown San Juan. According to Jorge Luis Arriola (Arriola 1973:209), "chua" is an apocope of "chuach" that means "in front of." Also, it means "above" or "over" in K'iche' and Ixil. Most of Aririola's examples are K'iche'. Also, J. Francisco Rubio (1982:208) says the mimosaceous tree, because of its attractiveness, is used as an ornamental.

According to Dayley et al. (1996:18) in the grammatical introduction of *Diccionario Tz'utujil*, a preposition proceeds the noun, but he spells "chuach" "chwach~chwech" (and "chua" "chwa," the apocope) and says it means "in front of," "on the surface of," and "on the face of." Also, in *Diccionario Tz'utujil*, Dayley et al. (1996:401) spell "suj" "suuj."

In a simple illustration of an apocope, Lorna Sinclair Knight et al. (2005:77) say "san" is an apocopated form of "santo."

Upon my query, Pedro wrote "when the exact day of the god or goddess of the enchanted hills arrives." Also, he told me Los Ki'che's, Kaqchikeles, and Tz'utujiles, and also the shamans, say that the Ajau I'x, day I'x, is a day of the Mayan calendar. I'x is the day of the Mother Earth, day of the enchanted hills. I'x comes from the word "Ixok," [or] woman in Spanish. Then Ixok' woman is the Mother Earth, Mother Nature. On the day I'x is when animals are seen in the enchanted places. But there is one thing—not all people see the things of Mother Nature.

Pedro's explanation is similar to Marco and Marcus De Paz (1991:32), who cite Rouanet Francisco Rodríguez, in *El Indígena Guatemateco*, Banco de Guatemala, when they define I'x as "[the] day dedicated to the divinities of the forests, hills and mountains, and most special places." They also add "Special day for rogations for rain and good harvests" and for "Attainment of forgiveness." They say the possible meaning of I'x is jaguar as did Pedro's informant, Manuel Teleguan, a K'iche' shaman living in a canton of San Juan la Laguna, in 1992. The shaman also told Pedro that the meanings of the names of the day lords are actually their naguales. That is, "the animals that carry the names of the day are naguales." El Batz is a monkey; his nagual is a monkey. Furthermore, Teleguan claimed that all the names of the day lords are actually naguales, including night air, cane, and flint, which was strange for Ignacio as well as for me.

However, this kind of information is similar to what Guatemalan historian Francisco Antonio de Fuentes y Guzmán was saying in the 1600s when he listed plants and objects as well as animals as naguales (Fuentes y Guzmán in Orellana 1987:33), and Orellana concluded he was confusing *nagual* with *tona*. For more information on these topics, see notes ten and thirteen in *Heart of Heaven, Heart of Earth* (Sexton and Bizarro 1999:133–36).

9. Here Pedro spelled "Oxlajuuj" as "Oxlajuj." I changed the spellings, which can be found in *Diccionario Tz'utujil* (Dayley et al. 1996:342, 621). Munro Edmonson (1988:262) used the older Tz'utujil spelling *iq'* for wind, which would be the same in K'iche'. I changed *iq'* to the standard Tz'utujil spelling *ik'*.

For another tale about rainmakers, see "The Story of the Poder [Power, Ability] of Persons When They are Born" in *Mayan Folktales: Folklore from Lake Atitlán, Guatemala* (Sexton 1992b:52–58). For more information about *taltuzas*, see "Story of the Gods of Corn" in *Mayan Folktales*" (Sexton 1992b:90–96) and "Story of the Dog and Cat" in *Heart of Heaven, Heart of Earth* (Sexton and Bizarro 1999:73–74).

10. On my query, Pedro said that "as for the ears of corn—yellow, white, and black, well, this is a creencia (traditional belief) of the grandparents. (It is not mine).

"The three kinds of ears of corn is a Mayan belief. The yellow ear of corn represents the color of the Mayan people (or indigenous) people. The white ear of corn represents the color of white people, and the black ear of corn represents the color of our black brothers.

"Another Mayan belief deals with the birth of children born white, brown, or black. When a dark-haired woman is pregnant and wants to have a white girl or boy, under her pillow she has to put a white ear of corn as a secreto so that she will give birth to a white baby. A pregnant woman, if she wishes to have a *morenito* [dark-skinned (Garcia-Pelayo et al. 1984:473)] baby, she needs to put a black ear of corn under her pillow. It was an ancient secreto; but now, this secreto about pregnancies is not accepted."

According to James Frazer (1963:12) writing in his book, *The Golden Bough*, this is a case of sympathetic magic in which "like produces like, or that an effect resembles its cause." Frazer adds that this "principle may be called the Law of Similarity." That is, a white object will produce another white object, and a black object will do likewise.

11. When I asked Pedro whether anyone in particular told him this story or whether it was a general tale that everybody knows, he replied that this tale is not a popular tale nor current. "One part my cousin Juan Upán Ovalle had told me. He has been dead for 50

years. This tale is not new. Juan Ujpán Ovalle, in peace may he rest, was older than I. With him, we went to cut firewood in the mountains. That's where he told me this story. I tidied (edited) it up a bit, and it seems it came out well. There is another story that the deceased Juan has told me, 'The Muleteer and Jealous Husband.' I have not wanted to write it. It is very vulgar."

This tale is a variant of "The Story of a Man [Devil] Who Was put Inside a *Tecomate*" in *Mayan Folktale* (Sexton 1992b:38–42). In this tale instead of the woman throwing the devil inside the tecomate and then into the garbage, where a drunk later lets him out on the condition that the devil help the man scheme to get money out of a king, the distressed wife buries him in the cemetery where he stays. In both versions, the way to deal with the devil is to entice him into a medium-sized gourd jar, or clay jar, cork it up, and throw it away.

The first version, Pedro says, was told by the old folks without giving anyone else specific authorship so the same applies to the current version.

12. "*Mees*" [*me's* in *Diccionario Tz'utujil* (Dayley et al. 1996:251)] is a Tz'utujil word used more in San Pablo. "*Mees*" is the common [gender neutral] of male and female cats. Now, in order to differentiate the masculine, the "a" is added to say "*amees* [*ame's*];" that is, male cat thief. Now in the feminine, the "t;" "*tames* [*tame's*]" is added to say female cat thief. Pedro says, "We in San Juan say 'mish.' In San Pedro, 'siaa' [sya] is said."

As Pedro and I reported (Sexton 1984:33–35), during the height of the civil war, the military commissioners were military veterans who gained and often abused power by spying on their fellow citizens and reporting to military commanders any prohibited behavior such as criticizing the government or army.

13. This story is a variant of "Temperament and Deeds of the Son of God" in *Heart of Heaven Heart of Earth and Other Mayan Folktales* (Sexton and Bizarro 1999:106–8).

14. Among the mountains of Sololá and Chichicastenango, there are two cantons [administrative units] that are called Churunel One and Churunel Two. The word "Churunel" is the surname of the Kaqchikeles. Pedro Sicayu tells: "The first who arrived were the Churuneles [who] established a caserío [hamlet]; later they gave it the name, Churunel One. In time, they say that another group migrated of the same surname [who] formed a caserio that now is called Churunel Two."

15. Pedro said that a teacher who understands and writes Tz'utujil Maya helped him with the present-day spelling of Xe' chimaay, Pa taam, Xe' kaq powoon, Pa chojoob', Chiriij kaq jaay, and Xe' cruz. Also, Pedro sent me a colored, hand-made map that illustrates the names and locations of these four places that are found in the region bordering the volcano of San Pedro la Laguna, collectively known by the Pedranos as Chua Nimajujú.

16. In the fourth volume of Pedro's life history, *Joseño: Another Mayan Voice Speaks from Guatemala*, I asked Pedro, "What is the *Ronda del mundo?*" Pedro answered, "It is a wind that passes four times a day—6 a.m., 12 noon, 6 p.m., 12 midnight. If a person is walking down the street, he or she has to move aside because he or she will die. The wind is to clean the world of sins of men and women. A person should not have two to three women because it is easy to fall to the *Ronda del mundo*. Another name for this is the *Mala hora del mundo* [Bad Hour of

the World]." This seems to be not a god but a force, or power (Sexton and Bizarro 2001:79–80). Later, he referred to this phenomenon as the *Pastor* [*del mundo*]. In the same episode, he provided other examples of this phenomenon, including mentioning that "at the moment an adulterer is having sex, the wind hits his back like a bullet, carried by the strong wind. The shot destroys his intestines, kidneys, and liver, and for that reason he vomits blood."

17. This is like in *Brigadoon*, the fictional Scottish village and the musical production by the same name, in which subjects lose their sense of time.

18. Pedro also wrote the following to me in a letter:

"The principal [dignitary] Sebastián Méndez came to my house before Christmas to give me some squash (pumpkins). I talked to him for an hour and a half. And he told me the same: the hills Xe' kaq powon, Pa chojoob', and Chiriij kaq jaay are enchanted and dangerous places.

"One time, he says that when he was a child, he went with his grandfather to take care of the milpa in Pa chojoob'. The pizotes [similar to coatis, carnivorous mammals with a long snout and tail that nimbly climb the trees] animals, squirrels, and raccoons did a lot of damage. They ate a lot of ears of corn.

"One time he says that his grandfather took a borrowed shotgun to kill the animals. They managed to arrive at Pa chojoob' as the animals were eating ears of corn. When his grandfather wanted to shoot the shotgun, two times they heard a voice that said, 'Be careful with killing the animals.' That is what they heard; they saw no one. It frightened them, and they began to return. I want to write a tale or legend about the sacred place Chiriij kaq jaay. I will have to go there and take don Sebastián so that he can explain it well. I am familiar with it and have visited it, but I don't know its origin."

19. For more on the dance of the deer, see "Story of the Dance of the Deer," in *Mayan Folktales: Folklore from Lake Atitlán, Guatemala* (Sexton 1992b: 58–64). Gertrude Prokosch Kurath (1967:180–182) offers more on the dance of the deer among other middle American Indians such as the Yaqui.

20. Pedro spells "aj-iitz" [witch, shaman] the same as Jo Ann Munson et al. (1991:3) *in Diccionario Cakchiquel Central y Españo*, whereas in *Diccionario Tz'utujil*, Dayley et al. (1996:7) spell it "aj'iitz." Thus, I changed the spelling to "aj-iitz."

Pedro did not give this tale a title. In a letter he sent to me, he just said "a very old tale or legend." I gave it a title using in part his description.

21. For another tale about sorcerers in Chichcastenango bewitching Santanecos, see "Dance of the Flying Monkey" (Sexton 1992b:153–57).

22. When I asked Pedro to give me the meaning of "Xuul," he said that "Xuul" means chirimía [traditional flute in Tz'utujil and in Spanish]. Also, he said "Xuul" means wind instrument for the saxophone and the trumpet. "Q'ojoom" is the drum that accompanies the chirimía. Then it is called "*xuul q'ojoom*" [chirimía drum, or drum of the chirimía]. But also, it is said "*q'ojoom*" to the marimba. That is, "q'ojoom" means marimba. It is a mixture of words in the Tz'utujil language.

Most of the literature on the origin of the Guatemalan marimba reports the theory that it was introduced to the Mayas by Bantu African slaves during the colonial period (Chenoweth 1964; Kurath, 1967; Garitas, 1983; Castro 2015). Kurath (1967:188) believes the marimba may derive from an African sansa.

According to Edwin Castro (15 September 2015), the Guatemalan folklorist, Marcial Armas Lara, says that in 1958 K'iche' Maya principals allowed him to copy a codex that shows a god playing the marimba with his arm. Although this is a popular theory, the codex is now lost. Another postulate of Mayan origins is based on the Ratinlinuxl ceramic vessel found in the Chamá area of Alta Verapaz, Guatemala, and now is in the Penn Museum of the University of Pennsylvania. It is believed to have an early form of a marimba painted on it called an *ojom*. It is not surprising that in both the K'iche' and Tz'utujil languages, the word for marimba is *q'ojoom*, and in Kaqchikel, *q'ojom*, because as Munro Edmonson (1967:250) points out, the Tz'utujil and Kaqchikel Maya are the closest linguistic relatives of the K'iche' Maya.

According to Edna Fergusson (1946:272), "The marimba is not native to Guatemala, though it is Guatemala." Although African slaves apparently introduced it in the colonial period, it was popular when she traveled there in the 1930s, and it still is.

Regardless of the ultimate point of origin of the marimba, the Mayas have had centuries to develop it according to their own needs as they have deeply engrained it in their culture over the years. The folktales, "Mayan Folktale: The Origin of the Marimba" and "A Mysterious Tale of the Matapalo Tree" help illustrate that whether the marimba is the result of African diffusion or Mayan independent invention, the ultimate origin is not as relevant as the significant role it plays in the lives of the people.

Also, Fergusson (1942:153–54) says "the Marimba comes [to Tehuantepec, Mexico] from Guatemala and has only recently come to Tehuantepec to stay."

23. In *Diccionario de la expresión popular guatemalteca*, Armas (1991:112) says that the hormigo is a "tree from warm lands, of hard and reddish wood, and from which marimba keyboards are made, especially for its sonority." Also, note that in Spanish the insect is spelled "hormiga" and the tree is spelled "hormigo." The former is feminine and the latter is masculine.

24. On December 14, 2019, Pedro sent me the following in a letter:

"I want to tell you, I Pedro wrote a story in the year 2005. It had the title, 'The Stonecutter and the Tree of Fortune' (Sexton et al. 2010:216–19). I took it from a matapalo tree, or amate [Ficusjimenezlii: tree of the most massive of the Guatemalan flower [Armas 1991:10] that was in the place Pachitez near the road that goes to San Pedro some 100 meters from the shore of Lake Atitlán. Well, many people said that within the matapalo there was a fortune because from the bottom comes a young man who is the dueño [owner; lord] of the enchanted tree; they say that he was seen in the mornings when the first rays of the sun appear, and in the afternoons before darkness.

"Well, I didn't much believe what the people said, that inside the great matapalo tree there is a fortune because there you could see an enchanted young man from underneath who appears and disappears at the foot of the great matapalo tree.

"Then, from that I got the idea of creating this tale, and it turned out well. The land where the great matapalo was, about twenty-five years, was sold to a señor of San Juan; the man was the richest in the town; thus, the matapalo tree was conserved. Many people said that that tree has its nagual, or owner.

"In February of 2018, the owner of the land felled, in other words, cut down, a tree and converted it into firewood to sell. The people of the town said something bad was going to happen to the owner of the land. Exactly a few days later, the owner of the land fell sick; they carried him to a private sanatorium in Quetzaltenago. His kin said that on the way, he began to vomit. They say that the vomit looked like milk. They believe that he was struck by Santo Mundo, or better said, by the lord of the enchanted place. There were comments [that] the vomit that the man threw up was the sap or liquid that gave life to the tree because the sap or liquid of the matapalo tree is the color white like milk.

"Thus, they took him to the best North American doctors and Spanish physicians, but none of them was able to do anything to help him. His family fought hard; they say they spent more than a million quetzals. They looked for witches and shamans who performed rituals or ceremonies in the place where the trunk of the enchanted tree is located. Nothing came of it. The señor was sick for a year and eight months. He died on 10 October of this year 2019, two months ago. There were comments in the town about this matapalo (amate) tree. In Tz'utujil [Dayley et al. 1996:309] and in Kaqchikel, it is called Po'j [Cojti Macario, Narciso et al.1998:232]."

In *Diccionario de voces usadas en Guatemala*, Rubio (1982:143) defines the matapalo tree: "When its seed germinates on a tree, it develops a [parasitic] plant that covers it until it completely surrounds it, feeding on its sap, while the roots of the new plant reach the ground. Absolutely nothing of the original tree is seen afterward. It has medicinal properties and is used to combat mezquinos [fake herpes, acne] and measles" (Rubio 1982:143).

# Notas

1. Como he dicho, la mezcla de la religión nativa y el catolicismo temprano introducido por los frailes españoles es más evidente en las cofradías, hermandades religiosas que tienen como una obligación importante de patrocinar a los santos y enterrar a los muertos (Sexton 1992b:xix–xx).

Cada cofradía tiene un alcalde (jefe), y las cofradías más activas tienen un juez (vicejefe) (y un primer mayordomo (un enlace entre el juez y los mayordomos secundarios que son los miembros de base). Los hombres suben de rango llevando periódicamente un cargo, u oficina, durante un año. Tener un cargo les obliga a redistribuir su riqueza porque se espera que gasten su dinero en comida y bebida para las fiestas que honran a los santos. Por lo tanto, las responsabilidades financieras de un miembro pueden hacerlo pobre en riqueza pero rico en estatus social. Así, es un mecanismo de nivelación de la riqueza. Pero debido a que las familias ricas logran que sus hijos asciendan más rápidamente que las familias pobres, puede ser un mecanismo de estratificación, especialmente en las comunidades ricas en tierras.

Los hombres que cumplen con éxito altos cargos religiosos y políticos pueden llegar ser conocidos como principales, o ancianos del pueblo, a quienes se consulta sobre asuntos civiles y religiosos. Aunque toda la familia del principal comparte el prestigio de su alto estatus, las esposas y los hijos disfrutan de este estatus sólo indirectamente.

2. Esto es lo que los antropólogos han identificado como la jerarquía cívico-religiosa en la que existe un servicio obligatorio no remunerado tanto en cargos religioso como civiles. En el momento en que los hombres ascienden a los rangos más altos, pueden ser financieramente pobre debido a todos los gastos que suponen estos cargos, pero ricos en estatus social en sus comunidades.

Pedro dijo que los trabajos más duro de un alguacil es ir a dejar y traer correspondencia a la gobernación departamental, Juzgado de Primera instancia o en administración de rentas. Ir y regresar a pie de San Juan a Sololá se necesitan 10 horas ida y regreso. También, dijo que tenía a ir hacer la leña de la familia del secretario municipal era un ladino.

En 6 de junio de 1976, Pedro también comenzó a servir como *síndico* (representante legal; fiduciario), el segundo cargo electo más alto después de alcalde de San Juan la Laguna (Sexton 1984:40). No mencionó este cargo en su resumen "Mi vida en la comunidad."

3. La siguiente cuenta de Pedro en 21 de noviembre de 2022 de la Virgen María, o Virgen de la Concepción, sanando su rodilla ayuda a explica su devoción a esta santa:

También, somos [yo y mi esposa Nicolasa] muy devotos de visitar a la madre del Señor

Jesús, María Santísima. Yo venía padeciendo de una rodilla. Fui con los médicos; me mandaron a hospital nacional de Sololá.

El resultado del examen me dijo que el cartílago de la rodilla está muy desgastado. Por eso, cuando camino los huesos se chocan. Me dieron un medicamento por 6 meses, y por último, me dijeron lo que me quedaba era una operación de la rodilla y me tendrían que poner prótesis. Pero el costo del material y la operación es de Q18.000, y me tendría que irme a un hospital de Antigua, Guatemala. Pero Q18.000 es muy caro. No puedo con esa cantidad de dinero; no tengo [el] dinero. Solo podía comprar la medicina para tomar nueve meses. Sufrí mucho; caminaba una cuadra, [y] luego descansaba. Por un tiempo, abandoné mis trabajos en el campo. Me dolía mucha la rodilla; no podía caminar bien.

Siempre con mis oraciones [era] pidiendo Jesús Sacramento y a Virgen María un Alivio de me enfermedad. En las oraciones, me acompañaba mi señora, Nicolasa.

Una noche soné cuando yo estaba dormido—una señora a me apareció en el sueño y me dijo: "Pedro, te veo muy preocupado y triste por el dolor de tu rodilla. Si quieres, yo te voy a curar. Conmigo tengo medicinas y varillas [varillas estrechas, agujas y las jeringas]."

En el sueño, yo le dije: "¿Señora, como sabe que yo estoy enfermo de la rodilla?"

Ella me dice en el sueño, "Yo te vi en el hospital cuando el doctor te dijo que la operación cuesta Q18.000—yo te voy a curar, [y] no cuesta ni cinco centavos para mirar tu rodilla."

Yo le enseñé mi rodilla estaba muy hinchada y me dolía mucho. La señora de su rebozo sacó una jeringa con una aguja de las agujas que usaban antes, pero no tenía líquido o medicamento, solamente la aguja con la jeringa introdujo en mi rodilla.

En el sueño, yo grité, [y] la señora me dijo "Cálmate ya estás curado." Palpó sus manos sobre mi rodilla.

En el sueño, yo le quería besar la mano. Ella me dijo "No me toques."

Cuando me desperté, me palpitaba mucho el corazón. Sentí que mi rodilla pesaba mucho, y [sentí] un dolor agudo.

En mi sueño dije, "¿Que es lo que pasó? ¿Quién es la mujer que me habló en el sueño? No es ladina." Una mujer diferente tenía puesta corte como usan las mujeres de la región. Tenía puesta una blusa blanca con cabello largo, no trenzada; me habló en tz'utujil.

Cuando se me quito el sueño, me quedé sentado en la orilla de mi cama a orar, ya no dormir nada. Cuando amaneció, le conté a mi familia lo que había soñado y lo que pasó conmigo.

A los pocos días, empecé a caminar. Abandoné el bastón. Ahora puedo caminar, puedo trabajar en el campo. Para mí, este fue un milagro de la Virgen María y de Jesús Sacramentado.

4. Para este cuento, vea "Francisco Sojuel y General Jorge Ubico: Cuento tz'utujil" en *The Dog Who Spoke and More Mayan Folktales* (Sexton et al. 2010:60–63). Para otro relato sobre los milagros de Sojuel y Ubico, vea "The Legend of Francisco Sojuel: a Tzutuhil Story" (Sexton y Bizzaro 1999:82–87).

Ni Diego Mendosa ni Pedro le pusieron título a "Caso Francisco Sojuel advierte del huracán Stan." Lo hice basándose en el contenido de la historia.

5. Hay 20 días en un mes del calendario maya, que van de 0 a19 o de 1 a 20, según la

fuente. En ese último, los nombres de los números van del 1 a 13 y luego se repiten, en orden consecutivo 7 veces más, sumado veinte. Cada día también tiene sus propios nombres individuales con posibles significados. Vea Marco y Marcus de Paz (1991:34) en *Calendario Maya: El camino infinito del tiempo*, y vea Monro S. Edmonson 1988:236) en *Book of the Year: Middle American Calendrical Systems*.

En repuesta a mi consulta, Pedro escribe que "los antiguos chamanes usaban [deletreada] "Ajpub." Hoy en día, usan [deletrean] "Ajpú." Para ambas grafías, también vea Juan Felipe Dayley et al. (1996:11) en *Diccionario Tz'utuijil*.

Para otro cuento que trata sobre el significado de Paruchi Abaj, vea "The Story of the Enchanted Place, Paruchi Abaj" en *Heart of Heaven, Heart of Earth and Other Mayan Folktales* (Sexton y Bizarro Ujpán 1999:67–70).

6. Para conocer otra historia interesante sobre un ciervo que se escapó de un cazador, vea "Otomi Parables, Folktales, and Jokes" (Russell Bernard y Jesús Salinas Pedraza 1976) en *International Journal of American Linguistics*, Native American Texts Series, 1, no. 2.

7. El pedazo es jade con oro. Es una fortuna que la dueña del cerro le regaló a la mujer. Se dice que no puede venderlo ni regalarlo a otra persona. Es como un talismán que se puede guardar adentro de la casa. Con esta fortuna, la mujer se curó de su enfermedad; todo se cambió en su familia. Su esposo comenzó a sembrar maíz y frijol y salió cosechar en abundancia. Y la señora comenzó con la crianza de gallinas y ovejas y los vendía a la gente. Con esos trabajos, obtuvieron buenas ganancias. En otras palabras, se puede decir el jade con oro era como un imán a traer a las personas para un negocio. También, se puede decir era un secreto (rito u objeto mágico o sagrado).

8. Chua-Suj parece ser un nombre k'iche' a pesar de que está en las afueras del centro de San Juan. Asegún Luis Arriola (1973:209), "chua" es una apócope de "chuach" que significa frente a. También significa "arriba" o "sobre" en k'iche' y ixil. La mayoría de los ejemplos de Arrirola son k'iche'. También, J. Francisco Rubio (1982:208) dice que el árbol mimosáceo, por su atractivo, se utiliza como ornamental.

Asegún Dayley (1996:18) en la introducción gramática de *Diccionario Tz'utujl*, una preposición precede al sustantivo, pero él deletrea "chuach" "chwach~chwech" y ("chua" "chwa," la apócope) y lo dice significa "enfrente de," "en la superficie de," y "en la faz de." También, en *Diccionario Tz'utujil*, Dayley et al. (1996:401) deletrean "suj" "suuj."

Para una simple ilustración de un apocope, Lorna Sinclair Knight et al. (2005:77) dicen "san" es una forma apocopada de "santo."

A mi consulta, Pedro escribió "cuando llega el mero día del dueño o dueña de los cerros encantados." También, me dijo que los ki'che's, kaqchikeles, y tz'utujiles, y también los chamanes dicen que el Ajau I'x, día I'x, [es un] día del calendario maya. I'x es el día de la madre tierra, día de los cerros encantados. I'x viene de la palabra ixok' [o] mujer en español. Entonces ixok' mujer es la madre tierra, madre de naturaleza. En el día I'x es cuando se ven animales en los lugares encantados. Pero hay una cosa—no todas las personas ven las cosas de la madre naturaleza.

La explicación de Pedro es semejante a la de Marco y Marcus de Paz (1991:33), quienes citan a Rouanet Francisco Rodríguez, en *El Indígena Guatemateco*, Banco de Guatemala, cuando definen que I'x es [el] día dedicado a las divinidades de los bosques, cerros, montañas, y los lugares más especiales (De Paz 1991:33). Ellos también agregan "Día especial para rogaciones por la lluvia y buenas cosechas" y para "Consecución de perdones." Dicen que el posible significado de I'x es tigre (jaguar) al igual que el informante de Pedro, Manual Teleguan, un chamán k'iche' residente en un cantón de San Juan la Laguna, en 1992. El chamán también le dijo a Pedro que los sentidos de los nombres de los señores del día son realidad sus naguales. Es decir, los animales que llevan los nombres de estés días son naguales. El Batz es un mono; su nagual es un mono. Además, Teleguan afirmó que todos los nombres de los señores del día son en realidad naguales, incluyendo aire noche, caña, pedernal, lo cual era extraño tanto para Ignacio como para mí.

Sin embargo, este tipo de información es semejante a lo que el historiador guatemalteco, Francisco Antonio de Fuentes y Guzmán, decía en el siglo XVII cuando enumeró plantes y objetos, así como animales, como naguales (Fuentes y Guzmán en Orellana 1987:33), y Orellana concluyó que estaba confundiendo nagual con tona. Para más información sobre estos temas, consulte las notas diez y trece en *Heart of Heaven, Heart of Earth* (Sexton y Bizarro 1999:133–36).

9. Aquí Pedro deletreó "Oxlajuuj" como 'Oxlajuj.' Cambié la ortografía que se puede encontrar en el *Dicccionario Tz'utjuil* (Daley et al. 1996:342, 621). Munro Edmonson 1988:262) usó la antigua ortografía tz'utujil *iq'* por la ortografía estándar tz'utujil *ik'*. Cambié *iq'* a la ortografía estándar tz'utujil *ik'*.

Para otro cuento sobre hacedores de lluvia, consulte "The Story of the Poder [Power, Ability] of Persons When They Are Born" en *Mayan Folktales: Folklore from Lake Atitlán, Guatemala* (Sexton 1992b:52–58). Para más información sobres taltuzas, vea "Story of the Gods of Corn" en *Mayan Folktales* (Sexton 1992b:90–96) y "Story of the Dog and Cat" en *Heart of Heaven, Heart of Earth* (Sexton y Bizarro 1999:73–74).

10. En mi consulta, Pedro dijo que en cuanto a las mazorcas de maíz—amarillo, blanca, y negro, pues, este es una creencia de los abuelos. (No es mía).

Las tres clases de mazorca de maíz, es una creencia maya. La mazorca de maíz amarillo representa el color de la gente maya (o indígena). La mazorca de maíz blanca representa el color de las personas blancas, y la mazorca de maíz negro representa el color de nuestros hermanos negros.

Otra creencia maya trata sobre el nacimiento de niños que nacen blancos, morenos, o negritos. Cuando una mujer morena está embarazada y quiere tener un blanquita o blanquito, debajo de su almohada tiene que poner una mazorca blanca como un *secreto* para que le nazca un bebé blanquito. Una mujer embarazada, si quiere tener un bebé morenito [negro (de raza negra) Garcia-Pelayo et al. 1984:473], tiene que poner una mazorca calor negra debajo de su almohada. Era un secreto antiguo; pero ahora, ya no se aceptado los [secretos de] embarazos.

Según James G. Frazer (1963:12), escribiendo en su libro, *The Golden Bough*, este es un caso de magia simpática en la que "los similar produce lo similar, o que un efecto se asemeja a su causa." Frazer agrega que este "principio puede llamarse Ley de Similitud." Es decir, un objeto blanco hará que otro objeto sea blanco, y un objeto negro hará lo mismo.

11. Cuando le pregunté a Pedo si alguien en particular le contó esta historia o si era un cuento general que todos conocen, respondió que este cuento no es un cuento popular ni actual. "Una parte me lo había contado mi primo Juan Upán Ovalle. Hace 50 años que falleció. Este cuento no es nuevo. Juan Ujpán Ovalle, en paz descanse, era mayor que yo. Con él, íbamos a cortar leña en la montaña. Allí es donde me contó este cuento. Yo arreglé (edité) un poco, y parece que salió bien. Hay otro cuento del fallecido Juan que me había contado, 'El arriero y marido celoso.' No he querido escribirlo. Es muy vulgar."

Este cuento es una variante de "La historia de un hombre [diablo] que fue puesto dentro de un tecomate" (Sexton 1992b:38–42) en *Mayan Folktales*. En este cuento, en lugar de que la mujer arrojando al diablo dentro del tecomate y entonces dentro a la basura, donde un borracho luego lo deja salir con la condición de que el diablo ayude al hombre a planear para sacarle dinero a un rey, la esposa angustiada lo entierra en el cementerio donde él se queda. En ambas versiones, la forma de lidiar con el diablo es atraerlo a un frasco de calabaza, o jarra de barro, de tamaño mediano, o jarra de barro, córchelo y deséchalo.

La primera versión, Pedro dice, fue contada por los viejos sin darle a nadie más la autoría específica, por lo que lo mismo se aplica a la versión actual.

12. "Mees" [*me's* en *Diccionario Tz'utujil* Dayley et al. (1996:251)] es una palabra tz'utujil más usado en San Pablo. Mees es el nombre común [genero neutral] de gatos y gatas. Ahora, para diferenciar el masculino, se agrega la "a" para decir "amees [ame's];" es decir, ladrón de gatos macho. Ahora en el femenino se agrega la "t;" "*tames* [*tame's*] para decir ladrona de gatos. Pedro dice, "Nosotros en San Juan decimos 'mish.' En San Pedro se dice 'siaa [sya].'"

Como informamos Pedro y yo (Sexton 1984:33–35), durante el apogeo de la guerra civil, los comisionados militares eran veteranos militares que ganaban poder y a menudo abusaban de él espiando a sus conciudadanos e informando a los comandantes militares de cualquier comportamiento prohibido, como criticar al gobierno o al ejército.

13. Este cuento es una variante de "Temperament and Deeds of the Son of God" en *Heart of Heaven Heart of Earth and Other Mayan Folktales* (Sexton y Bizarro 1999:106–8).

14. Entre las montañas de Sololá y Chichicastenango, hay dos cantones que se llama Churunel uno y Churunel dos. La palabra "Churunel" es el apellido de los kaqchikeles. Pedro Sicayu cuenta: los primeros que llegaron eran los Churuneles [que] formaron un caserío; más tarde le dieron el nombre, Churunel uno. Con el tiempo dicen que se migró otro grupo del mismo apellido [que] formaron caserío que ahora se llama Churunel dos.

15. Pedro dijo que un maestro que entiende y escribe maya tz'utujil lo ayudó con la ortografía actual de Xe' chimaay, Pa taam, Xe kaq powoon, Pa chojoob', Chiriij kaq jaay, y Xe' cruz. También, Pedro me envió un mapa a color hecho a mano que ilustra los nombres y ubicaciones de estos cuatro lugares que se encuentran en la región que bordea el volcán de San Pedro la Laguna, conocido colectivamente por los Pedranos como Cha Nimajujú.

16. En el cuarto volumen de la historia de vida de Pedro, *Joseño: Another Mayan Voice Speaks from Guatemala*, le pregunté a Pedro: "¿Qué es el *Ronda* del mundo?" Pedro

respondió, "Es un viento que pasa cuatro veces al día—6 a.m., 12 del mediodía, 6 p.m., 12 de la noche. Si una persona camina por la calle, debe hacerse a un lado porque morirá. El viento es para limpia el mundo de los pecados de hombres y mujeres. Una persona no debe tener dos o tres mujeres porque es fácil caer a la *Ronda* del mundo. Otro nombre para esto es Mala hora del mundo. Esto parece no ser un dios sino una fuerza o poder (Sexton y Bizarro 2001:79–80). Posteriormente, se refirió a este fenómeno como el Pastor [del mundo]. En el mismo episodio, proporcionó otros ejemplos de este fenómeno, incluyendo mencionar que "en el momento en que un adúltero tiene relaciones sexuales, el viento golpea su espalda como una bala, llevada por el fuerte viento. El disparo le destroza los intestinos, los riñones, y el hígado, por esta razón vomita sangre."

17. Esto es como en *Brigadoon*, la aldea escocesa ficcional y la producción musical del mismo nombre, en los que los sujetos pierden el sentido del tiempo.

18. Pedro también me escribió lo siguiente en una carta:

El principal [dignatario] Sebastián Méndez vino a mi casa antes de Navidad para darme unas calabazas. Hablé con él durante una hora y media. Y me dijo lo mismo: los cerros Xe' kaq powoon, Pa chojoob', y Chiriij kaq jaay son lugares encantados y peligrosos.

Una vez, dice que cuando era niño fue con su abuelo a cuidar a la milpa en Pa chojoob'. Los pizotes [similares a los coatíes, mamíferos carnívoros con un hocico y una cola largos que trepan ágilmente a los árboles] animales, ardillas, y mapaches hicieron mucho daño. Comieron muchas mazorcas de maíz.

Una vez dice que su abuelo tomó una escopeta prestada para matar a los animales. Consiguieron llegar a Pa chojoob' mientras los animales comían mazorcas de maíz. Cuando su abuelo quiso disparar la escopeta, dos veces escucharon una voz que decía 'Tenga cuidado con matar a los animales.' Eso es lo que escucharon; no vieron a nadie. Les asustó, y empezaron a regresar. Quiero escribir un cuento o leyenda sobre el lugar sagrado Chiiriij kaq jaay. Tendré que ir allí y llevarme a don Sebastián para que me lo explique bien. Lo conozco y lo he visitado, pero desconozco su origen.

19. Para más sobre la danza del venado, consulte "Story of the Dance of the Deer," en *Mayan Folktales: Folklore from Lake Atitlán, Guatemala* (Sexton 1992b:58–64). Gertrude Prokosch Kurath (1967:180–82) ofrece más sobre la danza del venado entre otros indios americanos medios como los yaquis.

20. Pedro lo deletrea "aj-iitz" [brujo, chamán] lo mismo que Jo Ann Munson et al. (1991:3) en *Diccionario Cakchiquel Central y Español*; mientras que en *Diccionario Tz'utujil*, Dayley et al. (1996:7) lo deletrean "aj'iitz." Por eso, cambié la ortografía a aj-iitz.

Pedro no le puso título a este cuento. En una carta que me envió, solo dijo "un cuento o una leyenda muy antigua." Por eso, le di un título usando en parte su descripción.

21. Para otro cuento sobre brujos en Chichcastenango hecizando a Santanecos, ver "Dance of the Flying Monkey" (Sexton 1992b:53–57).

22. Cuando pide Pedro a darme el sentido de "Xul," el dijo que "Xul" siente chirimía [flauta tradicional en tz'utujil y en español (flauta)]. También, dijo "Xul" significa instrumento de

viento para el saxofón y la trompeta. "O'ojoom" es el tambor [instrumento musical] que acompaña a la chirimía. Entonces se llama "*xuul q'ojoom*" [chrimia tambor, o tambor de la chirimía. Pero también, se dice "*q'ojoom* a la marimba. Es decir, "q'ojoom" significa marimba. Es un mescla de palabras en la lengua tz'utujil.

La mayor parte de la literatura sobre el origen de la marimba guatemalteca reporta la teoría de que fue introducida a los mayas por esclavos africanos bantúes durante el período colonial (Chenoweth 1964; Kurath 1967; Garitas, 1983; Castro 2015). Gertrude Prokosch Kurath (1967:188) cree que la marimba puede derivar de una sansa africana.

Según Edwin Castro (15 de septiembre de 2015), el folclorista guatemalteco Marcial Armas Lara, dice que los principales mayas k'iche' le permitieron copiar en 1958 un códice que muestra a un dios tocando la marimba con su brazo. Aunque se trata de una teoría popular, el códice ahora se ha perdido. Otro postulado de origen maya se basa en la vasija de cerámica Ratinlinuxl encontrada en el área Chamá de Alta Verapaz, Guatemala, y ahora se encuentra en el Museo Penn de la Universidad de Pensilvania. Se cree que tiene pintada una forma antigua de marimba llamada *ojom*. No es sorprendente que tanto en el idioma k'iche' como en el tz'utujil la palabra para marimba sea q'ojoom y en kaqchikel q'ojom porque, como señala Munro Edmonson (1967:250), los idiomas tz'utujil y kaqchikel. Los mayas son los parientes lingüísticos más cercanos de los mayas k'iche'.

Según Edna Fergusson (1946:272), "la marimba no es originaria de Guatemala, aunque sí lo es." Aunque los esclavos africanos aparentemente la introdujeron en el período colonial, era popular cuando ella viajó allí en la década de 1930, y todavía es.

Independientemente del punto de origen último de la marimba, los mayas han tenido siglos para desarrollarla según sus propias necesidades ya que la han arraigado profundamente en su cultura a lo largo de los años. Los cuentos populares "Cuento popular maya: El origen de la marimba" y "Un cuento misterioso del árbol Matapalo" ayudan a ilustrar que, ya sea que la marimba sea el resultado de la difusión africana o de una invención maya independiente, el origen último no es tan relevante como el significado significativo papel que desempeña en la vida de las personas.

También, Fergusson (1942:153–54) dice que "la Marimba viene [a Tehuantepec, México] desde Guatemala y solo recientemente ha llegado a Tehuantepec para quedarse."

23. En *Diccionario de la expresión popular guatemalteca*, Armas (1971:112) dice que el *hormigo* es un "árbol de las tierras cálidas, de madera dura y rojiza, y de la cual se hacen los teclados de marimba, especialmente por su sonoridad." También, tenga en cuenta que en español el insecto se deletrea "hormiga" y el árbol se deletrea "hormigo." La primera es femenina, y la segundo es masculino.

24. El 14 de diciembre de 2019, Pedro me envió lo siguiente en una carta:

"Quiero contarle, yo Pedro escribí un cuento en el año 2005. Yo venía padeciendo de una rodilla "El cantero y el árbol de fortuna" (Sexton et al. 2010:216–19). Lo saqué de un árbol de matapalo, o amate [Ficus jimenezlii: árbol de los más corpulentos de la flor guatemalteca (Armas 1991:10)] que estaba en el lugar Pachitez cerca de carretera que conduce a San Pablo a unos cien metros de la orilla del lago de Atitlán.

Pues, mucha de la gente decía adentro del matapalo había fortuna porque por debajo sale un jovencito que es el dueño del árbol encantado; decían que se miraba por las mañanas cuando salían los primeros rayos del sol, y por las tardes, antes de oscurecer.

Pues, no creía mucho lo que la gente decía que adentro del gran árbol matapalo hay fortuna porque allí se miraba un joven encantado aparece y desaparece al pie del gran árbol matapalo.

Entonces, de eso me nació la idea de formar este cuento, y me salió bien. El terreno donde estaba el gran matapalo era, más o menos hace veinticinco años, fue vendida a un señor de San Juan; el hombre era el más rico del pueblo; así, venía conservado el árbol de matapalo. Mucha de la gente decía que ese árbol tiene su nagual o dueño.

En febrero de 2018, el dueño del terreno botó, en otras palabras, cortó un árbol y lo convirtió en leña para vender. La gente del pueblo decía algo mal va a suceder con el dueño del terreno. Cabal a los pocos días, el dueño del terreno cayó enfermo; se lo llevaron en un sanatorio privado en Quetzaltenango. Decían los familiares que en el trayecto comenzó a vomitar. Dicen que el vómito se miraba como leche. Se cree que fue golpeado por Santo mundo, o vale más decir, por el dueño el lugar encantado. Hubo comentarios [que] el vómito que el señor sacaba era la savia o líquido que daba vida al árbol porque la savia o líquido del árbol de matapalo es de color blanco como la leche.

Así, fue se lo llevaron con los mejores médicos norteamericanos y médicos españoles, pero ninguno de ellos pudo hacer nada ayudarlo. Su familia luchó mucho; dice que gastaron más de un millón de quetzales. Buscaron brujos y samanes (chamanes) que hicieron costumbres o ceremonias en el lugar donde se encuentra el tronco del amate encantado. Nada se logró. El señor se enfermó un año con ocho meses. Se murió el 10 de octubre de este año 2019, dos meses pasado. Hubo comentarios en el pueblo de este árbol de matapalo (amate). En tz'utujil [Dayley et al. 1996:309] y en kaqchikel, se llama Po'j [Cojti Macario, Narciso et al. 1998:232]."

En *Diccionario de voces usadas en Guatemala*, J. Francisco Rubio define el matapalo tree: "Su semilla al germinar sobre un árbol, desarrolla una planta [parásita] que va cubriéndolo hasta rodearlo completamente, alimentándose de su savia, en tanto las raíces de nueva planta llegan a tierra. Del árbol original no se ve después absolutamente nada. Tiene propiedades medicinales y se le emplea combatir mezquinos [falso herpe, acné] y sarampión" (Rubio 1982:143).

# References Cited / Referencias citadas


Armas, Daniel. 1971. *Diccionario de la expresión popular guatemalteca*. Editorial Piedra Santa.

Arriola, Jorge Luis. 1973. *El libro de las Geonimas de Guatemala: Diccionario Etimológico*. Seminario de Integración Social Guatemalteco.

Cojti Macario, Narciso et al. 1998. *Diccionario Kaqchikel*. Proyecto Lingüístico Francisco Marroquín.

Chenoweth, Vida. 1964. *The Marimbas of Guatemala*. University of Kentucky Press.

Dayley, Juan Filipe et al. 1996. *Diccionario Tz'utujil*. Proyecto Lingüístico Francisco Marroquín.

De Paz, Marco and Marcus. 1991. *Calendario Maya: El camino infinito del tiempo, segunda edición*. Ediciones Gran Jaguar.

Edmonson, Munro S.1967. "Classical Quiche." In *Handbook of Middle American Indians*, vol. 5, *Linguistics*, edited by Norman A. McQuown.

Edmonson, Munro S. 1988. *Book of the Year: Middle American Calendrical Systems*. University of Utah Press.

Fergusson, Edna. 1942. *Fiesta in Mexico*. Alfred A. Knopf.

Fergusson, Edna. 1946. *Guatemala*. Alfred A. Knopf.

Frazer, James. 1963. *The Golden Bough: A Study in Magic and Religion*. Collier.

Garcia-Pelayo, Ramón et al. 1984. *Larousse Gran Diccionario: Español-Inglés*. Ediciones Larousse.

Knight, Lorna Sinclair et al. 2005. *HarperCollins Spanish Unabridged Dictionary, Eighth US Edition*. HarperCollins.

Kurath, Gertrude Prokosch. 1967. "Drama, Dance, and Music." In *Handbook of Middle American Indians*, vol. 6, *Social Anthropology*, edited by Manning Nash.

Munson, Jo Ann et al. 1991. *Diccionario Cakchiquel Central y Español*. Instituto Lingüístico de Verano de Centroamérica.

Orellana, Sandra L. 1987. *Indian Medicine in Highland Guatemala: The Pre-Hispanic and Colonial Periods*. University of New Mexico Press.

Richards, Julia Becker et al. 1996. *Nuestro primer diccionario K'iche' Castellano, segunda edición*. Ministerio de Educación, Dirección de Desarrollo Socio Educativo Rural. Available at https://aprendizaje.mec.edu.py/dw-recursos/system/content/c171493/Idiomas%20Mayas/Maya%20K'iche'/1er_diccionario_kiche.pdf.

Rubio, Francisco J. 1982. *Diccionario de voces usadas en Guatemala*. Editorial Piedra Santa.

Sexton, James D. 1972. *Education and Innovation in a Guatemala Community: San Juan la Laguna*. Latin American Center Studies, UCLA, vol. 19.

Sexton, James D. 1973. "Modernization among Tzutuhil and Cakchiquel Maya: A Comparative Analysis of Two Guatemala Towns, San Juan la Laguna and Panajachel." PhD diss., UCLA.

Sexton, James D. 1981. *Son of Tecún Umán: A Mayan Indian Tells His Life Story*. University of Arizona Press.

Sexton, James D. 1984. *Campesino: The Diary of a Guatemalan Indian*. University of Arizona Press.

Sexton, James D. 1992a. *Ignacio: The Diary of a Maya Indian of Guatemala*. University of Pennsylvania Press.

Sexton, James D. 1992b. *Mayan Folktales: Folklore from Lake Atitlán, Guatemala*. University of New Mexico Press.

Sexton, James D., and Ignacio Bizarro Ujpán. 1999. *Heart of Heaven, Heart of Earth and Other Mayan Folktales*. Smithsonian Institution Press.

Sexton, James D., and Ignacio Bizarro. 2001. *Joseño: Another Mayan Voice Speaks from Guatemala*. University of New Mexico Press.

Sexton, James D. et al. 2010. *The Dog Who Spoke and More Mayan Folktales / El perro que habló y más cuentos mayas*. University of Oklahoma Press.

# About the Authors / Sobre los authores

**James D. Sexton and Pedro Cholotío Temó** (Ignacio Bizarro Ujpán, former pen name) have worked together for fifty-four years, collaborating on seven other books, including *Mayan Folktales: Folklore from Lake Atitlán, Guatemala* (1992b, republished 1999). Sexton is Regents' Professor Emeritus of Anthropology at Northern Arizona University. Cholotío Temó is First Principal (Elder or Dignitary) of San Juan la Laguna on the shore of Lake Atitlán, Guatemala. He has served in a number of civil and religious offices in the town.

**James D. Sexton y Pedro Cholotío Temó** (Ignacio Bizarro Ujpán, antiguo seudónimo) han trabajado juntos durante 54 años, colaborando en otros siete libros, incluyendo *Mayan Folktales: Folklore from Lake Atitlañ, Guatemala* (1992b, 1999). Sexton es Professor Emérito de Anthropolgía de Regents en la Universidad del Norte de Arizona. Cholotío Temó es Primer Principal (Anciano o Dignitary) de San Juan la Laguna en la orilla de Lake Atitlán, Guatemala. Ha trabajado en varios cargos civiles y religiosos en el pueblo.

www.ingramcontent.com/pod-product-compliance
Lightning Source LLC
LaVergne TN
LVHW091122080826

845145LV00008B/2015

* 9 7 8 0 8 2 6 3 6 8 2 9 4 *